THE RESOLVED SOUL
A Study of Marvell's Major Poems

The Resolved Soul

A Study of Marvell's
Major Poems

By Ann E. Berthoff

Princeton University Press 1970
Princeton, New Jersey

Publication of this book has been aided
by the Whitney Darrow Publication Reserve Fund of
Princeton University Press

This book has been composed in Linotype Granjon

147529

Printed in the United States of America
by Princeton University Press
Princeton, New Jersey

To Rachel and Frederic

Time, then, and the heaven came into being at the same instant in order that, having been created together, if ever there was to be a dissolution of them, they might be dissolved together.

Plato, *Timaeus*, 38

. . . nothing can be recounted justly among the causes of our happiness, unless in some way it takes into consideration both that eternal life and this temporal life.

Milton, *Prolusion, VII*

. . . thus is man that great and true *Amphibium*, whose nature is disposed to live not onely like other creatures in divers elements, but in divided and distinguished worlds; for though there be but one [world] to sense there are two to reason; the one visible; the other invisible. . . .

Sir Thomas Browne, *Religio Medici*, I, 34

PREFACE

IN THE later years of the eighteenth century, an irate Philadelphian, writing a broadside protesting certain municipal building plans, could sign himself "Andrew Marvell" with the certainty that the claim thus made implicitly to courage and candor would be recognized.[1] Marvell's reputation as the scourge of a wicked age persisted and if Lamb remarked the poet's "witty delicacy," it was his moral vigor that Wordsworth saluted. Although the transcendentalists of Emerson's circle recognized the metaphysical poet, even as the English were hailing the Puritan polemicist and "the garden poet," the discovery of Marvell has really been a modern phenomenon. If we remember that it took over two hundred years to decide what kind of poet he was, it will be less astonishing that critics are still deciding what kind of poems he wrote.

This endeavor which one critic has called "the search for Andrew Marvell" has been described by another as the reenactment of the torture of Marvell's Unfortunate Lover:

> And as one Corm'rant fed him, still
> Another on his Heart did bill.
> Thus while they famish him, and feast,
> He both consumed, and increast.[2]

Both descriptions have their justifications. The search—the critical reassessment of Marvell's style and his themes—is legitimate because Marvell is properly identified neither as the chief of "the school of Donne" nor as the priest of a fabulous and conceited Hermetic cult. But the methods by which the search has been conducted are, if not destructive, often faulty or irrelevant.

[1] See Caroline Robbins, "Andrew Marvell in Philadelphia," *TLS*, Dec. 19, 1958, p. 737.

[2] Bruce King, "The Search for Andrew Marvell," *REL*, VIII (1967), 32-41; Frank Kermode, "Marvell Transprosed," *Encounter*, XXVII (1966), 77-84.

PREFACE

In my view, there are two critical problems: one is to define
the thematic unity of Marvell's poetry (excluding the Satires);
the other is to define the limits by which interpretations of his
metaphors should be guided. The poems are unified by the
master theme of the soul's response to temporality, but since
that resounding theme is not independent of metaphor, a
philosophical definition of the unity of the poems will be,
inescapably, stylistic as well.[3] The two critical problems define
one another so that although the chapters that follow are for
the most part entitled thematically, each is concerned centrally
with some problem of style. It is a sound premise that the
way a poet speaks determines the kind of meaning established:
to describe his manner, to identify the remarkably consistent
tone of Marvell's poetry, I have had recourse to the concept of
a *voice* of allegory. And I have described in some detail the
structure of the allegorical metaphor since the themes of the
major poems—incarnation, the operation of mind, the dangers
of love, the action of grace, the virtues of nature, the death
of innocence, the secret of power, the uses of time—live by
metaphor.

A critical interpretation of a poet's work must account for
the main features of style, but it should be explicitly recognized
that these are themselves the substance of a critical hypothesis:
the expectation of matter is determined by an appreciation of
manner, the manner judged in the light of what we take to
be the matter. This dialectic of definition, which Erwin Panof-
sky has called a *circulus methodicus*,[4] requires submitting the
interpretations of the theme and particulars of any one poem

[3] The unity of the poems has been obscured by the continuing at-
tempt to categorize by subject, with results both amusing, as when
Grosart listed "On a Drop of Dew" with "Poems of the Country" and
"The Coronet" with "Poems of Imagination and Love," and confusing,
as when John Press (*Andrew Marvell* [London, 1958]) differentiates
"Poems of retreat, contemplation and solitude" from "Poems on themes
of love and death."

[4] *Studies in Iconology* (New York, 1939), p. 7n.

to a continuing scrutiny in the light of the poet's complete works and, in turn, it requires a continuing reassessment of the whole body of work in light of particular analyses. No satisfactory account of Marvell's poems could ignore their philosophical dimension. Intellectual power and subtlety are as central to a definition of Marvell's style as grace of feeling and "witty delicacy." I have hoped to illuminate the philosophical character of Marvell's poetry by exploring the ways of his imagination, which I take to be conceptual in its resources and allegorical in its expression.

I have not attempted to account for all aspects of all the poems nor have I tried to summarize the immense bulk of scholarly findings and considerations. Articles cited are those from which I have learned or which are directly related to my purpose; there is no attempt to present a pocket bibliography for each poem. If "The Unfortunate Lover" needs complete exegesis, "To His Coy Mistress" needs little; the discrepancy in thoroughness of comment should not be construed as a sign of evaluation. I have no opinion on such matters as, for instance, the primacy of the Latin or the English version of poems which share a subject or on the Satires or the topical verse such as "Fleckno." I have nothing to add to the thorough investigation of prosody carried out by Legouis and Leishman. My scrutiny of the Cromwell poems is limited to the means by which Marvell establishes the character of the providential hero. Some matters in Marvell criticism have become very snarled indeed; where I have tried my hand at unsnarling, in several lengthy notes (relegated to an appendix), I have no doubt that in some instances I may well have only confounded confusion.

I have had recourse frequently to Marvell's prose, examining there the seams and joints of arguments which in the poems are all of a piece. The underlying philosophical conceptions, the habits of mind, and even the temperament

PREFACE

expressed in poetry and prose seem to me indivisible. Andrew Marvell—poet, Puritan, patriot—is not a tripartite being.

With the kind permission of the Clarendon Press, all quotations from the poems are taken from H. M. Margoliouth, *The Poems and Letters of Andrew Marvell* (Oxford, 1952), Volume I. All prose passages (except those from letters, which are from Margoliouth, Volume II) are printed as they appear in *The Complete Works in Verse and Prose of Andrew Marvell*, ed. A. B. Grosart (London, 1868-75), Volumes III and IV. I should like to thank the editors of *Modern Language Quarterly* and *The Review of English Studies* for permission to reprint as parts of Chapter III articles which appeared in somewhat different form in those journals. I am also grateful to the Harvard College Library for permission to reproduce the woodcut "An Orchard Plot" from the 1648 edition of William Lawson's *A New Orchard and Garden*.

I have been admonished and encouraged by many friends and colleagues in the course of writing this book. It grew from an interest in Renaissance iconography and an old affection for a poet whose voice had always seemed to me very little like Donne's and whose poetry seemed, as H. J. Massingham once put it, to bring "news and sounds of the eternal concords."[5] Charles Mitchell's iconological analysis of Alberti's program for the sculptural reliefs of the Tempio Malatestiano suggested to me the nature of the theme of "The Unfortunate Lover," a reading of which became my point of departure. Paul J. Alpers, Warner Berthoff, and Laurence Stapleton helped me in defining some of the problems which a study of the allegorical imagination must confront.

In the course of my explorations I have many times sought the advice of scholars who have been very generous. Professors Caroline Robbins and Pierre Legouis, to whom all students of Marvell are beholden, have been cordial and in-

[5] *Andrew Marvell, 1621-1678: Tercentenary Tributes*, ed. W. H. Bagguley (London, 1922), p. 109.

PREFACE

structive. I should like also to thank Gerald Ackerman, Charles Dempsey, Samuel Hynes, Eleanor W. Leach, William Loerke, Wallace T. MacCaffrey, Theodora S. McKay, Brunilde S. Ridgway, and Anne H. van Buren. I am especially grateful to Robert B. Burlin and Isabel G. MacCaffrey, who have saved me from more than one error of fact and judgment.

I am indebted to Roderick S. Webster, Curator of the Antique Instrument Collection of the Adler Planetarium and Astronomical Museum, Chicago, and Derek J. deSolla Price, Department of History of Science and Medicine, Yale University, for information about Renaissance planispheres.

I am grateful to have had the expert advice and friendly counsel of Eve Hanle and Linda Peterson of Princeton University Press.

This book is dedicated to persons whose good-humored forbearance has been vital to my endeavor.

Concord, Massachusetts   A. E. B.
March, 1969

CONTENTS

THE RESOLVED SOUL
A Study of Marvell's Major Poems

CHAPTER I

The Voice of Allegory

ARVELL is a poet for whom the overtones of experience attest to the true form of life more fully and more profoundly than the simple tune of a particular action or scene ever can. His style is in the service of an abiding concern for the universal and general character of experience: the hero of his poetry is, we might say, the soul in its temporal state. The tyrant may be Love or Heaven or Necessity (only once is it Honor); the battle may be won or lost; there may or may not be a lady involved; the poet may be somber or amused—or both; but the protagonist is resolute in opposition to fate, or Marvell urges such resolution, and the field is always time. Over against the brilliant apprehension of scene and the surely and finely modulated voice of the poet should be set this other commanding quality of Marvell's verse, its conceptual resonance.

Recognition of the voice of allegory, which accounts for this resonance, leads to a discovery of the thematic unity of the major poems. All critics pay homage to Marvell's mastery of so many genres, but the only writer to my knowledge who has looked beyond the variety of subject to this thematic unity is the English historian Christopher Hill: "Marvell's key ideas are linked in one symbol [the mower and the harvest], suggesting the possibility that all his poems really deal with a single complex of problems. . . . They are the problems of an individual in an age of revolutionary change. . . . Soul and body, Love and Fate, illusion and reality, escape or action—all the poems in the last analysis deal with the adjustment of individual conduct to external conditions and forces."[1] The emphasis on the fateful position of "an individual in an age

---

[1] *Puritanism and Revolution* (London, 1958), pp. 355, 363.

3

of revolutionary change" is perhaps necessary to the definition of the central motives of Marvell's life, but it should not distract us from the point that in his poetry the confrontation of the individual and history is dramatized in terms created by the allegorical imagination. In the figures of the major poems, Marvell has created guises in which the soul dances its life while it is "the Creations guest." Love's banneret, "angry Heavens flame," the Drop of Dew, the *"easie Philosopher,"* the shepherd Thyrsis, the mower Damon, the lover of the coy mistress, the man in the garden—the metaphysical character common to them all I have tried to define by referring to the role they play in their opposition to fate: each is the Resolved Soul.[2]

Such a description of character is inescapably a definition of theme which, by this *circulus methodicus,* determines our recognition that Little T. C. in a prospect of flowers and the Nymph complaining for the death of her fawn have as much in common as do Little T. C. and a child named Theophila Cornewall; that Marvell's Cromwell who "first put Armes into *Religions* hand,/ And tim'rous *Conscience* unto *Courage* man'd" is cousin to the "Resolved Soul" as much as he is a historical figure; that the lover of the Coy Mistress, the poet of "The Definition of Love," and the philosopher of the garden, each in his own kind of solitude, are confronting the realities of time; that in the Unfortunate Lover, body and soul are brought together in a dramatization of the metaphors of "A Dialogue Between the Soul and Body"; that the poet of "Upon Appleton House" and Damon the mower both make surveys of nature, considering their part in the temporal scheme; that the Shepherd of "The Coronet" could learn a lesson from the Drop of Dew.

To say that the major poems share the one grand theme of the soul's life in time, though it reestablishes what was for-

---

[2] Quotation marks will distinguish the "Resolved Soul" who is the dialogue partner of "Created Pleasure."

gotten or ignored in the exuberant reclamation of "the garden poet," might be thought too simple a formulation by some more recent critics. Until the last decade or so, Marvell was considered a dull case for the historian of ideas: the judgment was that his diction is conventional, his allusions generally commonplace, his wit in the familiar "metaphysical" vein; and the ideas which may be said to have provided the generative force for his poetry were considered the common coin of late Renaissance thought. But close reading (of a kind) and the determined effort to identify particular sources have resulted in a conception of Marvell as a philosopher of one sort or another who wrote poems. In dismissing such a notion, it is not enough to claim that as readers we attend to the voice rather than to the conceptualizing power. To say that it is not the poet's system-building that attracts us, or the possibility of our crystallizing a philosophy from his poetry, is not to deny that lyric poetry which takes as its theme the soul's life in time is philosophical. Grierson made this point long ago. In introducing the metaphysical poets in his famous edition of 1921 (*Metaphysical Lyrics and Poems of the Seventeenth Century*), he was quick to warn us that the English poets were neither so intellectual nor so systematic as Lucretius or Dante, but one of the defining characteristics of "high" metaphysical poetry he sets down holds true for much of seventeenth-century English poetry. Grierson wrote that "a philosophical conception . . . of the role assigned to the human spirit in the great drama of human existence . . . laid hold on the mind and imagination of a great poet, unified and illumined his comprehension of life, intensified and heightened his personal consciousness of joy and sorrow, of hope and fear, by broadening their significance, revealing to him in the history of his own soul a brief abstract of human destiny."

The idea that "laid hold on" Marvell's mind and imagination was that the absolute disparity of heaven and earth is mediated by the soul, that the separation of the realms of grace and nature, the discontinuity of time and eternity creates an opposition which the soul can resolutely seize upon, mitigating the terrible force of time through love, heroic action, and contemplation. Such re-creation is accomplished not by substituting earthly pleasures, solutions, advantages, and virtues for the grace of heaven, but by imitation. Celebrating the soul as it plays between the world of action and the world of idea, between time and eternity, Marvell asks, "What is our life?" He frames the question and the answers in terms provided by the allegorical imagination.

The Allegorical Imagination

Whether his source is the ocean of the mind, the garden of the world, or, occasionally, the life of his time, Marvell's imagination creates characters, landscapes, and narratives enlivened by a "philosophical conception . . . of the role assigned to the human spirit." His apprehension is brilliantly his own. (That Marvell is unmistakably Marvell is a judgment all readers make.) But the tone is neither intimate nor immediate. The generalized character of his personae, his swift and sure symbolic narratives, the strongly emblematic quality of all his verse, and the persistent use of traditional schemes and tropes argue that Marvell speaks habitually in the voice of allegory.

There is, of course, no need to argue the point that Marvell found the mode of allegory congenial. There are several poems which qualify as strict or generic allegories ("The Unfortunate Lover," "A Dialogue Between the Resolved Soul and Created Pleasure," "A Dialogue Between the Soul and Body," "The Coronet") and the poems which are actually continued metaphors or developed analogies include "Music's Empire," "Clorinda and Damon," "On a Drop of Dew," and "The Match." Allegorical figures abound: "Fair quiet" and "Innocence," "old Time," "the wanton Love," "Flora," Death the mower, Despair and Impossibility, Humility, and so forth.

6

All the major poems have centrally important allegorical metaphors, symbolic settings and characters. But my concern is with the operation of the allegorical imagination rather than the labeling of degrees of abstractness, with that balance of particular and general which results in what I have called the conceptual resonance of the major poems, the accommodation of the occasional to the universal which the allegorical mode allows.

Marvell contemplates the green world of time. He sees it brilliantly and he sees it emblematically; his response is both personal and prophetic. The point of departure may have been the idea of opposition or of sacrifice or of correspondence; or it may have been the violet air, a white fawn, or a fountain garden at Nunappleton. But as the poem proceeds, the simultaneity of emphasis is what we may chiefly note. There is a depth of field not accounted for in J. B. Leishman's comment that "the thing described still remains for [Marvell] the main thing, his real, not merely his ostensible, subject, and is not . . . a mere topic for wit, or a more or less accidentally encountered emblem or symbol of some truth, idea or experience which transcends it and which is the poet's real concern."[3] I do not argue that Marvell sacrifices the concrete detail, the particular moment, the actual occasion for the sake of generalized comment about the nature of life; his poetry involves neither the sacrifice nor the mere *use* of the particular, the actual, the occasional. But for Marvell, "the thing described" is itself exemplary; his scenes and occasions are essentially symbolic; his style gives equal time to idea and action, to picture and truth. This study is predicated on the belief that if we hear the voice of allegory in Marvell's poems we will be hearing Marvell more clearly and not an echo of Donne; we will be undistracted by a supposed adumbration of Keats or the ghostly presence of Hermes Trismegistus.

The allegorical imagination seeks an accommodation of the

[3] *The Art of Marvell's Poetry* (London, 1966), p. 57.

temporal scene and act to the conceptual. If it should be claimed that such accommodation is nothing more than the "metaphysical" manner, I would reply simply that in Marvell's case the accommodation is consistent and recurrent—some metaphysical poems are more metaphysical than others, Helen Gardner has remarked—and that his style, both in its general character and in its particulars, is the response to the requirements of his theme, which is best defined in terms of the "philosophical conception" which "laid hold on" his mind.

Perceiving the abstract character of reality and the reality of abstractions, the allegorical imagination creates a conceptual resonance which requires, as it were, sounding board as well as strings and bow. Imagery, rhetoric, and action may play either role, serving to transform the presence of the temporal world as well as to body forth idea. There follow several pairs of lines in which the point of departure is first a place or a moment (A, B, C) and then a notion of some kind (A', B', C').

A   He lands us on a grassy Stage;
Safe from the Storms, and Prelat's rage.
He gave us this eternal Spring,
Which here enamells every thing.
("Bermudas," ll. 11-14)

A'   But thou who only could'st the Serpent tame,
Either his slipp'ry knots at once untie,
And disentangle all his winding Snare:
Or shatter too with him my curious frame.
("The Coronet," ll. 19-22)

In A, though Marvell begins with the historical scene of the Puritans' exile in Bermuda, the idea with which the place is involved is represented from the first: Providence manages the life they play; the "eternal Spring"—the phrase announces one of the best known of Marvell's "sensuous" descriptions—

is as much an Eden as it is the New World. A' makes use of both Biblical and pastoral imagery to realize a concept of the different "obligations," as Marvell called them, of earth and heaven. The object itself (the garland meant to substitute for the crown of thorns), the rhetoric (the Shepherd's direct address to his Saviour and his self-directed exclamations), the narrative (the discovery of the serpent among the flowers) all contribute to the revelation of the poem's theme. Once we know what that theme is, we realize its presence from the first line of "The Coronet."

Simultaneous emphasis on scene and significance, though from different points of view, is illustrated in these opening passages from "The Picture of Little T. C. in a Prospect of Flowers" and "The Unfortunate Lover":

B   See with what simplicity
     This Nimph begins her golden daies!
     In the green Grass she loves to lie,
     And there with her fair Aspect tames
     The Wilder flow'rs, and gives them names. . . .

B'   Alas, how pleasant are their dayes
     With whom the Infant Love yet playes!
     Sorted by pairs, they still are seen
     By Fountains cool, and Shadows green.

The history of the Unfortunate Lover will explain the juxtaposition of "Alas" and "how pleasant"; and the warning to Little T. C. in that poem's final stanza will set up reverberations which reach back to the opening, lending an irony to "simplicity" and "golden daies." The lovely garden setting of each poem is a *paysage moralisé*, a scene which mediates between "flow'rs" and "Fountains" and the idea to which, as the poem unfolds, they are seen to give local habitation.

And then two actors, the poet in the woods at Nunappleton, and the "Resolved Soul," establish certain points of view:

9

C   And see how Chance's better Wit
         Could with a Mask my studies hit!
         The Oak-Leaves me embroyder all,
         Between which Caterpillars crawl. . . .

                               (ll. 585-88)

C'   Had I but any time to lose,
         On this I would it all dispose.
         Cease Tempter. None can chain a mind
         Whom this sweet Chordage cannot bind.

                               (ll. 41-44)

The *"easie Philosopher"* and the "Resolved Soul" wittily pursue their ways to positions of strength, the one creating pleasure with his "active Minde," the other balancing his sword in the fight against "Created Pleasure." Each character is compounded of image and idea, and what he says and does creates not only a persona but also the substance of argument.

Action, scene, character: each is metaphoric, with the particulars serving as vehicles for ideas which in turn enliven and determine the course of the poem. And it is this course which provides the vital context: these are continued metaphors—or they are metaphors which continue a passage of thought and feeling. If we detach them from what has gone before and what follows, we endanger the integrity of the poem, and it is of course the poem as a whole that reveals the significance of a figure.

If Marvell's allegorical metaphors are to be appreciated, they have to be recognized as metaphors in the first place. One result of the disregard for the place an image has in the discursive or narrative course of a poem is that metaphors are literalized, so that conceptual resonance is discounted altogether. When Clorinda says

     I have a grassy Scutcheon spy'd,
     Where *Flora* blazons all her pride.

> The Grass I aim to feast thy Sheep:
> The Flow'rs I for thy Temples keep . . . ,

she is not describing a coat of arms planted in flowers. The scutcheon is neither a planting some "Flora" has made nor an emblem with only a literary relevance. Flora and scutcheon together make up a fanciful image of a beautiful meadow. When Damon answers, "Grass withers; and the Flow'rs too fade," Clorinda's pleasant picture is no longer merely pretty: it is clearly an image of the evanescent beauties of nature which the shepherd finds inadequate for the needs of his soul.

Even though such an image may seem to serve no larger purpose than to provide visual delight, its complex character will be revealed if we attend to the context and to the rhetorical function of the image. The generally accepted reading of "this Dial new" at the close of "The Garden" is a case in point. The poet, having acclaimed the pleasures of solitude in the garden which has been seen as another Eden, "that happy Garden-state," sings the beauties of his surroundings thus:

> How well the skilful Gardner drew
> Of flow'rs and herbes this Dial new. . . .

The figure, it is assumed, simply refers to a planting of herbs and flowers in the design of a sundial. Editors since Grosart have offered hints about how such a "dial" is to be pictured (are the herbs and flowers planted in the shape of numerals, to which the shadow of a gnomon points? or do herbs and flowers, planted dialwise, open according to the sun's position?), their literalism nourished by delight in such a quaint fancy. But this planting is probably a creation of the nineteenth century. If we owe to Charles Lamb the charming phrase "witty delicacy," we must also blame him for reducing Marvell's grand and sonorous figure to a merely charming one. In "The Old Benchers of the Inner Temple," Lamb wrote: "It was a pretty device of the gardener recorded by Marvell, who, in the days of artificial gardening made a dial out of herbs and flowers." Lamb's tactless pursuit of the whimsical has taken us far from the ambience of Marvell's figure. "Herbs and flowers" is a common term for those plants whose annual growth and decline traditionally symbolizes the rhythms of man's life and time's course, to the celebration of which this stanza is devoted. "This Dial new" defines emblematically the beauties of the mutable world as they are represented by the garden. Rather than a "pretty device" with goatsbeard and chickweed opening from hour to hour on schedule, "this Dial new" is the garden of the earth, which the Creator has given to fallen man in lieu of "that happy Garden-state."

"This Dial new" is a metaphor which continues, follows out, an equivalence which has been developed in the preceding stanzas. It takes its place rhetorically and logically in a poetic discourse which has established a metaphoric relationship between this garden and Eden. It is precisely the rhetorical character of the allegorical metaphor which is not so well appreciated as that of the usual "metaphysical" conceit. In modern critical judgment there is a sophisticated understanding of that operation of wit by which the details of a particular object or scene—real or imagined—define and dramatize a thought or feeling. Modern criticism celebrates the skill, backed by the resources of irony and paradox, with which ideas, more or less abstract, are reconciled with images, more or less concrete. We admire the concision and speed of such images. But there is less appreciation of what is demanded in reading continued metaphor or metaphor which continues a complex equivalence. Compare, for instance, the reading of "this Dial new" as a floral horologue with our response to:

> My vegetable Love should grow
> Vaster than Empires, and more slow.

We hear the resonances that make it witty, the allusion to the vegetable soul which results in the counterbalancing of metaphysics and horticulture, the equivalence of personal passion and the history of states. We are saved from literalizing (seeing parsnips and turnips) by our awareness of the place the image has in the catalogue of hyperboles which makes up the opening of "To His Coy Mistress." Since the rhetorical character of the image is clear, we do not chide Marvell for a lack of taste nor are we tempted to stop the poem for a symbol chase. If the rhetorical character of "this Dial new" is understood, it will be no more visualized than "the Garlands of repose." "This Dial new" can thus become the instrument of our conception of Marvell's garden as another Eden.

The habit of mind which allowed men to conceive of the "Book of Nature" survived in Marvell's time. His image of "this Dial new" is properly read, I would argue, as a variant of that great and abiding trope: we read this dial and learn the life of time. The conceptual resonance of the figure is not a matter of the history of taste and style only but of the history of ideas.

To determine what was familiar to the audience of the past is perhaps the primary task of the historian of ideas who has turned his attention to poetry. But the investigation of highly particular ideas has sometimes seemed more important than the exploration of forms in which general conceptions were expressed.[4] For instance, the complications of judicial

---

[4] C. S. Lewis once observed in the course of a witty discussion of the Stock Response that some critics "talk as if improvement of our responses were always required in the direction of finer discriminations and greater particularity; never as if men needed responses more normal and more traditional than they now have " (*A Preface to 'Paradise Lost'* [London, 1942], p. 54). If the critical method by which we seek to define the nature of that "philosophical conception" which laid hold on Marvell's mind and imagination is confined on the one hand to the cataloguing of allusions and the labeling of images and on the other to the listing of specific notions which, it is alleged, he "must have"

astrology—the study of the positions of heavenly bodies in relation to earthly events—are of less importance, I think, to our understanding of Marvell's poems than the conception of "the stars which were necessary to the creation of Time," as it is put in the myth of creation recorded in the *Timaeus*. The concept of time's relation to fate and nature is given form in the most vital metaphors of Western thought. "The visible world and the relation of its parts is the dial plate of the universe" is a metaphor defining the world in terms of its temporality which we would not be surprised to find in Ralegh or Hooker or Blake, and we are not surprised to find Emerson quoting it from Swedenborg. The reader alert to the fundamental and universal concepts to which such radical metaphors give form can, if he hears the voice of allegory, discern their presence in the emblems and symbolic narratives of Marvell's poetry.

Metaphoric seeing is itself a conceptual act; the imagination working on radical, received metaphors is allegorical. Marvell reflects on natural scenes and on the words which have described them in a thousand poems, creating from these pictures and the old names new metaphors, emblems of his story of the soul's temporal life. His ideas are not independent of these metaphors; the ideas which inform his poetry are metaphorically conceived. To explore metaphor is thus to discover meaning; indeed, the philosophic insights offered by Marvell's poetry are often themselves incidental to his exploration of

---

had in mind, our appreciation of his poetry will not be advanced. The studied opinion of one editor that Marvell remained unimpressed by the scientific revolution of his day is not supported by the evidence offered, that though Marvell mentions microscopes, he takes fairies seriously. Unfortunately, Marvell's biography is not particularly helpful in the definition of his attitudes toward the life of his time; nor can philosophical influence be adduced by listing the books he "must have" seen on the parlor table, as it were, at Appleton House. Postulating or proving identifiable sources is, in any case, of less importance in the recovery of meaning than is the determination of fundamental assumptions.

language. The allegorical imagination sees the world meta-
phorically, acknowledges metaphors as they unfold in the
world. An appreciation of Marvell's metaphors is thus a pre-
requisite to understanding the philosophical conception of the
role assigned to the human spirit in the great drama of human
existence which laid hold on his mind and imagination.

Allegorical Metaphor

The habit of mind which allegory requires is not radically
different from that required by all figurative language. The
allegorical imagination creates metaphors which we must read
as we do all poetry. The essential rationale for all of man's
symbolic forms, including, of course, language itself, is that
the mind creates of every thing a symbol for that *kind* of
thing.[5] That the concept dwells in the percept defines the
nature of language as much as it describes the foundation for
rational thought. "Symbolization and consciousness," Owen
Barfield has written, "are simultaneous and correlative."[6] We
take it as a matter of course that this is true with regard to
things or creatures. One lamb is like another; it is representa-
tive of "lambness." And because a single lamb participates in
"lambness," it can be significant: its appearance, its attitude,
its character—what we make of it—is meaningful. A lamb is
white, and therefore "pure"; awkward, and therefore vul-
nerable; skittish and dumb and easily lost, and thus prey to
danger. The lamb can be a natural symbol of that-which-is-
innocent and therefore of innocence. But as it is the word that
enables us to conceive of the lamb as representative, so too it
is language whereby the range of more complex connotations
can be evolved and stored and transmitted.

The fact of mind which provides the rationale for language,

[5] See Susanne K. Langer, *Philosophy in a New Key* (Cambridge,
Mass., 1942), esp. Chap. X, "The Fabric of Meaning."
[6] "The Meaning of the Word 'Literal,'" in *Metaphor and Symbol*,
ed. L. C. Knights and Basil Cottle (London, 1960), p. 54.

that correlation of symbol-making and consciousness, is thus the ground of metaphor, which is our means of conceiving the fundamental facts of our experience. Metaphor creates the reality we know most profoundly. Allegory takes as a point of departure not "experience," not "life," but the symbols which language provides. It was an interpretive method before it was a mode of composition. Allegory is a reading of experience as it has been formed by mythic metaphor and by the conventions of language. The mind plays upon these mythic metaphors which, as rudimentary classifications, allow us to conceptualize the representative character of an act, an object, a scene: allegory is, as Roger Hinks wrote, essentially "the product of philosophic reflexion."[7] Allegory allows us to classify in terms not simply of appearance or function or of immediate feeling but in terms of concept.

The allegorical metaphor stands at a further remove from that reality which mythic metaphor has formed; it is, as it were, a meta-metaphor.[8] Creating a ratio of image to concept, the allegorical metaphor establishes an equivalence between an idea and an act, a scene, an object, a person. This equivalence generates a kind of wheeling, a circularity, but it remains an equivalence; it is not an identity.

The continued metaphor of the opening stanzas of "Upon Appleton House" is illustrative. It derives from the mythic identity of a man and his house, of spirit and habitation. Taking the conventional figures of speech in which this fundamental "figure of thought" has been expressed, Marvell deliberately literalizes the symbolic and symbolizes the literal, juggling architectural, mathematical, and physical terms with those of moral philosophy, punning his way to a witty statement of the equivalence of Fairfax and Appleton House. It is comic here, but the operation of the allegorical imagination is

[7] *Myth and Allegory in Ancient Art* (London, 1939), p. 4.

[8] Hinks speaks of the allegorical mode of thought and expression as a "paramythology" (p. 62).

the same as in other passages in "Upon Appleton House" where Marvell sets forth such equivalences with a high seriousness.

> *Humility* alone designs
> Those short but admirable Lines,
> By which, ungirt and unconstrain'd,
> Things greater are in less contain'd.
> Let others vainly strive t'immure
> The *Circle* in the *Quadrature!*
> These *holy Mathematicks* can
> In ev'ry Figure equal Man.
>
> Yet thus the laden House does sweat,
> And scarce indures the Master great:
> But where he comes the swelling Hall
> Stirs, and the *Square* grows *Spherical*;
> More by his *Magnitude* distrest,
> Then he is by its straitness prest:
> And too officiously it slights
> That in it self which him delights.
>
> (Stanzas 6-7)

Margoliouth's comment on "the *Square* grows *Spherical*" is as follows: "The roof of the hall was 'spherical.' Cf. the cupola in the quotation from Markham, supra. ['The central part of the house was surmounted by a cupola.']" His assumption seems to be that Marvell is working from the image which the actual manor house presents to his eye, exploiting an actual shape to get a very fanciful idea. But cogency does not depend on our having a visual image of Appleton House in mind. The "*Square* grows *Spherical*" probably derives not from the architectural details of Appleton House but from the implicit suggestions of the metaphor of the anthropomorphic house, which in turn is based not upon appearance but upon idea. (Just so, the cartoonist who drew the famous sketch of

New York's City Hall huffing and puffing, twisting and swelling upon the entrance of Mayor La Guardia—and subsiding as he exits—worked not from the architectural features of that building but from the concept of explosive energy which the mayor had come to represent.) To read "cupola" for "the *Square* grows *Spherical*" is to settle for whimsy.

Stanzas 1 through 9 are based on the concept of "equality" between the virtue of humility and unpretentious architecture. The description of the house, developed in figures drawn from geometry and the art of building ("square" is an architectural as well as a geometrical term), culminates in the lines declaring that the equivalence holds not only between virtue and architecture but between these and Lord Fairfax: "These *holy Mathematicks* can/ In ev'ry Figure equal Man." In the second stanza quoted, "Yet thus" signals a surprise: the implications of "ev'ry Figure" equaling "Man" will be dramatized. The operation of wit is to allow the metaphor to come to life: i.e., the deep-rooted correspondence between man and house will be taken literally. Physical and mathematical figures are counterpointed. Even though "ungirt" and "unconstrained," the "*Square*" sweats and swells, scarcely enduring "the *Master* great." (Those who read "cupola" would logically be led to assume that this is a reference to damp and sweating walls in a house built near a river.) And the figure of the spherical square reverses the earlier figure of "the *Circle* in the *Quadrature*." Mere earthly mathematics struggles vainly with the ancient problem set for plane figures; "these *holy Mathematicks*" undertake really difficult problems and with witty geometry solve them.

The physical relevance of the quadrature is less important than the pun it yields when Marvell uses the figure in ridiculing Mr. Bayes (his name for Bishop Parker in *The Rehearsal Transpros'd*) for the limitations of his academic self-interest, his narrowness of vision, etc.: ". . . coming out of the confinement of the square-cap and the quadrangle into the open air, the world began to turn round with him, which he imagined, though it were his own giddiness, to be nothing less than the quadrature of the circle." To the self-centered habitué of the quadrangle, that small world of the university,[9] "the open air" —that is, the real world, spacious, encompassing, "circular"— seems but another square. Mr. Bayes reduces the world as Lord Fairfax engrandizes the house. The quadrangle can figure forth either humility or dogmatism, but in either case, wit is a response to the metaphor itself.

There is no more characteristic aspect of Marvell's style than this witty responsiveness to language. Metaphors grow from one another, echo and reecho. Symbolic phrases come to life; actualities become translated into figures but then will suddenly rejoin the green world. There is frequent commerce across the semantic border and the reinforcement of idea and image is mutual. Like all important aspects of style, this instability—the shifting balance of particular and general, idea and image—has metaphysical significance. Observing that "the proleptic use of metaphor (the unapparent movement from the metaphoric to the literal) and the use of the converse are among the defining traits of Marvell's poetry," Geoffrey Hartman declares that such metaphors are "the signatures of a profoundly eschatological mind."[10] This "eschatological" motive is offered as the explanation for the "precarious realm" which Marvell's shifting metaphors create. The judgment seems to me misleading: eschatology looks to the end, looks beyond time, but Marvell looks to the green world as the scene of the recreation of eternity. His metaphors are "signatures" of a mind profoundly engaged in the world of temporality, which is indeed a "precarious realm" since mutability holds sway there. But Marvell's "proleptic" use of metaphor,

[9] Cf. "The Mower Against Gardens" for a comparable expression of scorn: "He first enclos'd within the Gardens square/ A dead and standing pool of Air."

[10] "Marvell, St. Paul, and the Body of Hope," *ELH*, XXXI (1964), 188.

like other aspects of his style, serves his conviction not only that man's life is full of "pitiful change" but that the immutable can be imitated, a motive foreign, I should think, to the eschatological mind. Thus Marvell's hyperbole is appropriate to the definition of the immeasurable;[11] pun and paradox are nets he casts to capture the ambiguities of incarnation; his symbolic narratives trap the elusive particularity of experience. The proleptic metaphor is best understood as a signature of a mind alert to the significances of things, of an active imagination involved in discovering the soul of reality in its mutable forms. It has an epistemological rather than an eschatological importance and is to be understood, I think, as a defining quality of a mind free in its inquiry and creative in its action.[12]

This "proleptical" character of metaphor—its instability, the circularity of first and second terms, the convertibility of tenor and vehicle—is a sign of mythic inheritance. In mythic ideation, thing and thing signified are indistinguishable and inseparable. In allegorical metaphor, identification is reborn as equivalence; ambiguity is thus assured. Wit plays with this uncertainty, creating from the equivalents new equations. The profound meanings of mythic conceptions are, as it were, spelled out in allegorical metaphor. The complexity of the referent—the multiplicity of meaning—is another sign of the development from radical figures. Thus the discursive nature of the allegorical mode has a twofold significance: it is *narrative*, as myths are, and it is *conceptual*, as myths, in their special way, are.

The kind of complexity represented by the equivalences created by allegorical metaphor in Marvell's poems is often misconceived. The equivalences derive from radical figures of

[11] Marvell's hyperbole stands in contrast to that figure as it is employed by the *libertin* poets. Odette de Mourgues comments: "The precieux's use of hyperbole is . . . characteristic of their wish to escape not only the complexity of reality but reality itself" (*Metaphysical, Baroque, and Precieux Poetry* [Oxford, 1953], p. 127).

[12] See Appendix, Note 1: "Prolepsis" and the Allegorical Imagination.

thought and their character is determined by the narrative in which they figure, the narrative which they create. Although the specialized use of an image and the development of conventions are legitimately the subject of historical inquiry, such historicism is misapplied in the assessment of allegorical metaphor if it is not held in check by a strict attention to context. "Quadrature" does not simply mean one thing or another, nor does it gather ambiguities *ad libitum*. The strictness of the square may suggest either humility or dogmatism, depending on the role the figure plays in the discourse. Such commonplaces have been neglected or forgotten in recent Marvell criticism.

Allegory and Myth

If Renaissance images do not float on the surface of the text like lilies (the phrase is Don Cameron Allen's), neither do they stare back at us like hieroglyphics which we can decode only by a study of literary forebears. Marvell's allusions are occasionally obscure: "the Black-bag of your Skin" has to be explained; the Lesser Ajax and Jubal have to be firmly identified; the nature of comets should be explored. Other obscurities are merely lexical: hewel, match, deodand, planisphere, saies. The destructive misreadings to which Marvell's poems have been subjected arise most frequently from a misconception of the relation of tone or manner to subject matter and of the relationship a figure bears to its referent, the result of reading metaphors wrenched from their setting. It is the logic of the metaphor which is thus destroyed and, with it, the poem's form.

In his learned study of the metaphoric tradition in the poetry of the English Renaissance, Professor Allen cites in a discussion of the water-meadow section of "Upon Appleton House" the floods which in Latin poetry represent civil strife.[13]

[13] *Image and Meaning: Metaphoric Traditions in Renaissance Poetry* (Baltimore, 1960), pp. 130-32.

Their relevance to Marvell's description is a debatable point, a question of interpretation. But when this critic argues that the wave as a metaphor of battling "begins" in classical literature, this is quite another matter. "The flood metaphor," he writes, "really begins with the fifth book of *The Iliad*." Does it not, rather, "begin with" language? Of the figure of the warrior/ reaper, of war as a harvest, Professor Allen writes that it "first appeared in the *Argonautica* of Apollonius of Rhodes." But the extended simile of war/harvest which he cites in examples from Latin literature grows from a verb (*metere*) which has both "to mow" and "to cut down, to strike off" as meanings. The most violent expression of destruction is the act of cutting. The one who cuts is the destroyer. Man cuts his wheat; Death cuts man. We are harvested at Death's command by the reaper War. The conception of war as a harvest is as old as the word for cutting-destroying.

Professor Allen's analysis of the figure of the mower continues: "To the metaphors of classical antiquity we must add those of Christian provenance, the reaping angel of the Revelation and the scriptural comparison of man to grass. The figure is now a cliché, but it was fresh enough for Marvell when he made it into allegory." The point essential for the historian of images to make here, it seems to me, is that for as long as men have cut their grain with scythes, every poet, every novelist, every painter has been free to rediscover the enormous vitality of the metaphor of Death the reaper, of Time the harvester, and to re-present it to an audience which could share the experience from which the metaphor springs. These figures which derive from man's life in nature—the sea of time, the fire of love, the harvest of death, and so forth— have histories because they are part of language and hence part of literature. But as root metaphors, they are figures of thought, means by which man has conceived the primal facts of his life. If we comprehend it at all—and of course that will require an imagination nourished by literature for most of us—the figure of Death as a reaper will be as fresh to us as it was to Marvell. This fundamental misconception concerning the alleged dullness of basic images (and attitudes and plots) derives from an historicist view of literature by which the grand original is seen to succumb progressively, as it were, to corruption and debasement.

A variant of this historicism is the notion that an image *is*, essentially, what it began as in the psychic life of the author (or of the reader). The quasi-Freudian reduction of meaning, regardless of the context, to that one theme with which all expression begins is particularly unhampered in reading allegory because, as C. S. Lewis remarked, Freudian representation is allegorical; it only remains to identify all figures in all allegories with the characters of the Oedipal plot.[14] We need to be reminded, as Freudian insights do remind us, that myths and poems begin with the stuff of unverbalized experience. Time with his scythe stands beyond all the figures of destruction not as a literary forebear but as an archetype of the imagination, not as a memory trace but as a mythic apprehension. He is, so to speak, the cause that strength is in those other equivalent images; but this is not to say that we therefore import him into any poem in which cutting or devouring or running appears. Such root metaphors derive from that complex of perception, attitude, and act which is the moment of naming.[15] Beyond "sources," psychological or literary, beyond tradition, we must look to experience as it is given form in language. The flow of water and the flow of time, for instance, have defined one another for as long as there has been language— and there is language because they could and did so define one another. The tonality in which the voice of allegory sounds must be invented afresh with every poem, play, epic,

[14] *The Allegory of Love* (Oxford, 1936), p. 61n.
[15] See Ernst Cassirer, *Language and Myth*, trans. S. K. Langer (New York, 1942), esp. Chap III, "Language and Conception," and Chap. VI, "The Power of Metaphor."

story. But the tropes themselves, by the ordered and expectable course they follow and by the picture they compose, express our experience of life as it is formed by language itself. Myth underlies allegory; it is the source from which the fountain of meaning springs.

Allegory is analogue: it presents to our understanding equivalences, not the original mythic conception itself. Thus, the mowers in the harvest scene of "Upon Appleton House" are not mythic figures, though what they are doing is described in terms of a mythic metaphor. The subject of Marvell's description is not war as a harvest of Death but mowing seen as a battle. Marvell's harvesters are not symbols of the New Model Army, but are described as if they were presenting a pageant in which the principal role the actors take is that of warriors. Marvell describes the harvest as a battle scene within the frame of another metaphor, the masque of nature. It is essential to the proper reading of the passage to understand that the harvest/war is, as it were, filtered through the figure of the harvest/masque. Filter or frame, there is a mediation which cannot be ignored. Interpretation of poetry in the allegorical mode requires something other than exegetical skill in reading figures in the context of their history. The semantics of allegorical metaphor demands attention to the narrative context as well. Allegory, be it remembered, is *continued* metaphor. The narrative matrix cannot be discounted in interpreting particular scenes or persons or acts. Narration is, of course, often checked —by confrontation in which the dialogue is mysteriously general; by soliloquy or frankly open address to the audience, which, like an aria, interrupts the story. Such static moments, I believe, are emblematic in character. An emblem is a narrative moment from which the particular occasion has, to various degrees, been refined.[16] Seen at a distance, the irrelevant details

---

[16] The degree of refinement may be quite extreme. The various forms of the Cross would appear as abstract designs to anyone who did not know how to read the symbol out into narrative form. Nonobjective

obscured, a huntsman stalking, a bold pirate boarding, a child weeping all become speaking pictures, shapes which say the meaning of what the figures do; and what they do tells what they are. The resultant abstractness facilitates application; indeed, it creates application. Nevertheless, an emblem has an actual particularity, and the history of which it is a transfiguration is still resonant in the image. It is, after all, a turtle which makes haste slowly (*Semper festina lente*) and he is quite certainly there, wrinkles and all. But it is not just the heavy shell, not the dull eyes that tell: it is "turtleness," the slow pace of perseverance.

Problems that arise in the analysis of the static allegorical figure are generally not more than troublesome. Often in the service of a political or religious cause, and always yielding to a nameable concept reached over the bridge of narrative, such figures lend themselves very satisfactorily to the kind of analysis which will happily settle for labeling. Even the immensely complicated, subtle, and abstruse symbolism of a *Melencolia I* will yield, finally, to inquiry which is aimed at the discovery of identifications. Panofsky's analysis of Dürer's engraving is not different in kind from the analysis we undertake as we explain to a child the significance of those accoutrements of Justice standing in front of the courthouse. The iconography of emblematic figures may inspire cleverness, but an emblem does not generally require complex rendering. It is meant to be explicit, or it is meant to be baffling to anyone who hasn't the key.

---

art is often explained by artist and interpreter alike in terms which are fundamentally temporal. The ultimate interdependence of spatial and temporal modes Roger Hinks describes in his explanation of Orphic and Olympian forms.

The emblem should not be confused with the rebus, as it is by Hartman ("Marvell, St. Paul, and the Body of Hope," p. 187). A rebus is a visual pun akin to such symbols as Dickensian names, wordplay made visible. The semantics of the rebus is absolutely different from that of the emblem, which always has a temporal ambience.

The failure to evaluate properly the narrative context which provides a vitally important check on the meaning of symbol, picture, emblem, the failure to appreciate the temporal aspect of allegory has led to such misconceptions as that allegory is essentially the expression of mystical vision; or that it is essentially hierarchical in structure. Or that the particular content of an allegory is made up of systematic allusions and that if it is meaningful at all it is therefore meaningful word by word. But the essential character of allegory is its instability, the tendency of emblem to explode into story, the tendency of narrative to freeze into attitude. This instability, like the proleptic character of the allegorical metaphor, is the effect of the recreation of mythic identification in the form of equivalence, the realization of the inherent ambiguity of mythic conception.[17]

If we read an emblem as a narrative fragment, if we keep in mind the temporal dimension of allegory, we may be closer to an understanding of how it is in this form that the particular participates in the general, of how the one becomes the many. For it is the becoming, the opening out into time

[17] It is the essential ambiguity of the radical metaphor which is responsible in part for subsequent confusions and misconceptions. Christine Brooke-Rose remarks that "it seems clear that no definition of metaphor can exclude confusion, errors or poetic gropings" (*The Grammar of Metaphor* [London, 1958], p. 13n.). On this score, see Walker Percy's entertaining and astute essay, "Metaphor as Mistake," *Sewanee Review*, LXVI (1958), 79-99.

Both the Greek *Kronos* and the Roman *Saturnus* are associated with knives, castration, and with the harvest. Whether a "mistake" or not, the identification suggests that the figures of destruction cited by Allen are also, in a sense, representations of time, because man's conception of his temporal existence is inextricably bound up with his experiences of the cycles of growth and decay, of seedtime and harvest. For a detailed discussion of the classical ambience of Kronos and Saturn (the stress is on the radical antitheses of character in each), see Raymond Klibansky, Erwin Panofsky, and Fritz Saxl, *Saturn and Melancholy* (New York, 1964), pp. 134-35.

that marks the dramatic apprehension of ultimate reality which it is the central purpose of allegory to discover and reveal.

"On a Drop of Dew"

The rhetorical and metaphysical character of the allegorical metaphor is especially well represented in Marvell's "On a Drop of Dew": the emblematic and narrative modes are counterbalanced; the elaboration of the figure is surely a "product of philosophic reflexion"; the imagery has a circular logic. Between the dewdrop and timeless, spiritual beauty there is a mythic identity which is drawn out into an allegorical equivalence; the Drop of Dew is a guise of the soul confronting its fate, which is time.

> See how the Orient Dew,
> Shed from the Bosom of the Morn
>   Into the blowing Roses,
> Yet careless of its Mansion new;
> For the clear Region where 'twas born
>   Round in its self incloses:
>   And in its little Globes Extent
> Frames as it can its native Element.
>   How it the purple flow'r does slight
>   Scarce touching where it lyes,
>   But gazing back upon the Skies,
>   Shines with a mournful Light;
>   Like its own Tear,
> Because so long divided from the Sphear.
>   Restless it roules and unsecure,
>   Trembling lest it grow impure:
>   Till the warm Sun pitty it's Pain,
> And to the Skies exhale it up again.
>   So the Soul, that Drop, that Ray
> Of the clear Fountain of Eternal Day,
> Could it within the humane flow'r be seen,

Remembring still its former height,
Shuns the sweat leaves and blossoms green;
And, recollecting its own Light,
Does, in its pure and circling thoughts, express
The greater Heaven in an Heaven less.
In how coy a Figure wound,
Every way it turns away
So the World excluding round,
Yet receiving in the Day.
Dark beneath, but bright above:
Here disdaining, there in Love,
How loose and easie hence to go
How girt and ready to ascend.
Moving but on a point below,
It all about does upward bend.
Such did the Manna's sacred Dew destil;
White, and intire, though congeal'd and chill.
Congeal'd on Earth: but does, dissolving, run
Into the Glories of th' Almighty Sun.

"See how": the opening words of the poem fuse the emblematic and the narrative modes. While it is admiringly described, as its history is being set forth, the dewdrop is recreated as the emblem of the soul. This equivalence of the dewdrop and the soul, explicitly announced only at one point (line 19), is developed in terms which we discover to be reciprocal. Even the purple flower, the most clearly actualized detail in the description of the dewdrop, is echoed by the "humane flow'r." The ground of reciprocity shifts continually (proleptically) from the physical to the metaphysical and back again. The dewdrop, "Scarce touching where it lyes," is "careless of its Mansion new"; and the soul, "Remembring still its former height,/ Shuns the sweat leaves and blossoms green." A term such as "mansion" provides a sounding board for the poem's conceptual resonance, establishing the equivalence of the dewdrop and the embodied soul. Both are alien to the earth, fearful of earthly corruption, yearning for home. The dewdrop's "Mansion new" is the purple flower; a "mansion" for the constellations is a station in their course through the zodiac: the shared term reminds us that the dewdrop is sister to the stars. And by its logic and rhetorical character, the allegorical metaphor "mansion" provides a gloss for the "former height" of "the Soul, that Drop, that Ray." It is because there are many mansions in heaven that the soul, like the dewdrop, can be "careless" of earthly beauty, much as the "Resolved Soul" is contemptuous of the bounties of "Created Pleasure."

In lines 27-36, the interpenetration is complete. "World," for instance, belongs to both dewdrop and the soul and is both literal and abstract, the physical balancing the metaphysical in an allegorical valence. Marvell's famous observation of "the hatching Thrastle's shining Eye" is framed with no greater care than is his description of the phenomenon of the dewdrop's changing appearance: its darkness when viewed from above, with the ground showing through, and its lightness when the perspective is heavenward. And yet the description is equally appropriate for the soul in its temporal state. Since light and darkness have secure connotations (they are mythic metaphors), this careful statement of particularity can reveal spiritual truth. So, too, the sphere of the dewdrop describes the essential limits of the soul's form, that is, its earthly point of rest and its heavenly reach: "Moving but on a point below,/ It all about does upwards bend." As the dewdrop by its perfect (spherical) form imitates its "native Element," so the embodied soul expresses its thoughts, pure and circling like the dewdrop, "The greater Heaven in an Heaven less."

The theme of the opposition to time afforded by contemplation has many variations in Marvell's poetry. In this great poem, alienation rather than accommodation is the keynote. The soul in all its guises (and the principal ones are to be found in "On a Drop of Dew") feels the distance from its heavenly home: the philosopher-poet whose contemplations of heaven imitate heaven; the would-be traveler-pilgrim whose journey is not done until time stops; the warrior prepared to ascend to that "Region beyond Time,"[18] just as the dewdrop waits to be drawn up to the skies by the force of the sun; and the lover, "here disdaining, there in Love." The dewdrop's gazing back upon the skies expresses the visionary character shared by the philosopher, the traveler/pilgrim/warrior, and the lover. Their passion for the "native Element" is the ground of their equivalence.

The presence of the dewdrop is described in terms which establish a metaphysical referent. These allegorical metaphors create a character for the dewdrop, just as they lend an appearance to the soul. Thus from the natural beauty of the dewdrop is fashioned an emblem of the hidden, fearful, yearning soul. The couplets which close the poem introduce a third term, "Manna's sacred dew," which is like a motto for the emblem. It sacramentally unites the soul and the dewdrop by a prophecy which gathers up the narrative discourse, moving beyond time. That recapitulation, for all its gravity, sounds less like a prayer than a madrigal. It is the music in which the voice of allegory sounds the poet's love for the truth.

Irony and Resolution

If the operation of the allegorical imagination is especially clear in "On a Drop of Dew," it is perhaps true that a careful reading of that poem can be helpful in assessing in other poems Marvell's "way of understanding"—one of Rosemond Tuve's most helpful definitions of the allegorical mode.[19] For it is not the complications of Marvell's ideas or the history of the images that he seizes upon with which a reader of his

---

[18] Cf. "An Horatian Ode Upon Cromwell's Return from Ireland," ll. 33-34 and "The Unfortunate Lover," ll. 7-8.

[19] *Images and Themes in Five Poems by Milton* (Cambridge, Mass., 1962), p. 109.

poetry should, I think, be concerned, but rather with the name and nature of his general conceptions, with his way of understanding, his way of using the received metaphors of Western thought.

The allegorical imagination is essential not only to the metaphysical conception of the soul's temporal life, but also to the description of certain problems of a social and political nature. The reason is that when social and political questions are entertained as variants of religious and philosophical questions, the language of metaphor is indispensable; for Marvell, the metaphysical and the political, the religious and the philosophical are mutually defining categories of understanding. Whatever is of philosophical interest to him has inevitably a religious dimension and all political conceptions have for him, as for his time, profound metaphysical implications. To paraphrase Marvell's description of the civil war, whichever was at the top of his poetry—history or philosophy—the other was at the bottom. And religion is everywhere the axletree of that polarity. The meaning of history, the definition of nature and of love, and the revelation of grace are all expressed by means which the allegorical imagination makes available to consecutive discourse. The mythic image and the visionary narrative are poetic forms by which the philosophical conception of the soul's temporal life can be set forth in terms of the dramatic confrontation of the Resolved Soul—as lover, as hero, philosopher, shepherd, the poet himself—and his fate. Man's life is the soul's journey, the soul's battle, the soul's tranquility: the temporal life of the soul is a life in nature. But it is, as well, a life in history. And precisely because the allegorical imagination can give form to the notion of permanence, it is well-fitted to describe the nature of change, the course of history. Entertaining a double perspective, the poet thus enjoys the opportunity for an "ironic" judgment of history, for the celebration of the hero as well as the acclamation of Providence. Because the allegorical imagination offers the means of conceiving of the opposition of two realms of being, it can express complex notions of causality. By identifying logical and temporal priorities,[20] Marvell can create emblems and symbolic narratives through which to speak feelingly of such paradoxes as the love born of despair and impossibility, of the conjunction contingent upon opposition, of the annihilation which is creation, of the ruin which is birth.

In short, the allegorical imagination, deploying mythic ambiguity, is a mode of conception especially congenial to the ironic temper;[21] however, so much has been written of Marvell's detachment, his "ironic vision," his remarkable capacity to remain aloof, that it might be useful to stress the conviction that underlies the disinterest, for it is only an unquestioned fundamental assumption that can be the fertile ground of irony. Marvell's recognition of the inescapable ironies attendant upon the fact of matter's limiting spirit is the spur not only of humor but of definition and judgment. His critical spirit invigorates because it is confident, because it springs not from hatred but from despair, the only ground of action; not from resignation but from resolution. *Resolution* is the generative power as much of Marvell's acceptance of Cromwell as it is of the lover's recognition of the "rough strife" which is passion; or of the poet's definition of the love of his soul as the child of despair and impossibility; or of the Shepherd's discovery that grace is not to be reduced to "meer Morality." Love, heroic action, and contemplation are all

[20] See Kenneth Burke's discussion of the narrative and philosophical modes of discourse in *A Rhetoric of Motives* (New York, 1950), pp. 13-15.

[21] Ruth Wallerstein, among others, has written perceptively of Swift's debt to Marvell, finding in Swift's irony "a deep intellectual parallel, as well as a historical filiation, with Marvell's paradoxes, with Marvell's focus upon ethical intuition. And it is not fantastic to compare . . . Swift's symbolic use of the popular literary forms—project, traveller's tale, fable—to express his paradoxes with Marvell's use of the emblem image" (*Studies in Seventeenth Century Poetic* [Madison, 1950], p. 341).

modes of the mediating heart and mind, acts of the Resolved Soul confronting his fate, which is time. If separation is the condition, resolution is the predicate: the wedges that separate are the wedges that join. Marvell throughout his poetry confronts with resolute imagination the absolute contingency of freedom and necessity, transforming that philosophical conception into the drama, the "story," of the Resolved Soul.

CHAPTER II

Knowledge and Resolution

HE poet, Sidney tells us in *The Defense of Poesie*, surpasses as a teacher of moral virtue both the philosopher and the historian. They both instruct man, the one by precept, the other by example, "but both, not having both, do both halt." The "peerlesse Poet" performs both, "for whatsoever the *Philosopher* saith should be done, he gives a perfect picture of it by some one, by whom he presupposeth it was done, so as he coupleth the generall notion and the particuler example."[1]

Marvell surely had no such exalted sense of his role as poet. The personal or psychological motives for his composition remain entirely obscure, nor can we point to any poetic theory or aesthetic which he elaborated or even announced. There is no record in letter or reported conversation of Marvell's attitudes toward his art. We know only what Aubrey tells us: "He kept bottles of wine at his lodgeing, and many times he would drinke liberally by himselfe to refresh his spirits and exalt his Muse." Leishman's suggestion that he bought all the new books of verse upon his return from the Continent and sat down to see what he could do himself is as good (and as useful) a surmise as any. It is not to make up for the lack of a Marvellian theory of composition that I am suggesting that he creates characters, scenes, and stories which set forth a theme of moral and philosophical significance resounding in the major poems. In describing the action of Marvell's poetry in terms of an "allegorical imagination," I mean only to offer a critical hypothesis which can account for

[1] *The Complete Works of Sir Philip Sidney*, ed. Albert Feuillerat (3 vols.; Cambridge, Eng., 1923), III, 14.

certain traits, among them the coupling of "the generall notion with the particuler example."

Marvell accommodates the philosophical conception and the historical or particular instance, one to the other, by balancing emblem and narrative in continued metaphors. Thus the characters of his poems—some, like the Nymph and Damon, realized more dramatically than others—are symbolic figures; scenes are often brilliantly actualized, but they are all, as well, representative; the stories which unfold are narratives whose burden we may define in metaphysical terms. The allegorical imagination by so mediating between "the generall notion and the particuler example" assures the soul, whose existence is conceived metaphorically, a presence in the world we experience. Narration is an expressive form answering to the temporality of experience; emblem gives voice momentarily to the abstract. In Marvell's poems, the created picture is resonant with the history it bespeaks and the unfolding story discovers significance in the world of time.

In this chapter I will consider "The Nymph Complaining for the Death of Her Fawn," "The Coronet," "Bermudas," and the Cromwell poems in an attempt to analyze how, in these very different poems, allegorical metaphor in emblematic and narrative modes sets forth the soul's life in time, a continuing confrontation of fate. In "The Nymph," the particular example is displayed in a highlighted foreground, but Marvell offers a double perspective by which we may discover more of the significance of the Nymph's experience than it is given to her to understand. "The Coronet" tells of the Shepherd's discovery of the limitations of human power and the limitless power of grace; "Bermudas" sets forth God's will in history. In the Cromwell poems, the Resolved Soul in the person of the Puritan leader acts in freedom to make the Lord's will and the Lord's work his own. Action and discovery *take time;* they demand narrative. But whether the action is set in "a little Wilderness" or "in th' Oceans bosome," in "the Watry maze" of man's life or amongst the ruined works of time, the story that unfolds has a quiet constancy of meaning, for the allegorical imagination creates images that simultaneously present to us earth and heaven, eternity and time.

"The Nymph Complaining"

"The Nymph Complaining for the Death of Her Fawn" has a remarkable complexity of tone. The quickly established and consistently developed correspondence of personal feeling and moral quality makes it clear that the poem, so touching, is about more than the death of a pet. Discovering what this is has led critics to storm the magic circle guarding the poem's intention with generic definitions: it is the only major poem of Marvell's in the mode of direct address by someone other than a poet; it is a dramatic monologue; it is "pastoral," if not a pastoral; it is an epicedium; it is a complaint. Critics, asking persistently what is symbolized by the Nymph's complaint, have constructed one new poem after another, failing to return the image seized upon to its narrative setting, to the tale being told.[2]

[2] Douglas Bush suggests (in a pointedly casual way) that the poem may signify "an Anglican's grief for the stricken Church" (*English Literature in the Earlier Seventeenth Century* [Oxford, 1945], p. 161). The suggestion—it does not appear in the second edition, 1962—is carried to a ludicrous extreme by E. H. Emerson in "Andrew Marvell's 'The Nymph complaining for the Death of her Faun,'" *Études anglaises*, VIII, 2 (1955), 109. E. S. Le Comte asserts that "the overtones of the poem have to do with the Eden (or Nature) versus Civilization issue" ("Marvell's 'Nymph . . . ,'" *MP*, L [1952], 98). Leo Spitzer is amazed that everybody has overlooked the identification of the Nymph and Niobe ("Marvell's 'Nymph . . .': Sources versus Meaning," *MLQ*, XIX [1957] 232). Muriel C. Bradbrook's and M. G. Lloyd Thomas' claim that "the love of the girl for her fawn is taken to be the reflection of the love of the Church for Christ" (*Andrew Marvell* [Cambridge, Eng., 1940], p. 50) is the hare that started many hounds. Perhaps Karina Williamson has most helpfully recalled us to the essential character of the poem, that "it is somehow about more than the death of a pet, but that the [religious] overtones are intended

The lament is sounded both in the personal narrative of the Nymph's account of the fawn's life and in the epigrammatic contemplation of the meaning of that life and of the consequences of a cruel death. The Nymph is a girl suffering, speaking in fits and starts; she also calmly and wittily considers the nature of the fawn. There is a story to be told, a history to be reviewed, but the story evokes grave meditations and the history has more than a local significance. The dramatic presence of the maiden, the temporal character of her account, the fact that it is in progress during the death of the fawn, all strengthen the occasional element so that we cannot without violence to the whole of the poem neglect it. Indeed, it is the particular that leads unfailingly to the general: salutations of the dying beast and the remembrances of its life and manner become the stuff of metaphysical consideration. The discovery of the dying fawn is followed by a discourse on justice; the loving remembrance of the nursling leads to an account of the perfidious Silvio and the betrayal of trust; the lyrical account of the early days of the innocent, pure animal modulates to a hymn to beauty. The hyperbole which in every case sets its mark upon these meditations is the chief rhetorical means of suggesting a correspondence between the lowly and

---

as overtones" ("Marvell's 'The Nymph . . .': A Reply," *MP*, LI [1954], 268). That is essentially T. S. Eliot's view: ". . . Marvell takes a slight affair, the feeling of a girl for her pet, and gives it a connexion with that inexhaustible and terrible nebula of emotion which surrounds all our exact and practical passions and mingles with them" ("Andrew Marvell," in *Selected Essays* [New York, 1932], p. 259).

In recent articles, Geoffrey Hartman (" 'The Nymph Complaining for the Death of Her Fawn': A Brief Allegory," *Essays in Criticism*, XVIII [1968], 113-35) and Ruth Nevo ("Marvell's Songs of Innocence and Experience," *SEL*, V [1965], 1-21) have stressed the fact that the poem is a narrative, that the foreground and background signify different worlds of meaning. Although both critics attend to the symbolic nature of the story told, each tends to neglect the particulars in order to establish one identification or another, either of the fawn as a surrogate for Christ the comforter (Hartman) or the garden as the scene of the soul's contemplations (Nevo).

the high, between the mere animal and beauty and innocence. Thus the death of the fawn becomes the occasion for a monody on the death of innocence. The Nymph again and again in her lament sounds the note of a universal sadness, but she is returned to herself by the poet who though he sings of death, celebrates nonetheless that one death which is the subject of his poem. This counterbalancing is the manner we must tolerate if the poem is to be wholly enjoyed.

Literalism, rather than tolerance of counterbalancing, is, however, the more common response. It is the "nothing but" of the critic grown weary of the pursuit of the esoteric, unnatural, sinister, or (merely) clever significance. Thus Leo Spitzer dismisses the suggestion of religious overtones in the Nymph's exclamation "It had so sweet a Breath!" because he has found lines from du Bellay in which a healthy dog's sweet breath is acclaimed as a sign simply of its strength and soundness.[3] Of course, one of the chief delights poetry can provide is the exact and telling detail, but in allegorical writing, such images, exact as they may be, serve as well to body forth ideas. "Sweet breath" is in a family of images which symbolize the beauties of holiness (indeed, "sweet" is the adjective perhaps most frequently found in Puritan descriptions of the soul), so that to settle for a clean fawn's tooth is to settle for half the account.

But ignoring the symbolic referent is no more destructive of the balance of particular and general than that urge to which critics set to discover "sources" are prone, to identify an image divorced from its narrative context. Professor Allen tells us that the Nymph's garden is the *hortus mentis*.[4] In support of this contention, he is driven to assert that the " 'little wilderness' is not a wilderness at all." We need not, of course, picture a primeval thicket; we are meant to imagine a miniature representation of nature "pure and plain."

[3] "Marvell's 'Nymph . . .': Sources versus Meaning," p. 235.
[4] *Image and Meaning*, p. 107.

Marvell probably intends a witty allusion to that part of a garden which was deliberately kept in its natural state and which was called a "wilderness." The identification of the nymph's garden as the *hortus mentis* adds an unnecessary dimension, one which is not useful in accounting for the tone or particulars of the poem; and indeed, this identification renders the actual points of emphasis illogical.

The Nymph, whose "solitary time" and "idle Life" have been enlivened by the fawn, tells us of pleasures now forever gone. She describes the games they played, races and hide-and-seek.

> I have a Garden of my own,
> But so with Roses over grown,
> And Lillies, that you would it guess
> To be a little Wilderness.
> And all the Spring time of the year
> It onely loved to be there.
> Among the beds of Lillyes, I
> Have sought it oft, where it should lye;
> Yet could not, till it self would rise,
> Find it, although before mine Eyes.
> For, in the flaxen Lillies shade,
> It like a bank of Lillies laid.
> Upon the Roses it would feed,
> Until its Lips ev'n seem'd to bleed. . . .

The white fawn and the lilies (dulled to a flaxen shade by the brilliance of the animal's whiteness), the fawn's reddened lips and the roses: the remembered picture of the fawn lying amongst the flowers, nibbling them, becomes an emblem of the truth that the fawn was part of that garden, a secret, dearly loved part of the place the Nymph inhabits. "Of my own" reminds us that though the Nymph may be the daughter of a leading country family or of a shepherd, she is, as well, a woodland creature: she is as complex a figure as the fawn.

This garden, amid parks, fields, pastures, is hers, a preserve in which she is mistress, if not a presiding deity. But it is not her mind. The garden which is the *hortus mentis* is not secret and it is certainly not a wilderness! The point of that ancient image is that it suggests by the order that the garden imposes on wild nature the order of the mind's understanding. It is a symbol of man's ordering of his experience. Marvell seems quite clearly to stress here the privacy and innocence of the garden, its simplicity, not its design; its natural state, not its artful order.

There is comparable damage done to the integrity of a poem when the rehabilitation of mythic allusions is ignored and figurative description is confused with mystical metamorphosis. What happens when part of a myth is used descriptively? Transposed from the parent narrative, the mythic element becomes an allegorical metaphor standing at two removes from its subject. In Marvell's allusion to the Heliades, for instance, the referent is already a metaphor.[5] In the Nymph's evocative description of the fawn's tears, Marvell proceeds from nature to ritual to myth, each figure in the sequence supporting the others, becoming part of a new whole:

> See how it weeps. The Tears do come
> Sad, slowly dropping like a Gumme.

[5] Marvell's use of Ovid here is justified in ways which have not always been recognized in comment on the passage. Allen's implicit judgment is that Marvell is being "literary": "the Heliades are *brought into* the garden" (*Image and Meaning*, p. 113; italics mine). As trees, they are already there. When Empson writes (*Seven Types of Ambiguity* [Norfolk, 1947], p. 168), that "if you had expected . . . that Marvell had made the myth up . . . you would want the *brother* to be more relevant to the matter at hand," he leaves unremarked the fact that the brother is, in this context, as irrelevant as the unmetamorphosed Heliades. Marvell needs an analogy relatively free of sexuality; the loss of a brother strikes the right note in defining the relationship of the Nymph and her fawn. *Brotherlessness* is a state generalized enough to allow the Nymph to transfer her feelings of loss and to impute that feeling of being forsaken to the dying fawn.

So weeps the wounded Balsome: so
The holy Frankincense doth flow.
The brotherless *Heliades*
Melt in such Amber Tears as these.

The tears have not been changed into "liquid substances" nor are they "represented anthropomorphically";[6] it is the "Gumme" to which they have been compared which is so represented by Ovid. The "sad, slowly dropping" tears recall resin in appearance and the resin is in turn expressive, like them, of hurt, as it is expressive, in its slow, endless fall, of limitless grief. Ovid's trees are not wounded, but Marvell, as we should expect of him, insists upon the poignant nature of a tree's wounds; it is an act of mythopoeic imagination to transfer the animal's hurt to the tree. The tree's wound is a metaphoric bridge to the notion of the inarticulate pain which characterizes the holy, sacrificial suffering of a dumb and helpless being. Thus in the next figure, the rising smoke of incense is like the fawn's tears because it is the sign of sacrifice.[7] The mythic allusion takes its place with the other images of the sequence, deepening the significance of the tears by identifying the Nymph's grief and the fawn's hurt. Ovid's myth, already metaphor, has helped to widen the range of feeling conveyed.

The temporal pattern of the poem, as much as the counter-balancing of tones, accounts for Marvell's success in fusing the particular and the general. As the narrative draws to a close, the history done, we are brought back to the present and then the poem, increasingly emblematic, opens to the future. It concludes with a sculptural, pictorial image of a kind Marvell elsewhere employs as a grand and solemn ending to a fitful, personal, or highly graphic narrative. The Nymph, remembering their games, cries to the dying fawn, "vanish'd to/ Whether the Swans and Turtles go,"

[6] Spitzer, "Marvell's 'Nymph . . . ,'" p. 241.
[7] There is a similar cluster of images in "Eyes and Tears," stanza 11.

O do not run too fast: for I
Will but bespeak thy Grave, and dye.

The Nymph uses language appropriate to Niobe in describing her statue, as Spitzer notes.[8] She foresees that the statue will be humanized by weeping, a metamorphosis comparable to that bemusedly considered for the fawn, which might have become "Lillies without, Roses within." The hyperbole is appropriate to pastoral and works here as it does throughout the poem to suggest the boundless energy of youthful grief. If the fawn can be described in terms appropriate to the dying Christ, the Nymph can have her moment too. The homage the young girl pays is her willingness to die and, beyond that, the felt certainty that she will die of grief. "It seem'd to bless/ Its self in me": this is the central truth of the fawn's life with the Nymph, that they were bound by a mutual love which was at once a game and a sacrament. The statue is a vision of that identity, an emblem of the history of the Nymph and her fawn. The emblem's power thus to represent the historical even as it simultaneously transcends it is suggested by the fact that a seventeenth-century term for a sculptural group was "story."

The Nymph steps back into a mythic silence in which the story seems still to be happening. The lament, expressive of personal grief, dies in a symbol of grief. The statue functions like the close of a dramatic ballad, where the riderless horse or the bank, strewn with bodies, the lone woman in the castle tower or the red rose round the briar not only sums the whole of the story but symbolizes its deeper significance. We can read forward from the wounded Acis to the bloody stream

[8] He proceeds, however, to *identify* the Nymph and Niobe, leaving out of account the narration as a whole and misconstruing a metaphor, which represents an attitude, as the description of an actual change about to occur: "this warm life-blood" he takes as referring to the Nymph. Despite Legouis' corrective note ("Marvell's 'Nymph' . . . : A Mise au Point," *MLQ*, XXI [1960], 31), Spitzer's construction is being perpetuated, by Allen for one, who writes: "The Nymph . . . cries that even her own blood which flows from her broken heart, is also not enough" (*Image and Meaning*, p. 103).

becoming the fresh-flowing river; or we can look back from the river to the boy suffering mortal hurt: whether representative of river or boy, emblem makes the narrative immediate and present. And it is just this immediacy that makes manifest the universality of the theme. The Nymph's personal anguish becomes the agency of a universal feeling. Indeed, it is so from the first: "The Nymph Complaining for the Death of Her Fawn" is a poem whose particularity is so balanced with the figurative that we can call it "continued metaphor." The resonance we hear is the voice of allegory and it depends not on allusions to classical myth but on the characters and the story itself.

In "The Nymph Complaining" Marvell has created his own version of pastoral, a story with many elements of a mythic character: the broken taboo, the sacrifice of the innocent, the false lover, the woodland setting, the memorial which will symbolize the story and, of course, the totemic animal itself. But these elements do not any more than the allusions to Ovid account for the mythic dimension of the poem, which bears the same relation to mythic motif as the *Lied* bears to folk song. It is, we might say, an art-myth. Professor Allen has shown how ancient and honorable is the lineage of nymph, deer, and garden. Such genealogies can provide the literary reasons why gardens, for instance, are expressive. And the aura of significance an animal has, deriving in part from its literary existence, is one factor which can make it less a beast than a metaphor. Marvell, of all poets, would appreciate the ambience of his characters and their story. But to feel the immediacy of these images and, indeed, to understand their conceptual significance, we must return them to the story of which they are a part. We are concerned not with nymph, garden, fawn, but with a narrative in which the Nymph complains for the death of her fawn.

Innocence is, surely, the central truth of the Nymph's life. The Nymph and her fawn have lived in a world with which they are identified in a holy, sacramental unity. Discord is absent, because since Silvio's betrayal the Nymph has lived entirely in the present, from day to day—that is, virtually out of time. The freshness of the garden, the happiness of her life there recalls another of Marvell's poems of a strongly emblematic character. "The Picture of Little T. C. in a Prospect of Flowers":

> See with what simplicity
> This Nimph begins her golden daies!
> In the green Grass she loves to lie,
> And there with her fair Aspect tames
> The Wilder flow'rs, and gives them names. . . .

In time to come, Little T. C. will by her chastity defeat "the wanton Love." Nevertheless, she might herself become an early victim of that other tyrant, Death. By the end of the poem, the "simplicity" of these "golden daies" is denied: knowledge of fate is alone enough to kill innocence. The expectation of Death in such a setting is an attitude sharpened by—indeed, created by—the picture of Little T. C. in a prospect of flowers. This motif of Death encountering the "young beauty of the Woods," as congenial to the medieval temperament which created the *memento mori* as it is to the Romantic sensibility that produced "Der Tod und das Mädchen," makes manifest a mythic apprehension of the power of time and fate. The Nymph has had a warning: counterfeit Silvio should have been enough. But she has not understood that such betrayal is exemplary of our fateful lives. The Nymph has yet to suffer the knowledge, even with the death of her fawn, that the loss of beauty and innocence is the cruel necessity not of fortune but of fate. Still, a dawning sense of fatefulness seems to inform the determination of the Nymph to forgive, her promise to prevail with heaven to forget. (We may note that the murder is immediately not a matter for revenge nor, later, for atonement.) The Nymph grieves as innocents must, but her resolution to forgive only bespeaks a wisdom whose

44

comfort she can not yet enjoy. Thus the weighty significance of this incipient knowledge of fate is balanced by a compelling actuality of striking psychological validity, for is it not the most poignant characteristic of youth, this melancholy that weeps for dead pets and cruel elders and knows not that it weeps for "Death, Hell, and Sin/ That Adam's transgression involved us in"? Fate is a background for the sacrifice of the fawn, though it is we who are free to see it; the Nymph expatiates instead on the cruelty of the wanton troopers and of Silvio. Does the poem concern "a slight affair"? The nature of temporal life is not for the Nymph the subject of this complaint. But it may be for us, because the form of the poem is testimony that it was for Marvell.

"The Coronet"

"The Nymph Complaining for the Death of Her Fawn" tells Marvell's favorite story: temporal life necessarily incurs corruption; perfection cannot hold; fate demands sacrifice and sacrifice becomes beautiful. The theme of the confrontation of the soul and its fate sounds here in the voice of allegory which allows us to discover the nature of that confrontation, though for the Nymph it amounts only to a desire to escape from the world of suffering. The Nymph resolves to forgive, to remember, to commemorate, but her discovery of the necessities of fate is only nascent. The poignancy of the poem is to a degree dependent on our understanding of how much the Nymph has to learn;[9] the poem's metaphysical significance, too, lies in the discrepancy between experience and understanding. The Nymph is an innocent, but the Shepherd of "The Coronet" has been willfully ignorant. Expecting sacrifice to do

[9] One thing the Nymph must learn is the Christian duty of transcending grief. In a letter (printed in the 1681 folio) written in 1667 to Sir John Trott, whose son's death he commemorated with a Latin epigraph, Marvell analyzes the nature of grief in religious terms: "I know the contagion of grief, and infection of Tears, and especially when it runs in a blood. And I my self could sooner imitate then blame those innocent

the work of grace, he discovers, at a cost, the Christian mean-
ing of the opposition of the two orders of reality. The concept
of opposition was centrally important for Marvell; it had for
him profound political implications which were inescapably
religious as well, as this accusation directed toward Bishop
Parker attests: "your ignorance of divine and humane things
. . . makes you jumble them so together that you cannot
distinguish of their several obligations" (III, 393). In "The
Coronet," Marvell defines the "several obligations" in terms
provided by pastoral.

The voice of the poem is not that of Marvell speaking as
"Andrew Marvell, Poet and Puritan" but the voice of fallen
man seeking the means of salvation in the scheme of nature.
Critics (especially Professor Legouis) have read the poem al-
most as a *mea culpa* uttered by the conscience-stricken artist
in rejection of his art.[10] But Marvell nowhere exhibits any
degree of self-consciousness as an artist, or any interest in him-
self as a creator of beauty; he nowhere expresses any conflict,
pride, devotion, or fear concerning his art.[11] To ascribe to him

relentings of Nature, so that they spring from tenderness only and
humanity, not from an implacable sorrow. . . . But the dissoluteness
of grief, the prodigality of sorrow is neither to be indulg'd in a mans
self, nor comply'd with in others. . . . Upon a private loss . . . to be
impatient, to be uncomfortable, would be to dispute with God and beg
the question" (Margoliouth, II, 298).

[10] A notable exception is Joseph H. Summers, who writes: "When
we have understood what the 'prospect of flowers' implies, 'The Coro-
net' does not seem a churchly recantation of all Marvell valued, but an
artful recognition of the ultimate issues" ("Marvell's 'Nature,'" *ELH*,
XX, [1953], 134).

[11] Unless we wish to consider that "Upon an Eunuch: a Poet" (given
below in translation) is self-addressed. Supporters of Parker in the
controversy following publication of *The Rehearsal Transpros'd* made
slanderous charges against Marvell, among them the claim that he had
been castrated (Pierre Legouis, *Andrew Marvell: Poet, Puritan, Patriot*
[Oxford, 1965], p. 199). In view of Marvell's high-minded (and actually
very funny) contempt for certain remarks of Parker's which he consid-
ered (or pretended to consider) salacious, this countercharge could
have been expected. (A kind of literary McCarthyism has led a modern

these allegedly "Puritanical" attitudes toward beauty is unwarranted. "The Coronet" concerns a more fundamental antithesis than that of art and religion. Such an interpretation of the theme leaves out of account the action of the poem, and it is precisely the action that makes the object telling. For the Shepherd attempts to replace the crown of thorns with the garland, and that is a debasement of "Heavens Diadem."

The discursive, quasi-narrative form of the poem converts the garland to an emblem: the narrative follows the story of the Shepherd's discovery, as the creation and destruction of the emblematic garland represents it. The garland is beautiful and artful, but it is being used for purposes for which "mortal Glory" is inadequate because irrelevant. The poem asks, "Which is the coronet: the garland or the crown of thorns?" The Shepherd means the garland to supplant the crown of thorns; the question of motivation and purpose is central to the poem. The Shepherd seeks other means of redemption, but the Christian cannot substitute the garland for the crown of thorns: the coronet which is "Heavens Diadem" cannot be made of "mortal Glory." Only that which crowns the Cross can be the coronet: *no Cross, no crown.*[12]

Weaving anew headdresses once given in token of earthly

---

critic, who has allegorized the coy mistress as Marvell's muse, to repeat the allegations as "well-known" facts.)

It is conceivable that Marvell wrote this epigram for his own satisfaction, saving more effective answers for subsequent pamphlets.

Don't believe yourself sterile, although, an exile from women,
You cannot thrust a sickle at the virgin harvest,
And sin in our fashion. Fame will be continually pregnant by you,
And you will snatch the Nine Sisters from the mountain;
Echo too, often struck, will bring forth musical offering.

This and all other translations from Marvell's Latin poetry which I will cite are taken from William A. McQueen and Kiffin A. Rockwell, *The Latin Poetry of Andrew Marvell* (Chapel Hill, 1964).

[12] The scriptural epigraphs that William Penn chose for his work bearing this title could stand too for Marvell's poem: Luke 9:23 and 2 Tim. 4:7, 8.

love, the Shepherd thinks to turn from the profane to the sacred, much as the poet of "The Garden" turns from the worldly to the private.

> When for the Thorns with which I long, too long,
>> With many a piercing wound,
>> My Saviours head have crown'd,
> I seek with Garlands to redress that Wrong:
>> Through every Garden, every Mead,
> I gather flow'rs (my fruits are only flow'rs)
>> Dismantling all the fragrant Towers
> That once adorn'd my Shepherdesses head.
> And now when I have summ'd up all my store,
>> Thinking (so I myself deceive)
>> So rich a Chaplet thence to weave
> As never yet the king of Glory wore:
>> Alas I find the Serpent old
>> That, twining in his speckled breast,
>> About the flow'rs disguis'd does fold,
>> With wreaths of Fame and Interest.

The resounding pronoun—"*My* Saviours," "*my* Shepherdesses head," "*my* store," "*my*self,"—underlines the willed action of the sacrifice, for love has been transformed as it has been redirected. But it is a foolish delusion (and the present tense dramatizes the fact that it is recurrent), this notion that man can work out his own salvation without fear and trembling. The two parenthetical phrases reinforce one another: the deception is that the flowers will suffice. Marvell has brought to life a conventional metaphor, for "fruit" is the yield of God's grace. Not all of nature's store is fruitful of salvation, which is through grace and grace alone. God cannot be made part of the natural scheme, not even of the moral universe of mortal man. This is the Christian meaning of necessity and it depends on that careful distinction between grace and

48

morality which Marvell called "the most serious subject perhaps in all Christianity" (III, 412).

The narration is not continuous: the historical present yields to exclamation:

> Ah, foolish Man, that would'st debase with them
> And mortal Glory, Heavens Diadem!

and then to humble petition:

> Either his slipp'ry knots at once untie,
> And disentangle all his winding Snare:
> Or shatter too with him my curious frame:
> And let these wither, so that he may die,
> Though set with Skill and chosen out with Care.
> That they, while Thou on both their Spoils dost tread,
> May crown thy Feet, that could not crown thy Head.

The beauties of nature have their uses, as the lover of gardens and of women knows, but nature cannot yield the stuff of "Heavens Diadem," for the serpent is always there. The intention of substituting sacrifice for grace must itself be sacrificed, the act for which the destruction of the garland is an emblem. The Shepherd, be it noted, does not himself destroy his offering; he prays that Christ will untie, disentangle, or, realizing that it is a tinsel-winged and feeble Hope to expect such measures against Evil to be successful, that He will "shatter too with him my curious frame."[13] The poem tells of sacrificing sacrifice, a paradox by which is set forth the

---

[13] I doubt that the emphasis on the "Skill" and "Care" with which the "curious frame" has been fashioned is intended to suggest a perversion of nature comparable to the seductions of "Luxurious Man" which are held in contempt in "The Mower Against Gardens." The phrase "all my store" would suggest that it is the misuse of nature, whether "pure and plain" or artificialized, that is the object of the Shepherd's discovery. Marvell elsewhere shows no scorn for pictures made of feathers, which would certainly seem a grotesque "seduction." It is not imitation per se which he condemns, but the prideful intention that accompanies it.

yielding to Christ's power, the forsaking of the prideful attempt to use nature, the discovery of the "several obligations" of earth and heaven.

The political and religious significances of that theme are, as I have noted, inseparable. In his interpretation of the limits of civil and religious authority in *The Rehearsal Transpros'd*, Marvell again turns to the superior power of grace over sacrifice, making it analogous to the superiority of mercy over law. He cites Hosea 6: 6 in the following passage: "whatsoever obligations may be put upon mankind, they are to be expounded by that great and fundamental law of mercy. And therefore it was that our Saviour . . . interpreted the meaning of 'I will have mercy and not sacrifice' as a general dispensation in all things that were within that respect and consideration" (III, 397-98). The Book of Hosea, like all prophetic works an emblematic narrative, tells us that the knowledge of the Lord is redemptive. Marvell's Shepherd could say with Ephraim: "What have I to do any more with idols? I have heard [the Lord] and observed him: I am like a green fir tree. From me is thy fruit found."

An analogue of "The Coronet" is that remarkable quatrain in "Eyes and Tears":

> So *Magdalen*, in Tears more Wise
> Dissolv'd those captivating Eyes,
> Whose liquid Chaines could flowing meet
> To fetter her Redeemers feet.[14]

The Magdalen's tears of joy at her conversion are victorious over her beauty, which is inseparable from her sin, as the

---

[14] The Latin version of this stanza (the only stanza of the poem which is matched in the Latin) brings out the conversion from earthly to heavenly love more clearly:

> Magdala, lascivos sic quum dimisit Amantes,
> Fervidaque in castas lumina solvit aquas;
> Haesit in irriguo lachrymarum compede Christus
> Et tenuit sacros uda Catena pedes.

garland and the serpent are scarcely distinguishable. Her tears dissolve "those captivating Eyes" and become fetters themselves. The Shepherd of "The Coronet" awakens to self-deception when he finds the serpent and discovers that his Saviour (as he has been captivated by the Magdalen's penitence) may be honored by the humility of Christian devotion. The only way to "redress that Wrong" is to accept the Cross. The Shepherd is "more Wise" in the knowledge that the love of the Lord is a cup of suffering. That is ever the hard-won wisdom of the Resolved Soul.

For all its religious overtones, "The Nymph Complaining" does not concern the Christian meaning of necessity. The Nymph forgives, but she is resolute only in her decision to seek the death which will reunite her with the fawn. She has no knowledge of the redemptive power of suffering or of the merciful power of grace. But the Shepherd, willfully ignorant in his prideful attempt to be himself the agency of salvation, discovers that heaven may bend to him, though he cannot reach so high. The revelation is signaled by a change in tense—"Ah, foolish Man, that would'st debase with them/ And mortal Glory, Heavens Diadem!"—and is itself an act of grace. The Shepherd then wills to offer the garland to be sacrificed; his resolution is the human correlative of grace.

One could argue from this poem that Marvell held to the doctrine of *gratia cooperans*. Indeed, the cooperation of grace and will is central to Marvell's conception of the Resolved Soul, to his view of history and his understanding of human freedom, a concern which is at the heart of his prose and, I believe, of his poetry. But what we hear there is the voice of allegory, not sectarian argument. The major poems are not theology in disguise but stories of the soul's temporal life, the discovery of the limitations of human power and knowledge, the experience of necessity. The counterpointing of meditation and narration, of ceremonial salutation and historical account, of pastoral setting and symbolic action creates the conceptual resonance of the major poems.

The soul opens itself to grace; just so, the providential hero, Marvell tells us, makes his destiny his choice. Providence is God's will in history, as grace is God's dispensation to the soul. It is the relationship of emblematic narrative and the historical sense that I shall consider in discussing Marvell's providential view of history in "Bermudas" and the Cromwell poems.

"Bermudas"

The occasion which "Bermudas" celebrates is made clear by the title and the song from "the English boat"—a "Puritan canticle," Professor Bush calls it.[15] Such phrases as "Safe from the Storms, and Prelat's rage" invite us to consider that the event set forth is a matter of history, of public record. The references, more numerous if not more substantial than that to "the wanton Troopers," establish a historical, not a fictional context. But if the Puritans escaping Laudian repression are not creatures of Marvell's imagination, the narrative nevertheless tells a story which is mythologized, so to speak, as the picture of the exiles and the saving shore merges with images of paradise. The historical is itself transformed. With respect to its "mythological" character, then, "Bermudas" is close to "The Nymph Complaining," as with respect to its historicity it is close to the Cromwell poems.

Neither the Puritans nor what happens to them is an invention, but the emblematic narrative which constitutes Marvell's poem is as much an invention as the allegorical metaphor of "Music's Empire." There, the progress of sound has a history which is set forth in a continued metaphor in which colonization is the vehicle. In "Bermudas," the exiled Puritans are themselves colonials whose song tells their history, but the relationship of the figurative to the literal is more complex

[15] *English Literature*, p. 161.

because the historical event is a part of a larger story, itself conceptual. What happens to the Puritans is exemplary of the soul's search for salvation.

What we treasure, surely, is the picture the poem gives us, the catalogue of delights which is so peculiarly Marvellian. No poem of Marvell's has a more brilliant surface. But we misconceive those images if we read them as if they were concocted in the manner of *precieux* poetry, for the enamel creates depths; it does not merely cover brass with exquisite colors.[16] Like "Kubla Khan," "Bermudas" is a fragment suggesting infinite riches. We know that Marvell's imagination, like Coleridge's, was fed by accounts of exotic places.[17] But for Marvell that new world was not an image which answered to his private dreams; it was a metaphor coming to life.

> Where the remote *Bermudas* ride
> In th' Oceans bosome unespy'd,
> From a small Boat, that row'd along,
> The listning Winds receiv'd this Song.
>   What should we do but sing his Praise
> That led us through the watry Maze,
> Unto an Isle so long unknown,
> And yet far kinder than our own?
> Where he the huge Sea-Monsters wracks,
> That lift the Deep upon their Backs.
> He lands us on a grassy Stage;
> Safe from the Storms, and Prelat's rage.
> He gave us this eternal Spring,
> Which here enamells every thing;

---

[16] The libertine manner seems to me diametrically opposed to the allegorical. Such poets as Theophile and Saint-Amant, with whom Marvell has often been compared, have an entirely different attitude toward experience. Odette de Mourgues has described the libertine "use" of nature in her study *Metaphysical, Baroque, and Precieux Poetry*, in which, by the way, Marvell does not figure. See esp. pp. 93, 97.

[17] See Bush's discussion of the probable sources in *English Literature*, pp. 161, 177.

And sends the Fowl's to us in care,
On daily Visits through the Air.
He hangs in shades the Orange bright,
Like golden Lamps in a green Night.
And does in the Pom granates close,
Jewels more rich than *Ormus* show's.
He makes the Figs our mouths to meet;
And throws the Melons at our feet.
But Apples plants of such a price,
No Tree could ever bear them twice.
With Cedars, chosen by his hand,
From *Lebanon*, he stores the Land.
And makes the hollow Seas, that roar,
Proclaime the Ambergris on shoar.
He cast (of which we rather boast)
The Gospels Pearl upon our Coast.
And in these Rocks for us did frame
A Temple, where to sound his Name.
Oh let our Voice his Praise exalt,
Till it arrive at Heavens Vault:
Which thence (perhaps) rebounding, may
Eccho beyond the *Mexique Bay*.
Thus sung they, in the *English* boat,
An holy and a chearful Note,
And all the way, to guide their Chime,
With falling Oars they kept the time.

In her excellent commentary on the poem, Rosalie Colie remarks: "Earthly paradises are always static. Marvell's oarsmen go about no special business, do not arrive anywhere, are 'In th' Oceans bosom unespy'd. . . .' Their Puritan paradise, even in the Bermudas, must be, like Eden and like Marvell's other garden, a state of mind rather than the specific island of Captain John Smith or of Lewis Hughes. Richard Norwood could and did survey the island belonging to the Virginia

54

Company: Marvell's 'Bermudas' has metaphysical dimensions whose measure can be taken only by the poet."[18] There is indeed a "static" quality in the poem: it is the emblematic character of a scene which is being mythologized before our very eyes. But like all transformations, the process is temporal, as it is in "The Nymph Complaining," and it is recounted in narrative form. A song of thanksgiving and a hymn of praise framed by a few descriptive lines (among the most beautiful Marvell ever wrote), the poem is a tale told again, the *reenactment* of a providential rescue, for the song tells us that the exiles have landed, have been provided for, have established themselves anew in Eden. Rather than enjoying the scene as a reenactment, we may wish to consider that, as in a medieval painting (in that style called "continuous narration"), two scenes are being presented simultaneously: the approach to the shore and the discovery there of the abundant comforts and pleasures which the Lord has provided. The tenses are as subtly deployed as they are in "The Coronet." They help to create an emblematic narrative reaching beyond the dramatic moment which is its focus, as prophetic as it is historical.

The Cromwell Poems

In a sense, Marvell's poems about Cromwell tell the story of England's providential rescue. Were the tribulations which preceded that rescue any greater than the costs of the rescue itself? Marvell's task in these poems—and surely in his heart and mind—was to justify the ways of certain men and thus to account for the paradox of the shipwreck into health (to borrow a figure that the Soul uses in its dialogue with the Body). He tells a story in which the ruinous history of the times can be seen in transcendent terms. It is an emblematic narrative whose action is the meaning of history; whose theme is the conquest of time (the achievement of Cromwell); whose

[18] "Marvell's 'Bermudas' and the Puritan Paradise," *Renaissance News*, X (1957), 79.

plot is the mediation of earth and heaven by Providence; and whose hero is the Resolved Soul in the guise of the soldier-statesman, the Lord Protector of England.

The Cromwell poems are, of course, on a vaster scale than "Bermudas," but in them as well the historical moment is conceived allegorically. Mythology and the Bible and actual historical events themselves furnish the stuff of that conception as Marvell creates scenes and figures that transcend history in the telling. They sum in themselves attitudes or principles of action, becoming thereby images of history, emblems of truth.[19] The focus shifts within each poem and from poem to poem, so that, taken together, the Cromwell poems make up a narrative which has as complex a tonality as "The Nymph Complaining." The central theme, however, is unchanging. It is that upon Cromwell's acts has been set the seal of heaven.[20]

Marvell's judgment of history in the Cromwell poems is prophetic. The emphasis throughout is on what is to come, on the effect of acts whose cost has been great. Thus the uses of time, which is a theme found in "A Poem upon the Death of O. C.," is first sounded in "An Horatian Ode Upon Cromwell's Return from Ireland" and is taken up in "The First Anniversary of the Government under O. C." Marvell's Cromwell races the sun and, having ruined "the great Work of Time," ("Horatian Ode," line 34), "he the force of scatter'd Time contracts,/ And in one Year the work of Ages acts" ("First Anniversary," lines 13-14). Marvell again and again confirms the judgment that the effect of all that has been done must be for the good. There is a continuous double emphasis on ruin and creation, cause and effect, what has been accomplished and

[19] In reference to the painting of Marathon by Panainos, Hinks remarks, "The art of Panainos should . . . be called 'mythistorical': his composition refers to a specific historical event, but he treats it as a 'symbolic situation' by alluding to the moral conflict of which the political clash is the outward and contingent expression" (*Myth and Allegory*, p. 65).

[20] See Appendix, Note 2: The Providential Hero.

what is to come, each pair of opposites being unified by the conception of the ways of Providence. Marvell does not seek to avoid the confrontation of "the antient Rights" and "the forc'd Pow'r," of fate and justice, nor to present that confrontation as any less harrowing than it in fact was. Since his aim is to justify and celebrate Cromwell's career, he must create images convincingly portraying the providential hero, but it is not to be an easy praise. Marvell's tirelessly dialectical intelligence invents ways to advance by seeming to undercut, ways to leap ahead by rearing backwards. There is, perhaps, something of that habit of mind which is expressed in the epitaph he wrote for Edmund Trott, in which outrageous insults are excused thus. "(Ut verae Laudis Invidiam ficto Convitio levemus)" (That we may lighten the envy of true praise with a feigned reproof). The burden of "true praise" Marvell probably felt strongly in the Cromwell poems; he certainly wished to make a case which could not be considered perfunctory.

Correlative with the resolute acceptance of his acts is Marvell's recognition that only the highest authority could justify the magnitude of the sacrifices Cromwell has exacted. A man of such destructive force and passion, if he is not to be castigated as a prideful tyrant, must be accepted as the embodiment of the will of heaven. Clearly, what he has done is not to be judged by earthly measures: if he is not Lucifer, he must be "angry Heavens flame." He transcends the limitations of earthly men:

> And thou, great *Cromwell*, for whose happy birth
> A Mold was chosen out of better Earth.
> ("First Anniversary," ll. 159-60)

He is identified with nature. When he dies,

> . . . as through Air his wasting Spirits flow'd
> The Universe labour'd beneath his load.
> ("Death of O. C.," ll. 131-32)

He is identified with the nation, as in the words of the embittered foreign prince who speaks toward the end of the "First Anniversary":

> "And still his Sword seems hanging o're my head.
> The Nation had been ours, but his one Soul
> Moves the great Bulk, and animates the whole."

His enemies know that his acts are guided by a wisdom of unearthly dimension:

> "Where did he learn those Arts that cost us dear?
> Where below Earth, or where above the Sphere?"
> ("First Anniversary," ll. 385-86)

Clearly, if Cromwell's career is providential, then merely moral judgment of him, like merely political judgment, becomes irrelevant:

> 'Tis Madness to resist or blame
> The force of angry Heavens flame.

The confrontation of "antient Rights" and "greater Spirits" is described in language which creates the pathos of that violence in all its immediacy, but it does not reflect upon Cromwell. There is open condemnation of the witnesses of the execution: the *"Royal Actor"* mounts the *"Tragick Scaffold,"*

> While round the armed Bands
> Did clap their bloody hands.[21]

But Cromwell himself is not held to this account. The stage upon which he acts is grand and universal: the civil war,

[21] There is a curious echo in "A Poem on the Death of O. C." Marvell is describing the reactions of the people when Cromwell, after such a violent life, dies peacefully:

> The People, which what most they fear esteem,
> Death when more horrid so more noble deem;
> And blame the last *Act*, like *Spectators* vain,
> Unless the *Prince* whom they applaud be slain.
> (ll. 7-10)

where he is concerned, is conceived of as a climactic event in the unfolding order of creation. The difference between Cromwell and the "armed Bands" is that Cromwell has been translated to another realm, whereas the people remain angry men whose acts are judged, as they are described, in earthly terms.[22] It is a double standard, but it is not simply *ad hominem* and it derives from high principle.

Marvell is never more a Puritan than in his conception of Providence. To see in the unfolding of the moment the very course of history and its meaning is the prime motive of the allegorical imagination. Emblematic seeing is the intaglio of prophetic judgment: the Puritan imagination, it is well to remember, is an allegorical imagination. The perception of crisis and the sense of the especial scene are characteristics of minds haunted by the conception of Divine Providence. A dramatic sense of the historical moment is, of course, allied to the apocalyptic or eschatological temper and among the Puritans there were visionaries for whom the present simply disappeared. But in the main, the Puritans were men whose sense of history led them not to mystic transcendence or to a passive reckoning of the Second Coming, but to acts of will. If the Puritan imagination, playing upon the passing scene, perceived "the future Time," it also conceived the necessity of action which would determine its form. Such action, violent as it often was, could be sanctioned only by an appeal to the doctrine of the Divine Providence.

The prophetic judgment is that ruin is the precedent of order. It is a judgment that requires the vantage point of heaven and freedom from the confinement of the present. Cromwell is in opposition to "the antient Rights," to justice,

[22] In view of his commendation in later Latin poems of those who go beyond the law, even to the point of murderous assault, we must conclude that Marvell drew the line only at regicide and that he exonerates all who rebel on behalf of liberty of conscience, even if they are not to be labeled as agents of Providence.

but as the agent of heaven his opposition is in the service of a higher need, for he is to "cast the Kingdome old/ Into another Mold." What is to come is the sanction of what has come to pass. A point of view limited to the immediacy of Cromwell's acts would have been disastrous to the cause of defining them, to say nothing of justification. The execution of Charles, as it is represented in the pageant-like scene of the "Horatian Ode," cannot be excused; such ruinous acts as the regicide must be cast in higher terms if they are to be judged necessary and right. Marvell is not so high-minded that he contemplates the actual course of events from the heavenly point of view exclusively: that superiority is a Puritan habit of mind which he derides. He presents the earthly man in all his vigor, but his judgment is of great Cromwell as heaven's viceregent.

By his allegorical metaphors, Marvell in a sense philosophizes history. If the historian, as Sidney says, is wanting precept, that lack the philosopher can remedy. But the philosopher, too, has his limitations. Sidney remarks that he may, with his learned definitions, replenish the memory "with many infallible grounds of wisdom, but they will lie dark before the imaginative and judging power, if they be not illuminated or figured forth by the speaking picture of Poesie."[23] The precept is stated in the "Horatian Ode" thus:

> Though Justice against Fate complain,
> And plead the antient Rights in vain:
>   But those do hold or break
>   As Men are strong or weak.
> Nature that hateth emptiness,
> Allows of penetration less:
>   And therefore must make room
>   Where greater Spirits come.
>
> (ll. 37-44)

[23] *Defence*, in *Works*, III, 14.

Principle depends upon strong men and even nature must accommodate them; the alliance with nature converts the willful act to the providential act. Judgment of Cromwell as the providential hero demands that action be sanctified by heaven-sent knowledge. The absolute contingency of action and knowledge, of power and wisdom is at the heart of each of the Cromwell poems, though the terms are most intensely counterpointed in the "Horatian Ode," since the acts celebrated there dramatize most immediately the terrible nature of the confrontation of justice and fate. Marvell's Cromwell makes his destiny his choice, that virtuous act hailed in "Upon Appleton House" (line 774). He is a man of destiny, but he is also a man of will, in terms of Renaissance astrology, a *virtuoso*:[24] he "does both act and know." Cromwell's knowledge is, like his will, heavenly. Knowledge and power, destiny and choice, fate and will: each pair of opposites is unified by the concept of the providential hero.

At the close of the "Horatian Ode," for instance, Marvell, having saluted the military prowess of the conquering hero—this Caesar, this Hannibal—looks beyond, to the wise action and careful regard for danger which will be necessary:

> But thou the Wars and Fortunes Son
> March indefatigably on;
>   And for the last effect
>   Still keep thy Sword erect:
> Besides the force it has to fright
> The Spirits of the shady Night,
>   The same *Arts* that did *gain*
>   A *Pow'r* must it *maintain*.
>
> (ll. 113-20)

---

[24] For a discussion of the role of free will in the character of the *virtuoso* and of the *fortunato*, see Benedetto Soldati, *La Poesia Astrologica nel Quattrocento* (Firenze, 1906), pp. 243-52. (Professor Charles Mitchell kindly drew my attention to this study.) Pontanus argued in

The figure of the soldier with his drawn sword is an emblem which bespeaks past and future: what has happened is that power has been "assur'd" by acts of blood; times to come will require the resolute use of the new power as well as "the same Arts," including that "wiser Art" (line 48), by which it has been won.[25] Knowledge and power have ruined "the great Work of Time"; knowledge and power must act "the work of Ages": the phrase is from the "First Anniversary" (written in 1654, four years after the "Horatian Ode") and it suggests, as do other echoes, that Marvell is sounding again the theme of the "Ode," that ruin is right and necessary if it leads to creation. The prophecy of the final stanza is answered in this passage from the "First Anniversary":

> . . . I think, if in some happy Hour
> High Grace should meet in one with highest Pow'r,
> And then a seasonable People still
> Should bend to his, as he to Heavens will,
> What we might hope, what wonderful Effect
> From such a wish'd Conjuncture might reflect.
> Sure, the mysterious Work, where none withstand,
> Would forthwith finish under such a Hand:
> Fore-shortned Time its useless Course would stay,
> And soon precipitate the latest Day.
> But a thick Cloud about that Morning lyes,
> And intercepts the Beams of Mortal eyes,
> That 'tis the most we determine can,
> If these be the Times, then this must be the Man.
>
> (ll. 132-44)

"The last effect" ("Horatian Ode," line 115), which was to

---

his *De Rebus Coelestibus* that knowledge of astrology made modifications of influence possible by several agencies, including free will. Marvell, of course, supposes the hero's knowledge to be of the Lord.

[25] See Appendix, Note 3: "Still keep thy Sword erect."

be secured by art and sword, cannot even now be assured, because it is uncertain that the people will be "seasonable." Prudence, therefore, is still in order:

> And well he therefore does, and well has guest,
> Who in his Age has always forward prest:
> And not knowing where Heavens choice may light,
> Girds yet his Sword, and ready stands to fight.
>
> (ll. 145-48)

"Indefatigable" is the word for Cromwell in both poems.[26] First to last, successful statecraft demands not only power but also the knowledge of the limits of tyranny and freedom:

> 'Tis not a Freedome, that where All command;
> Nor Tyranny, where One does them withstand:
> But who of both the Bounders knows to lay
> Him as their Father must the State obey.
>
> ("First Anniversary," ll. 279-82)

In the "Horatian Ode," the allegorical metaphor of the falcon who obeys the falconer, responsive to the lure which is the law of the Commonwealth (lines 91-96), puts the burden on Cromwell; here, the burden is on the people to obey the man who "does both act and know." He who threatened "The Spirits of the shady Night" with the sword now converts them to the uses of the state:

> The Common-wealth does through their Centers all
> Draw the Circumf'rence of the publique Wall;

[26] As Marvell wrote many years later: "in this World a good Cause signifys little, unless it be well defended. A Man may starve at the Feast of good Conscience" (Margoliouth, II, 309). This is the famous letter "To a Friend in Persia," written in 1671. Two years later Marvell would be arguing in *The Rehearsal Transpros'd* (Part II) that in the case of the civil war fought over liberty and religion, the cause was too good to have been fought for. The contradiction is real: twenty years after the "Horatian Ode," Marvell was still examining the grounds of his judgment.

The crossest Spirits here do take their part,
Fast'ning the Contignation which they thwart.
                    ("First Anniversary," ll. 87-90)

Along with the military prowess of the soldier whose very name in times to come shall "armyes fright," Marvell praises in "A Poem on the Death of O. C." the exercise of wiser arts: "What prudence more than humane did he need/ To keep so deare, so diff'ring minds agreed?" (lines 217-18). He is saddened that those Cromwell leaves behind "No more shall heare that powerful language charm,/ Whose force oft spar'd the labour of his arm" (lines 237-38). The providential hero who "does both act and know" has in his accomplishments effected the conquest of time: "No part of time but bore his mark away/ Of honour; all the Year was *Cromwell's* day" (lines 141-42).

Thus the themes and motifs of the "Horatian Ode" are heard again in "A Poem on the Death of O. C." The serene and generous ruler whose tact and humility have saved the nation from itself is the object both of praise and affectionate regard expressed in a quite personal manner, but the keynote of the commemorative poem is the hero's magnanimity. The mysterious power of the man is that while his soul animates his very person, his person tempers his great soul. The emblematic narrative which the three poems constitute bodies forth Cromwell's providential power, his heavenly knowledge. The allegorical figures of the sun, the lusty mate, the obedient falcon, the creating architect, the flame of Heaven, the soul of the nation and of nature, and those passages in which Marvell sets down what he has seen and heard as a witness of the historical enactment of heaven's will, substantiate a prophetic figure, the Resolved Soul confronting his fate, conquering time, knowing necessity, choosing his destiny. And the disjunction between Oliver Cromwell and his great spirit, between the Lord Protector and his tenderness, between the ruiner and the creator, between "angry Heavens flame" and the humble David is made a unity by the story which Marvell's allegorical imagination creates.

Loyalty to the republican cause may have been a harrowing choice for Marvell; the fact that his whereabouts during the period of the wars are unknown suggests at least that it was not an automatic one. But once he had decided that the rebellion was necessary, there was a tremendous amount of energy expended in the justification of the usurping power. Violence, ruin, chaos are judged necessary precedents of order. "Marvell is not hovering between two ways of looking at Cromwell," L. D. Lerner has written. "His greatness is unthinkable without the damage he does."[27] Necessity is Marvell's theme. But necessity, in Milton's words, is "the tyrant's plea"; it is for this reason that Marvell associates necessity with the will of heaven, dramatizing the providential nature of the hero's acts. The key metaphor Marvell borrows from St. John: Cromwell is "the *Angel* of our Commonweal," who "troubling the Waters, yearly mak'st them Heal."

"If the republican spirit consists essentially in preferring principles to men," Professor Legouis has written, "no one was ever less of a Republican than Marvell."[28] Was Marvell willing to lay principle aside when he could justify a course of action on personal grounds? Are principles merely abstract concerns for Marvell, or do they motivate and inspire? Surely it was principle that drove Marvell to conceive of the ruin of "the great Work of Time," not just of "decrepit institutions."[29] It was principle that allowed him to translate Cromwell to a figure larger than life. Marvell persuaded himself that what Cromwell had done was in the service of a

[27] "An Horatian Ode," in *Interpretations*, ed. John Wain (London, 1955), p. 71.
[28] *Andrew Marvell*, p. 242.
[29] Legouis, *Andrew Marvell*, p. 16.

principle dearer to him than life and thus he loved the man.

To identify wrathful, ruinous acts with the will of God is to risk self-righteousness and to prepare the way for the denial of the fundamental freedom. Marvell's later consideration of the judgment that Cromwell acted providentially, which I will consider in the next chapter, attests to his awareness of that danger. But the judgment in 1650 had its justification. If we define Marvell's judgment in terms of the Puritan-Royalist antithesis, we limit it to a matter of sympathy; whereas the defense of the principle of liberty of conscience he considered an act of the whole being, the sacred duty of all Christians, of the monarch and of the supporters of the Good Old Cause.

THE APPEAL the Cromwell poems make to our imagination is fundamentally the same as that made by the other poems I have been considering. The mediation of the two realms of being is accomplished by a Horatian conception of the ambiguities of power and a Puritan conception of the ways of Providence. It is expressed in figures created by the allegorical imagination whereby man's freedom to make his destiny his choice is defined. In each of the poems considered in this chapter we are given more than one perspective. The historical present is set over against the mythical past or the prophetic future; the climactic moment forecasts even as it summarizes; the continued metaphors are broken in upon by exclamation and exhortation; pictures distill the essential meanings of the unfolding story, as the continuing story transcends the ambiguities of momentary scenes. Marvell's allegorical imagination creates poetic forms which allow for enacting the discovery of the meaning of necessity. The Nymph loses some of her innocence and the Lord Protector learns magnanimity; the willfully ignorant Shepherd is chastened and the Puritan exiles are redeemed: their experiences, their discoveries take time. The power of grace, the requirements of statecraft, the way of the world, the redemptive power of suffering—all that man learns of the nature of necessity is learned not by soulful introspection or by the dictates of faith, but through his experiences of temporality, his discoveries in the world of time.

The central figures of these poems enjoy some sort of actuality, whether it is developed into a personality, as in the case of the Nymph and the serene conqueror, or is merely conventional, as in the case of the Shepherd. As figures in their landscapes, they are sharply differentiated. But their resolve makes of them a company. For Marvell, the knowledge of necessity is the essential motive of resolve; resolution is choice, the free exercise of the will whose agent is the soul. Thus these figures search out the secrets of history, opposing fate, discovering, always, the fallen world and the cost of redemption. They are the particular examples by which the general notion of the Resolved Soul is given form.

CHAPTER III

Love, Time, and Necessity

The Families of the Necessities

OME twenty years after the Cromwell poems, Marvell was to damn the appeal to necessity as an unholy sanction of unlawful power. There are no letters dating from the time of the "Horatian Ode" to which we might turn for substantiation of whatever political views he held then,[1] but there are passages in the later prose pamphlets written with an intensity of feeling which suggests not so much a reversal of opinion as a return to principles deeper still than those by which he had justified Cromwell. The dangers of the providential view of history had become manifest in a way which must have tempted Marvell to self-righteousness, given the bitterness with which he attacked those who in the 1650's appealed to necessity with an awareness of its ambiguities somewhat less acute than his own. But his attack on those who appeal to necessity now, in the years after the Restoration, though it is relentless, is remarkably free of that "knowing" tone, the exasperating sanctimony both of former true believers who reject a doctrine once held unquestioningly and of men whose guiding principle is expediency. There is no attempt to excuse faculty judgments and Cromwell is not mentioned; the Good Old Cause is not impugned.

One of the chief motives of the prose pamphlets seems to

[1] Masson speculates interestingly that Milton's "Letter written to a Gentleman in the Country" (1653), in which he exonerates Cromwell for the dissolution of Parliament by claiming that the "ways of Providence are unscrutable," was probably addressed to Marvell, who might have occasioned this exercise in rationalization by an expression of dismay (*The Life of John Milton* [6 vols.; London, 1859-80], IV, 519ff.).

68

be to explain to his very wide audience, and perhaps to himself as well, how it is that the appeal to the concept of necessity, though it had at one time seemed justified, is not generally to be sanctioned. Indeed, the perverse appeal to necessity becomes in Marvell's account the chief cause of the terrible course of events: he lays the blame for the king's undoing at the door of those "Archidiaconal preachers" (III, 354) who seduced Charles into believing that his power was *necessarily* unlimited. In effect, what Marvell does is, first of all, to associate the appeal to necessity with those who simply wish to defend what they have decreed or instituted, namely the absolute power of the magistrate and the impossibility of dissent; and, secondly, to dissociate the Good Old Cause from a defense based explicitly on this same appeal, which he does by differentiating the cause from the rebellion as skillfully as he had Cromwell from his fellows. Marvell's rhetorical powers serve him in this endeavor as brilliantly as did his allegorical imagination in creating the emblematic narrative in which his earlier judgment was declared.

Almost the full energy of his argumentation goes not to a defense of Providence but to an attack on his adversaries; but Marvell, although he is contemptuous, is nonetheless philosophically rigorous. The philosophical basis for the attack on the argument from necessity is the concept of the two orders of reality. With considerable skill he differentiates these two orders, identified in one instance as "temporal interests" and "every man's eternity and salvation" (IV, 127). He derides those who would not distinguish between " 'the natural and politique capacity,' " arguing that "without that distinction there would be no law nor reason of law left in England" (IV, 305-06). Necessity belongs to heaven—or both heaven and earth belong to necessity, and man is vain to call upon its name in self-defense.

To his chief adversary, Samuel Parker, Marvell gives the

title "Mr. Necessity Bayes,"[2] ridiculing his attempt to justify his ways by an appeal to necessity. Marvell's principal rhetorical strategy is to badger his opponents with requests for definition and demonstration, meanwhile supplying his own. He defines a position out of existence by showing up contradictions and faulty analogies, using, as he admits, "definition in effect against definition" (IV, 185). He sets out with a Coleridgean zeal to differentiate the "several families of the Necessities" (III, 365). We are led to expect a genealogy, but with an impatience as Coleridgean as the zeal, Marvell avoids explaining the "genus" which his definition of definition[3] requires, and instead proceeds to identify only two families, after which, with a satirist's fantasy, he lists at will the "necessity" of the neck ("that is, that the whole body of the people should have but one neck . . . very useful and virtuous toward the attainment of 'publick tranquillity' ") and, shifting from the metaphoric to the physiological, the "necessity" of the calf (which should be in front of the leg to protect those who tend to bark their shins, but, alas, it is where it is), and so forth. They are all, it is soon clear, cousins-german to Necessity II and there are no close relatives to Necessity I: "[It] was pre-eternal to all things, and exercised dominion not only over all humane things, but over Jupiter himself and the rest of the Deities, and drove the great iron nail thorough the axletree of Nature" (III, 366). Marvell follows this stunning definition with another in the form of an accusation directed toward Parker: "I have some suspicion that you would have men understand it of yourself, and that you are that necessity [i.e., the "pre-eternal" necessity]. For what can you be less or other . . . who have obliged Providence to dispense power to the magistrate according to your good

---

[2] See Legouis, *Andrew Marvell*, p. 194.

[3] Definition "alwaies consists, as being a dialectick animal, of a body, which is the genus, and a difference, which is the soul of the thing defined" (IV, 183).

pleasure, and herein have claim'd to yourself that universal dictatorship of necessity over God and man, though it were but *clavi figendi causa*, and to strike thorow all government, humane and divine, with the great hammer." "Mr. Necessity Bayes" has deliberately and falsely identified his own manipulation, his own earthly necessities, with the pre-eternal necessity. Proof of his insolence is that the hammer he claims to wield has, in his hands, struck only to join (*figendi causa*), whereas Necessity, in wielding the hammer, joins by separating. "You have taken it upon yourself," Marvell is saying, "to act the part of Necessity, but in your hands the wedges [*clavi*] are used only for the purpose of joining; you nail together what the great hammer is meant not only to join but to separate."

The profound secret of the universe is that polarity creates unity: the fateful power of necessity is not to be demeaned by an easy identification with sublunary concerns. Marvell holds that what necessity explains and justifies is not particular acts and earthly contingencies but the general conditions of existence itself. In his latterday arguments from necessity, he is cautious in developing the idea that civil disorder is, in an important sense, a result of the fall:

[The] state of perfection was dissolv'd in the first instance, and was shorter-liv'd than anarchy, scarce of one day's continuance. . . . God has hitherto, instead of an eternal Spring, a standing serenity, and perpetual sunshine, subjected mankind to the dismal influence of comets from above, to thunder, and its lightning, and tempests from the middle region, and from the lower surface to the raging of the seas and the tottering of earthquakes, beside all the other innumerable calamities to which humane life is exposed, He has in like manner distinguish'd the government of the world by the intermitting seasons of discord, war and publick disturbance. (III, 368-69)

And when he frames his thought in pragmatic rather than theodicean terms, the imagery is comparable: "Tranquillity in government is by all just means to be sought after. . . . But men have oftentimes . . . other ends of government. . . . How should such persons arrive at their design'd port but by disturbance? For if there were a dead calm always, and the wind blew from no corner, there would be no navigation" (III, 369). But if "disturbance" is necessary for "navigation," that is not to say that we therefore may clearly prefer one wind to another, claiming that it is "necessary." There is here no rationale provided for that identification by which Marvell was emboldened to sing: " 'Tis Madness to resist or blame/ The force of angry Heavens flame."

Marvell needs at every point to exploit the rhetorical strengths of his definition of necessity, since the argument deriving from it is never unambiguous. Leaving undefined the role of human agency, he bravely allies the Good Old Cause with nature's own. Its defense is made to seem an inevitable concomitant of Christian acceptance of the separation of the natural and the civil orders. In the best-known passage of his prose he explains why men should have trusted the king: "For men may spare their pains where nature is at work, and the world will not go the faster for our driving. . . . [A]ll things . . . happen in their best and proper time, without any need of our officiousness" (III, 212-13). He identifies the causes of liberty and justice with nature and thus can argue that extra force—"our driving"—is no more relevant than counterforce: so much for the providential hero. Still, he manages to have it both ways, for this inevitability of change is nevertheless contingent on the fact, as Marvell sees it, that the king, because he was "of so accurate and piercing a judgment," would have seen the righteousness of the cause, would have responded to the petitions of his patient subjects. "Would have" saves Marvell from appealing directly to necessity, but it is an ex post facto expediency and it bespeaks a troubled heart. Marvell, for as long as he lived and wrote, seems to have continued to weigh the judgment that men were led to rebellion by Providence.

MARVELL's definition of necessity provides the rhetorical means by which he asserts the prerogative of heaven, claims the inviolability of man's freedom, and attests to the power of grace. The creation of the universe, defined by a metaphor which makes being contingent upon separation, becomes a paradigm of sound government in which the social order depends upon the distinction between " 'the natural and politique capacity.' " From that distinction stems the proper "owning of God's jurisdiction" (III, 403) and the protection of liberty of conscience, which is the only guarantor of the soul's access to grace.[4] In short, the definition of necessity has its political and its religious uses; but its metaphysical meaning is the chief motive, I believe, of Marvell's poetry.

Necessity ordains the separation of the soul in its sublunary state from its heavenly home, its true source. But, as "On a Drop of Dew" declares, that separation, that opposition is the ground of resolution, for the modes in which the soul enjoys and suffers its temporal being—love, heroic action, contemplation—are acts of will. Resolution springs from the confrontation of will and fate. Conditioned by time, the will is free: the ambiguities of necessity are solved by the paradoxical acts of the Resolved Soul, the agent of will.

In Marvell's poetry, the choices are dialectically conceived. There is no mystic celebration of an escape from time. Central to the major poems is the notion that the opposition of fate and will, the confrontation of the pre-eternal necessity, entails sacrifice: form is born of annihilation, beauty of suffering; renewal builds on ruin; love and heroic action create from chaos. The range of attitudes assumed by Marvell toward the force that destroys one condition as it creates other conditions

---

[4] See Appendix, Note 4: The " 'natural and politique capacity.' "

anew, toward the servitude which determines freedom, toward the choice which is obedience, extends from the jocular to the intense and moving expression of piety and loyalty.

For the "Resolved Soul," that anti-Faust of such reserve and hauteur who spurns "Created Pleasure" with an exhilarating ease—"I sup above, and cannot stay/ To bait so long upon the way"—choice is easy to the point of being no choice at all. Resolution is elsewhere in the major poems marked by passion. Even in the "Dialogue Between the Soul and Body" the tone bespeaks not the cold disdain (or colorless righteousness) of the "Resolved Soul," but impatience and, we might say, anger. Sentient being, which the "Resolved Soul" denies or simply transcends, provides for the Soul the very source of energy for the opposition to fate. The pain the Soul suffers by being sentient, the Body suffers by being possessed. Each lives by the other. To the Body is given the final word:

> What but a Soul could have the wit
> To build me up for Sin so fit?
> So Architects do square and hew,
> Green Trees that in the Forest grew.

Questions concerning which one "wins" the debate are out of order because the Body is the guise of the Soul. The poem's close recreates the unity which was put asunder; the form of the dialogue separates for dialectical purposes that which is metaphysically inseparable: what the great hammer has separated it has joined. It is not the most profound statement of Marvell's conception of the limits of temporal being, but it is perhaps the most succinct.[5]

---

[5] Christopher Hill comments: "The symbolism . . . is a favorite of Marvell's: the loss of certain natural qualities that the symbolizing process makes inevitable" (*Puritanism and Revolution*, p. 346). In Marvell's description of the framing of government, "square" and "hew" represent different methods and stages of forming and are opposed to one another, rather than being paired (IV, 281). The figure as it applies to the soul Marvell may have borrowed from Hooker,

Passionate resolution, then, is at the heart of each of the major poems. Choices are defined, defended, celebrated. The three poems I will consider in this chapter—"The Unfortunate Lover," "The Definition of Love," and "To His Coy Mistress" —all concern the necessities of temporal life and the opposition of the Resolved Soul to which they give rise.

"The Unfortunate Lover"

In "The Unfortunate Lover," paradigmatic in so many ways of all his poems celebrating (or, often as not, decrying) love, Marvell establishes an equivalence between the lover and the soul: the poem is a continued metaphor by which is figured the necessary suffering of the time-bound soul, the lover in his world of sacrifice and redemption.[6] To tell this story, poets generally do speak in the voice of allegory. Given the imagery of the paradisiacal garden, the raging sea and pitiless storm, the solitary shipwreck, and the continuing battle, we should expect not a personal legend or a private poem plastered with an unusual assortment of "metaphysical" conceits, but the commonplace themes of allegory. Given this rhetoric, we should recognize the Unfortunate Lover as the soul in its most usual guise. It is precisely on the score of the poem's rhetoric that criticism has failed. Although the Marvellian cadence sounds here most masterfully, although the complexly con-

---

who compares the sacraments to instruments by which God's mercy works, "even as the axe and saw do serve to bring timber into that fashion which the mind of the artificer intendeth" (*The Laws of Ecclesiastical Polity* VI, vi, 9). The architect's art provides in Marvell's poetry an imagery suggestive of forming, of useful construction (as of the state in the Cromwell poems) rather than of artful production. Mrs. Bennett limits the philosophical significance of these lines when she writes that "Marvell suggests a parallel with the artificer who transforms nature into art, for instance, the gardener's topiary art" (*Five Metaphysical Poets* [Cambridge, Eng., 1964], p. 114). Hedges, be it remarked, are not squared or hewn but clipped and trimmed.

[6] A version of this discussion of "The Unfortunate Lover" appeared in *MLQ*, XXVII (1966), 41-50.

sistent tone and the handsome symmetry of its form make this poem representative of some of the strengths of Marvell's art, "The Unfortunate Lover" has provoked critical responses ranging from discomfiture to doubts concerning its authenticity. It has been dismissed wholly or in part as "preposterous rubbish," "a mixture of magnificence and foolery"; it has been tolerated as parody.[7] The rhetoric of the poem has embarrassed or simply amused most commentators. But the circumstances of the birth and career of the Unfortunate Lover can be deduced from the rhetoric; given those circumstances, the rhetoric is plausible. This *circulus methodicus* assures that if we know what kind of poem we are reading we can be prepared for the kind of language we find. We do not complain that the characters of *Everyman* have no names other than "Goods" or "Cousin" or that the grotesques of early comedy are grotesque. Nor do we trouble to note that Rodomonte speaks rodomontade. "The Unfortunate Lover" is an allegory by which is figured the soul's resolute opposition as exemplified in the lover's fate. It is an allegory not because it is a political tract camouflaged by Spanish emblems; nor because it is a hieratic symbol to be translated at three or four levels; nor because labeling it "allegory" would be a simple way to allow for larger meanings. "The Unfortunate Lover" is an allegory because mythic imagery serves a metaphysical idea, because the Unfortunate Lover's career in the world of passion corresponds to the temporal life of the soul.

The mysterious compromise by which the temporal and the timeless, the particular and the abstract may consort on equal terms is effected by those tropes that picture our life as a battle, a journey, a play, in images which are at once dramatic and abstract. Marvell's allegory sets forth this story of the Unfortunate Lover in grand figures that seem to portend

[7] See, for example, V. Sackville-West, *Andrew Marvell* (London, 1929), p. 44 and F. L. Lucas, *Authors Living and Dead* (London, 1926), p. 78.

much more. The poem is like a scenario for an epic. The garden scene is a condensation of paradise; the shipwreck is a journey in miniature; the birth and ghastly nurture summarize the history of a soul's rearing; the battle with storm and fire depicts man's lifelong war with fortune; and the heraldic banner, which is the emblematic equivalent of the image that the poem itself presents, sums the pageant, the essential drama of the life of the lover. Each figure of the poem—shipwreck, battle, banner—is an image which is also a history.

> Alas, how pleasant are their dayes
> With whom the Infant Love yet playes!
> Sorted by pairs, they still are seen
> By Fountains cool, and Shadows green.
> But soon these Flames do lose their light,
> Like Meteors of a Summers night:
> Nor can they to that Region climb,
> To make impression upon Time.
>
> 'Twas in a Shipwrack, when the Seas
> Rul'd, and the Winds did what they please,
> That my poor Lover floting lay,
> And, e're brought forth, was cast away:
> Till at the last the master-Wave
> Upon the Rock his Mother drave;
> And there she split against the Stone,
> In a *Cesarian Section*.
>
> The Sea him lent these bitter Tears
> Which at his Eyes he alwaies bears.
> And from the Winds the Sighs he bore,
> Which through his surging Breast do roar.
> No Day he saw but that which breaks,
> Through frighted Clouds in forked streaks.

While round the ratling Thunder hurl'd,
As at the Fun'ral of the World.

While Nature to his Birth presents
This masque of quarrelling Elements;
A num'rous fleet of Com'rants black,
That sail'd insulting o're the Wrack,
Receiv'd into their cruel Care,
Th' unfortunate and abject Heir:
Guardians most fit to entertain
The Orphan of the *Hurricane*.

They fed him up with Hopes and Air,
Which soon digested to Despair.
And as one Corm'rant fed him, still
Another on his Heart did bill.
Thus while they famish him, and feast,
He both consumed, and increast:
And languished with doubtful Breath,
Th' *Amphibium* of Life and Death.

And now, when angry Heaven wou'd
Behold a spectacle of Blood,
Fortune and He are call'd to play
At sharp before it all the day:
And Tyrant Love his brest does ply
With all his wing'd Artillery.
Whilst he, betwixt the Flames and Waves,
Like *Ajax*, the mad Tempest braves.

See how he nak'd and fierce does stand,
Cuffing the Thunder with one hand;
While with the other he does lock,
And grapple, with the stubborn Rock:
From which he with each Wave rebounds,
Torn into Flames, and ragg'd with Wounds.

And all he saies, a Lover drest
In his own Blood does relish best.

This is the only *Banneret*
That ever Love created yet:
Who though, by the Malignant Starrs,
Forced to live in Storms and Warrs:
Yet dying leaves a Perfume here,
And Musick within every Ear:
And he in Story only rules,
In a Field *Sable* a Lover *Gules*.

The first and final stanzas frame a narrative of the Lover's birth into the world of passion and his fight there with fortune under heaven's eye, beleaguered by love. The setting of the first stanza provides several images which serve to emphasize the chaos of the world of passion which awaits. There, in the garden, lovers are paired; Love, an infant, plays with them "By Fountains cool, and Shadows green." The imagery of place thus suggests the quietude and peace of innocent, soulful love: love without passion is like love in paradise. But the fire which shines and lights becomes the fire that burns and wastes; those flames which now only shine are like meteors that fall to earth in self-destruction: "Nor can they to that Region climb,/ To make impression upon Time." Once fallen, those comets cannot restore themselves to that timeless realm from which time could be assaulted. ("To make impression" is to attack [*OED*, 1, b]; as a noun, "impression" can mean a comet or meteor [*OED*, 5], so that there is a pun of sorts.) The final couplet of the first stanza states the paradox that will sound throughout the poem. Only in this heavenly state are the flames invincible (and therefore a threat), but flames by necessity burn out; meteors are not meteors until they fall.

The poet turns from the green and pastoral perfection of the ideal state to darkness and elemental strife. The tone of this first stanza is thus comparable to the smooth voice of a movie narrator describing the opposite of what his story will be, so that the trumpets and drums and blinding flashes of lightning to come will be the more exciting. The device can be comic or it can be melodramatic: allegory is halfsister to melodrama.

A tale will be told: " 'Twas in a Shipwrack. . . ." The subject has shifted from the generalized plural "[those] With whom the Infant Love yet playes" to the singular "my poor Lover," an epithet akin to "our hero." And the hero, by that slight, individualizing "my," is given a persona comparable to that, say, of the unhappy third son at the opening of a folk tale.

Aboard a ship at the mercy of wind and waves, the hero "floting lay"; that is, I suppose, he was in the ship that lay floating, though the phrase refers, strong and clear, to the Lover and suggests a prenatal helplessness. "And, e're brought forth, was cast away" is a parenthetical, summarizing riddle which is then immediately answered. At last the vessel was driven upon the rocks, where it split amidships and was thus delivered of a son by *"Cesarian Section"*—in the poem's most fanciful figure.

With the third stanza, the sudden intrusion of the present tense serves to underline the character of the action which Marvell is defining, that it continues still: "The Sea him lent these bitter Tears/ Which at his Eyes he alwaies bears." The shifting tenses, here as elsewhere in the poem, emphasize that "my poor Lover" (our hero) is caught in an everlasting struggle. His kinship with the elements, too, works to define his character in universal terms. He has his tears given him by the sea, and his sighs roar from the very wind. His struggle is in darkness and hideous noise, "As at the Fun'ral of the World." This hero, this demigod, survives his birth only to become the heir to misfortune. Into their "cruel Care," black cormorants receive "The Orphan of the *Hurricane.*" His torture begins. He is fed in order to be famished; hope, digested, is despair. This Promethean suffering produces "Th' *Amphibium* of Life and Death."

Nature has presented a "masque of quarrelling Elements" to celebrate his birth, as she has provided these guardians to nurse her charge: it is natural for vultures to appear at the scene of death, and the Lover's birth is, as we see, a kind of death. Now Heaven asks for sport, "a spectacle of Blood." Nature complies and arranges a tournament. The fight, which first was for survival, now is against an enemy. The Unfortunate Lover, set against Fortune, who is joined by the Tyrant Love, must fight both flames (Love) and waves (Fortune): he, "Like *Ajax*, the mad Tempest braves."[8] The tense is now clearly in the present: the fight is on, and we are called to witness how he cuffs the Thunder, grapples with the Rock, how he rebounds, though

> Torn into Flames, and ragg'd with Wounds.
> And all he saies, a Lover drest
> In his own Blood does relish best.

Among those called to witness this battle ("See how he nak'd and fierce does stand"), it is the lover who will best appreciate what the combatant attempts because, "drest/ In his own Blood," he will find there the image of his own battle.[9]

In the final stanza the battlefield is left behind. Love does not retire the Unfortunate Lover from the field, for that combat is unending as long as there are lovers: the Unfortunate Lover, though he is singular and before our very eyes, is, after

---

[8] This is the Lesser Ajax, punished by Athena because he had molested Cassandra. After wrecking his ship, Athena transfixed his breast with a thunderbolt, so that he breathed flame, and then impaled him on a rock (*Aeneid* I, 39ff.).

[9] "Saies" I read as the aphetic form of "assay," which is "to test," "to taste," "to try to do the difficult" (*OED*, "say" 2, 4, 5). "To relish" is to take delight in something that is pleasant to the taste—and to appreciate, to understand (*OED*, 3). Because of the shared concept of "taste," the two words "saies" and "relish" stand in rather witty conjunction.

all, representative and general. His end must be as charged with meaning as his beginning, or he would suddenly become more actual than symbolic. It is not in his bravery and spirited battling that he is an honored victor, but in his apotheosis. The figure of his dying into art looks back to the metaphor of his birth. The only conquest of the *"Banneret"* is in that story which has been narrated and which the heraldic standard itself symbolizes. "In a Field *Sable* a Lover *Gules"*: the static, timeless banner is therefore comparable both to the "story" of the Nymph and her fawn, which she so lovingly describes, and to the sculpted tomb that Damon describes at the close of his song:

> And thus, ye Meadows, which have been
> Companions of my thoughts more green,
> Shall now the Heraldry become
> With which I shall adorn my Tomb. . . .

In his dying, the Lover "leaves a Perfume here,/ And Musick within every Ear." Sweet odors[10] and sweet sounds, the sensory delights of the contemplative mind, are the earthly counterparts of the beauties of heavenly life. The Lover's sacrifice assures our enjoyment of them.

Transfigured, the Lover lives in an ideal state not essentially different from that green paradise of the soul with which the poem begins. In the serene timelessness of that emblem (as in the historical present of the narrative), he has, indeed, climbed to that "Region" from which he is able "To make impression upon Time."

THE FRAMING stanzas, then, present images which are beyond time, which in their lineaments suggest the contempla-

---

[10] Cf. the lines spoken by the "Resolved Soul": "A Soul that knowes not to presume/ Is Heaven's and its own perfume." Perfume is identified with incense from the altar in "Eyes and Tears." Perhaps here it rises in sign of the lover's sacrifice.

tive rather than the active. The first stanza is no puzzle: the pastoral scene (confounded, of course, by irony as many times as not) is an appropriate setting for the presentation of innocence and the soul's nontemporal life. Though the final stanza is more complex syntactically, it is certainly about art as a kind of timeless "field" above or beyond the field of battle which is human passion—or human life: the equivalence is, I think, one that the poem confirms.

The battle imagery is more substantial in "The Unfortunate Lover" than in other poems of Marvell, where it appears largely as decorative reinforcement rather than dramatic metaphor. The battle is, of course, one of the two or three principal tropes by which allegory proceeds. And Marvell, I think we can say, is neither inventive[11] nor obscure in his use of it. It is the birth of the Unfortunate Lover and the circumstances of his upbringing that have been felt to be strange to the point of distaste. But this small narrative is of a piece with the garden and the heraldic emblem. It has character, setting, conflict, and each can be assigned a significance when the burden of the narration is gathered.

Wind and waves: weather, not climate. Time in contrast to the timeless will necessarily appear dynamic. As the summer comets of the opening scene suggest the shock and sur-

---

[11] Even for the striking term "Banneret" and its metaphoric use, Margoliouth finds precedent in Lovelace's lines in "Dialogue—Lucasta, Alexis": "Love nee're his Standard when his Hoste he sets,/ Creates alone fresh-bleeding Bannerets." (The emphasis is on "fresh-bleeding"; only those who suffer are honored.) There are other echoes of Lovelace in "The Unfortunate Lover," especially of these lines from "To the Genius of Mr. John Hall":

> . . . that Soldier Conquest doubted not,
> Who but one Splinter had of Castriot,
> But would assault ev'n death so strongly charmd,
> And naked oppose rocks with his Love arm'd.

(*The Poems of Richard Lovelace*, ed. C. H. Wilkinson [Oxford, 1930], p. 191.) See also L. N. Wall, "Some Notes on Marvell's Sources," *N&Q*, CCII (1957), 171-72.

prise of the change from an ideal state, so the storm signals the terror and pain that will accompany involvement in another state. The character of water which Marvell stresses in "The Unfortunate Lover" is its violent action, its danger; not water, but stormy water, symbolizes the dynamic character of temporal life and of passionate love.

The shipwreck that takes place in this storm brings to birth the Lover. The boat is driven onto the rocks, where it splits amidships. This "*Cesarian Section*" and the son who is "brought forth" imply a mother. There is no need to puzzle out the identity of a ship-mother, for "she" is really a mother-*ship*: her relationship to her son is not personal but linguistic. The double metaphor of the "*Cesarian Section*" and the "Shipwrack" is fanciful, but it should not be obscure. It is a typically Marvellian development of the implications of a received metaphor, a commonplace figure. "To miscarry" is, of course, used with reference to any catastrophe which might be so described, especially a nautical disaster. When Sir Harry Vane remarked that the republicans "miscarried . . . then shipwrecked," he used a nautical metaphor to describe a political course. What Marvell has done, relying on the deeply rooted association of *ship* and *woman* (of which a recollection of the figureheads of clipper ships can easily remind us), is to elaborate "miscarry" into "*Cesarian Section*," reconverting the nautical metaphor and juxtaposing it with "Shipwrack." The shipwreck is a metaphor expressing the "birth" of the Lover into the world of passion. That "birth," which signals the images to come—"Th' unfortunate . . . Heir," the "Orphan of the *Hurricane*"—is the first of the dreadful paradoxes which characterize the Unfortunate Lover's career. It sets forth the knowledge that disaster and the existence of passionate love are absolutely contingent on one another: that is the answer to the riddle "And, e're brought forth, was cast away."

A case can be made, I believe, for the appropriateness of the figure of the "*Cesarian Section*" to its subject. It is, first of all, a description of the splitting of the ship. The basis of the metaphor is clear and it is singular: the breaking of a side. Any mention of an infant "from his mother's womb untimely ripped" would be inappropriate to a ship; it would reinforce the imagery of birth, but at the cost of emphasizing a relationship which is not to be developed in this allegory. (See Appendix, Note 5.) The mother-ship must remain just that; "*Cesarian Section*" is therefore unmodified and unaccompanied. Like *Hurricane, Amphibium, Ajax,* and *Banneret,* the phrase is italicized and capitalized—devices, perhaps, for emphasizing the complexly abstract character of these metaphors. They are complex because the significances they bear are already symbolic. The figure of the Caesarian section describes not just an incident, but an idea which that incident represents: the splitting of the ship is already metaphoric. The equivalences may be represented thus:

$$\frac{\text{splitting of ship}}{\text{``Cesarian Section''}} = \frac{\text{``Cesarian Section''}}{\text{birth of Lover}} = \frac{\text{birth of Lover}}{\text{emergence of love into time}}$$

The common term is *birth,* and it is a birth whose violence underlines the contrast between the ideal garden of innocent love and passion's storms, the contrast between eternity and time.

A strikingly comparable figure is to be found in the "Horatian Ode." When he describes Cromwell's emergence from a peaceful state into "adventurous War," Marvell compares that career to lightning:

> And, like the three-fork'd Lightning, first
> Breaking the Clouds where it was nurst,
>   Did thorough his own Side
>   His fiery way divide.

The lightning is, like the summer meteors of "The Unfortunate Lover," a fiery impression; its descent is described in the additive (and disruptive) metaphor of a Caesarian birth, which here stresses a relationship of complex political interdependence. The figure is as appropriate to the emergent leader as it is to the shipwrecked lover because (1) this birth seems a kind of self-generation; (2) it is violent, semi-natural, and unexpected; (3) it is an heroic entrance into the world, at least since the nativity of Julius Caesar.

Just as we have meteors, not stars; waves, not water; so there is shipwreck, not just ship: the active, kinetic character of these images gives them a temporality by which may be figured the leaving of the timeless realm for the earth. The shipwreck is actually a violent condensation of the journey, the archetype of all such figures. And the sea, its patterns of change a measure of time, its restless energy the very image of action, is a prime symbol of life in its temporal aspect. A violent sea is, of course, symbolic of life in its passionate aspect, so that the shipwreck is, as it were, doubly emblematic of the power of life and love. Finally, the "Shipwrack" and the *"Cesarian Section"* are equivalent metaphors for the passage from one mode of existence to another.

The mythic cluster of shipwreck/birth/rescue is a rich source of allegorical metaphors depicting the emergence of the soul into time and the retreat into eternity.[12] Marvell's Unfortunate Lover—he who loves outside the garden of innocence—is born into the violent world of passion as the soul is born into temporal existence. The figure of the shipwreck Marvell uses again in "Dialogue Between Soul and Body" in describing the disaster which is paradoxically a salvation, which then becomes disastrous (the Soul is complaining of its fateful relation to the Body):

> Constrain'd not only to indure
> Diseases, but, whats worse, the Cure:

---

[12] See Appendix, Note 5: Shipwreck, Storm, and the Birth Into Time.

>   And ready oft the Port to gain,
>   Am Shipwrackt into Health again.

Though the Soul must share the Body's sickness, it is life's continuance, the cure of disease, which is a far worse burden. Shipwrecked into temporal life, the Soul suffers that kind of death which the Unfortunate Lover suffers in his shipwreck into passion, that birth which the cormorants "That sail'd insulting o're the Wrack" know portends a death.

NOT ONLY the Unfortunate Lover's birth but also his rearing, his struggle, and his apotheosis are resonant with the theme of the soul's life. The Lover's sufferings in the field are like the soul's sufferings in the prison of the body; the Lover's battle is a dramatic analogue of the debate of the Body and Soul, and in some instances, there is an enactment of certain of the metaphors of the two dialogues. Indeed, would we be surprised if "Th' *Amphibium* of Life and Death" should speak the words of the Body: "O who shall deliver me whole,/ From bonds of this Tyrannic Soul?/ Which . . . has made me live to let me dye"? The lover is the most renowned type of the soul, for it is the Tyrant Love who by his challenges brings the soul and body into liveliest conflict. Or, in terms of the color symbolism of the armorial emblem, it is the bleeding, martyred figure of the lover which shows up most brilliantly against the black field of life.[13] The poem's emblematic images are representative of a history, itself symbolic. The

---

[13] Robert L. Brandt cites Marvell's stanza as a possible source for Hawthorne's closing description of the scarlet letter, stressing that "The Unfortunate Lover," besides suggesting "an aesthetic distance, an elevation of the story to the realm of legend, would imply a redeeming light in the beauty of the tragedy" ("Hawthorne and Marvell," *American Literature*, XXX [1958], 366).

Edward Arlington Robinson in "The Man Against the Sky" depicts a lone heroic figure, "Black-drawn against wild red . . . unawed by fiery gules," in language which in several instances recalls Marvell's poem.

history the poem recounts is the history of the Unfortunate Lover, cursed by "the Malignant Starrs." But these are the stars that shine on all who live and love outside the timeless garden, the stars necessary to the creation of time. The lover's misfortune, we might say, is only his soul's fate.

From the standpoint of eternity and art, we look down upon the temporal sea, the field of battle which is the scene of human passion—but what a curious representation of passion it is, without the dialectic of courtship! We witness a battle more elemental than the sexual contest. Violence and bravery and spirit and feeling, represented to the mind's eye by storm and battle, bespeak not only passion as lust but also passion as suffering. This passion the lover and the soul share. We look down upon—as Lord Hastings in Marvell's commemorative poem looks down from heaven upon—"the *Turnaments*/ Of all these Sublunary *Elements*."

"The Definition of Love"

Enlisted in the tournaments of love, the Unfortunate Lover opposes his fate resolutely, creating the legend we all admire, winning the rewards due to those who suffer willingly. In "The Definition of Love," the master theme of opposition sounds again as Marvell addresses himself to the necessities of temporal being, speaking in the voice of allegory to define the love of the embodied soul for its heavenly life.[14]

"The Definition of Love" has been a casualty of the fundamental misconception of Marvell as an imitator of Donne. The poem proceeds by way of figures which in the context of a "love" poem would be expressions of the power of the poet's love for his lady. And such they are generally taken to be: the poem is commonly read either as an ingeniously abstract declaration of love or as a description of Platonic love. But if we entertain for a moment the notion that these figures are

[14] A version of this discussion of "The Definition of Love" appeared in *RES*, XVII (1966), 16-29.

not hyperboles, that what we are presented with is, indeed, a definition of a kind of love, the poem can be seen as something other than a brilliant exercise in Donne's wittiest manner.

The metaphors of this poem have, I think, been underrated; they have been misunderstood as "scientific" figures ironically serving the extreme expression of feeling. But they are emblematic in character. The images of "The Definition of Love" are allegorical metaphors drawn from the experience of sublunary passion, the language of philosophy, the geometry of necessity, and the fatal form of the world. They serve as bridges to what is otherwise incommunicable. The expression throughout is allegorical, the mode necessary to the very conception of metaphysical abstractions such as purity and perfection of being, identity and unity, immortality and incarnation. As we should expect from Marvell, the ambiguities of language are fully exploited so that by the time we come to "Conjunction" and "Opposition" in the concluding stanza, we discover not only that each term defines the other with an algebraic complexity but also that each term is at once sexual, logical, astrological, and geometrical. Counterpointing the austere scientific and philosophic figures is the language of love, but this is not to say that the theme of the poem is the love of a luckless man for a woman. The personal tone is generated by the poem's continued metaphor of sexual love. Marvell has proceeded in a characteristic manner, reversing theme and image so that the soul, often in attendance upon the theme of earthly love as the poet sings "soulfully" of his desire, becomes itself the subject whose dilemma the language of earthly passion serves to define. There is no extended contrast between earthly and heavenly love. Nor is it the case that the imagery is drawn from heavenly love to describe in hyperbole an earthly passion; it is the other way around: the state of the soul, the conditions of its temporal being, the nature of its heavenly character are defined by way of a philosophical disquisition spoken in the voice of allegory by the poet in love with his soul.

This particular "dialectick animal"—Marvell's name for definition—is as rigorous and well-made as his definition of necessity. The metaphors which define this love are all, in a sense, riddles, for the love defined cannot be separated from its figurative state. One riddle therefore only begets another. Since the logic of the imagery, the attitude expressed, and the argument are all of a piece, to characterize one is to define all. The key to the poem is its abstractness: the imagery is highly intellectualized; the expression is reserved; the argument is unrelievedly paradoxical. The poem's abstractness is always acknowledged by critics, but is often then simply ignored, or else its implications are not fully taken into account. Frank Kermode is so perplexed at the disparities he finds between Marvell's poem and other poems in the genre of the "definition" that he proposes the theory that Marvell's poem has had the wrong title affixed.[15] But the title is appropriate and exact. The poet will define; his subject will be love. The riddling definition with which the poem opens is answered in images which are consistently, relentlessly abstract. The function of that abstractness is twofold: it maintains the generality of the referent and guards the absolute character of the definition, the paradox of a love created by despair and impossibility. Consider any one phrase to be only expressive and not, literally, definitive, and the tone becomes more precious than grand, the rigorous paradox collapses. The necessity of deciding whether Marvell's poem is indeed a "description" or a "definition" is obviated if it is recognized to be allegory, for an allegorical *description* setting forth the character of the soul's love for its heavenly being will *define* that love. And the definition will necessarily be metaphoric, since identification is impossible. This love lives by metaphor

[15] Frank Kermode, "Definitions of Love," *RES*, VII (1956), 185.

and thus it is that definition, as much as love, is the subject of Marvell's poem.

Professor Kermode is right to doubt that the poem is a "definition" if he takes the subject to be a mortal passion which Marvell sets about to distinguish from other, baser loves. For in that case the metaphors are overstatements, not of much use in a definition; they are merely personal. He comments that Marvell's poem "distinguishes but it does not define" and that "it is the rarity, the unusual qualities of his particular love, that the poem deals with."[16] This assertion is based upon Marvell's phrase "My Love" and it is not convincing. Whatever particularity there is in "The Definition of Love" is not actual but virtual: "*My* Love" lends a personal tone to offset— or perhaps to set off—the curious phrase "strange and high." When Marvell writes of a mistress fair, the figures may be ornate and abstract, but they will at some point give way to actuality—to eyes, voice, a glimpse of bosom, flower-crowned hair, to a name. But the love which Marvell defines in this poem could not be so represented without risk to its integrity. Certainly it is *his* love, but the strong implication is that the poet's love is directed toward the unearthly, that the love being defined is not the poet's "particular love" but a particular *kind* of love. The generality of the referent controls the tone.

The argument of the poem, too, depends on abstractness. Most critical difficulties stem, I believe, from a misapprehension of the terms of that argument as they are introduced in the first stanza:

> My Love is of a birth as rare
> As 'tis for object strange and high:
> It was begotten by despair
> Upon Impossibility.

In terms of Marvell's definition of definition, the poem addresses itself immediately to "the soul of the thing defined":

[16] *Ibid.*, p. 184.

"My Love" is to be distinguished from other kinds both by the character of its origin—mythically speaking, its birth—and by the character of its object, also mythically conceived in terms of place. Here and throughout the following stanzas, the separation that the poem celebrates seems to call for a degree of abstractness in its definition beyond that which earthly passion, no matter how intellectualized, can legitimately claim. And yet John Press can write: " 'The Definition of Love,' though far less sensuous than 'To his Coy Mistress,' conveys with equal force the longing of two lovers to be united."[17] Since there is rather contemptuously expressed in this poem the notion that "longing" is beside the point—"feeble Hope could ne'er have flown"—that the situation in which the poet finds himself is incommensurate with longing, this comment seems to me unsupportable. The love here being defined has been fathered by despair; and though Press, along with most readers, identifies this love with earthly passion, it is notable that the love of a woman, though it may generate despair and be nourished by despair, is *fathered* by hope and desire.[18]

Criticism of the poem has been concentrated on finding a source or at least an analogy for the paradox of a love which is generated by impossibility. Insofar as it is a logical term and not simply an exaggeration, "impossibility" defines that which is contrary to the nature of reality. It is so used in this poem from Philip Ayres's *Emblems of Love*, entitled "The Impossibility":

[17] John Press, *Andrew Marvell*, p. 30.

[18] Pierre Legouis, noting that Massinger has hope and impossibility as neighbors, remarks that Marvell "improved" upon this figure by substituting despair for hope and making those neighbors the parents of his love ("Marvell and Massinger," *RES*, XXII [1947], 63-65). But this is not an "improvement," it is a change of the figure, and a radical change: the logical basis is entirely different. If Marvell writes that Despair has fathered this love, that Impossibility is its mother, this is saying something other than that they are simply "related" to his love a little more closely than neighbors would be.

Who warmly courts the cold and awkward dame
    Whose breast the living soul does scarce inspire
With them an equal folly may proclaim
    Who without fuel strive to kindle fire.[19]

The emblem *defines* an impossible state of affairs; it is not an expression of hopelessness or misery. In contrast, a lover who sighs at the "impossibility" of his love sighs because there is no response, not because there can be none. If he should speak of "impossibility," the term would be hyperbolic, for he does not, in his heart, lose the faith that "Fortune relieves the cruelties of Fate."[20] Thus Cowley in his "Impossibilities," a poem cited by Margoliouth and others as a possible source for Marvell's poem, is claiming that nothing else *would be* impossible, "could mine bring thy *Heart Captive* home." Cowley's is a passionate boast in which "impossibility" remains subjunctive; the term does not here designate a present and absolute state of affairs.

A lover—*by definition*, we might say—could not argue the absolute impossibility of his love. Thus Sidney's Philoclea soon persuades herself that "impossibility" is for a lover impossible. Her appeal to the stars and her own reason to help her out of an impossible situation has been cited as an analogue to Marvell's declaration: "O then, o tenne times unhappie that I am, since where in all other hope kindleth love; in my despaire should be the bellowes of my affection; and of all despaires the most miserable, which is drawn from impossibilitie."[21] She is declaring that she loves "Zelmane," a supposed Amazon whom we (and Philoclea's perspicacious mother) know to be the disguised knight Pyrocles, smitten with love for the lady

[19] *Minor Poets of the Caroline Period*, ed. George Saintsbury (Oxford, 1906), II, 356.

[20] *The Poems and Translations of Thomas Stanley*, ed. G. M. Crump (Oxford, 1962), p. 58.

[21] *The Countess of Pembrokes Arcadia*, ed. Albert Feuillerat (Cambridge, 1912), p. 174.

Philoclea. Her despair, therefore, is a tease for the reader, who knows that what Philoclea claims to be impossible is not that at all. Rhetorically, that "impossibilitie" is hyperbole, as Philoclea herself decides once she has drawn up these two analogies, truly intolerable in their absoluteness: "The most covetous man longs not to get riches out of a ground which never can bear anything; Why? because it is impossible. The most ambitious wight vexeth not his wittes to clime into heaven; Why? because it is impossible." Sidney's analogy is Marvell's theme and if Marvell found inspiration in Philoclea's distraught exclamations it was in the logic of her supporting argument, not in the rhetorical description of her supposed situation.

When the abstractness of the imagery and the cold, grand tone of "The Definition of Love" have been appreciated, they have often been taken as evidence that the poem is a celebration of Platonic love rather than a definition of the more usual variety of earthly love. But Marvell's "Definition," though it expresses that stoic awe which often characterizes the Platonic lover, defines a love "begotten by despair," and with despair the Platonic lover has naught to do. Caroline poems which set forth the marvels of Platonic love are full of a self-conscious wonder, indeed of self-satisfaction; "holier-than-thou" is almost unavoidable. If not scorn, there is pitying distaste for those lovers who are enchained by the senses:

> Let our mutual thoughts betray,
> And in our wils our minds display;
>
> .   .   .   .
>
> Thus we (my Dear) of these may learn
> A Passion others not discern.[22]

Despair is appropriate to Platonic love neither as motive nor as consequence, for that form of affection is deliberately chosen with the conviction that it is less harrowing, more enjoyable than sexual love:

[22] *Stanley* (ed. Crump), p. 27.

What human passion does with tears implore
The intellect enjoys, when 'tis in love
With the eternal soul, which here does move
In mortal closet, where 'tis kept in store.[23]

"The Definition of Love" cannot be read as a poem about Platonic love if the absolute character of the paradox of a love created by impossibility and despair is granted. This is not a concession to be made in the interest of simplifying the reading of the poem: it is a consequence of taking metaphoric definition seriously. Impossibility's mate, in Marvell's metaphor, is *Despair*, not the mystical enjoyment of another's soul. Despair is essential to the dialectic of Marvell's definition. It is carefully differentiated from misery[24] and defined as the fallow ground of a resolute acceptance of fate.

Fate is not the way things go but the way things are. Fate is not a mode of happening but the fact of being. Fate is necessity and the prime necessity of temporal life is that the soul must be, *for the time being*, displaced, separated from its true home. The caged bird, the shipwreck, the prisoner are all dramatic symbols of the soul in time, figures that are, after all, only the literary expression of those mythic metaphors which grow from man's most primal feeling, that he is lost: "the world's an orphans' home." The feelings which are awakened by this knowledge—a knowledge which, in the circle of time, itself grows from an awareness of the feelings—are hope, despair, and fear: fear of corruption and the rough strife; hope for the discovery of paradise on earth; despair of such discovery. But from that despair bursts resolution. Such renewal is a theme

[23] Philip Ayres, "Platonic Love," in *Minor Poets*, II, 318.
[24] Kermode rightly dismisses Dennis Davison's reading of the poem ("Marvell's 'The Definition of Love,'" *RES*, VI [1955], 141-46) as "an alternation of hope and despair," claiming that hope has no place in the poem. He then seeks to compare Marvell's "Definition" with a French poem in which the misery of a lover is expressed. But misery has no more place in "The Definition of Love" than hope. "Despair in love" is not the poem's subject.

found in Herbert and Hopkins. "The Definition of Love" belongs, I think, with poems in which resolution is the keynote.

Whether it is that of the lover or the philosopher, despair is, of course, primarily an empty thing. It is only when it creates something else that it comes into its own. The lover's despair, if it becomes the resolute acceptance of fate, is no longer earthbound; it is no longer merely the antithesis of hope, as it is so often represented in poems of Marvell's contemporaries. The Caroline sport of writing a brace of poems on hope and despair may be symptomatic of an energetic delight in metaphysical antithesis, but the poems are not notable for a subtlety of definition, because, indeed, subtlety is not required. These poems are generally limited to the notion of hope as the well-spring of desire, of despair as the sorrow which the hapless lover must bear. Definition is formulated according to a graduated scale, with despair below hope and above fear. The easy paradoxes—Cowley's "'Tis Hope is the most hopeless thing of all," for instance—stand between the poet and the possibility of moving statement. But when, in his despair, the lover or the philosopher resolutely accepts fate, then despair becomes the conqueror of all earthly passion. It is no longer a substanceless, negative feeling but takes on character and spirit and becomes the very type of the soul which discovers joy in contemplating its separation from heaven.

Marvell's "Magnanimous Despair"—like Bunyan's Giant Despair it is beyond a mere personal hopelessness—has shown the poet the nature of his love because it is equal to it, as the epithet suggests:

> Magnanimous Despair alone
> Could show me so divine a thing,
> Where feeble Hope could ne'r have flown
> But vainly flapt its Tinsel Wing.

This *divine thing*—"that thing Divine" is Marvell's name for the soul in "A Dialogue Between the Resolved Soul and Created Pleasure"—has not been revealed by hopeful desire nor by a melancholic, peevish malcontent; for with these it is entirely incommensurate.

Magnanimous Despair and the Love it creates form a dialectical unity, just as the Drop of Dew represents in itself the incomparable joy of contemplation of heaven and despair of the life that makes such contemplation possible. It is the kind of paradox found when two modes of being are contrasted. It shares the profundity of those sacramental metaphors by which Christ describes and defines for His disciples the love of God for those who love His Son.[25]

THE abstractness of the poem, I have said, works to maintain both generality of reference and the absolute paradox of the love which is at once the creator and the progeny of despair.[26] The secret of the poem's difficulty is that the metaphors by which that abstractness is effected do not define "real" things or actual relationships. They are allegorical metaphors and they refer to metaphysical concepts which, though they are indeed derived from human experience, are themselves abstract. The poem's metaphors are meta-metaphors. As they succeed one another there is a gradual revelation of significance in an argument whose discursive development provides the scheme of the poem. And yet, because the referent is constant,

[25] See, especially, John 14-15, where the imagery is comparable to Marvell's here. The tone of that colloquy is analogous too: joy and certainty pitted against despair.

[26] Harold Toliver is the only critic I have read who confronts the real difficulties of the poem: the identification of the object "strange and high" and the absolute nature of the paradox of the love born of impossibility and despair. His reading, stressing love's ambivalent need for union and separateness, makes as good a case as can be made for the poem's being "concerned with the essential nature of love as well as the personal experience of the speaker" (*Marvell's Ironic Vision* [New Haven, 1965], p. 48). But Professor Toliver finds "the emphasis gradually shifting from an uncompleted, continuous yearning to a closed and defined experience" (p. 53n.), an interpretation gainsaid by his recognition of the creative power of despair.

there is, as well, a static quality about the poem's imagery. It is this fusion of the discursive—the quasi-narrative—and the emblematic which the allegorical mode achieves.

The eight stanzas of "The Definition of Love" present an argument as strictly formal in its design as the "Had we . . ./ But I . . ./ Let us . . ." of "To His Coy Mistress." The complex relationship between love and despair is described in the first two stanzas; the next five describe the action of fate; the final stanza defines the consequence. I propose to follow that argument by analyzing the allegorical metaphors by means of which it is presented.

The assertion that hope is feeble in the case of the "divine thing" which despair has revealed is tautological, since despair certainly itself defines that hopelessness. But this tautology strengthens the paradox on which the whole poem pivots. Since the riddle of the "divine thing" holds little promise for development, Marvell turns to the primal metaphor of the journey:

> And yet I quickly might arrive
> Where my extended Soul is fixt,
> But Fate does Iron wedges drive,
> And alwaies crouds it self betwixt.

My contention is that the poet stands in the same relation to the place where his "extended Soul is fixt" as he does to the "divine thing," that his soul and the object of his despair-created love are the same.

"Extended Soul" means just what it says: this is a metaphoric definition, not just a simple euphemism like Ayres's "mortal closet." The soul is heavenly in essence but it has a temporal life: the definition of incarnation requires just such an ambiguous term as "extension." "Extended" and "fixt" are both geometrical terms and they point ahead to stanza 7, but geometry has a physical as well as an abstract aspect and Marvell exploits it by the same operation of wit as that by which he has the Body complain that "this Tyrannic Soul/ Which, stretcht upright, impales me so,/ That mine own Precipice I go." Here, he develops "stretcht" out of the notion of extension, combining the physical and the metaphysical as surely as they are combined in the more obvious metaphor, "Cramp of Hope."[27]

The spatial metaphor created by "extended" and "fixt" repeats and reinforces the trope implied in "arrives." The journey of the soul to its home or the flight of the soul heavenward is the commonest figure in descriptions of the soul's return: it is impossible to dispense with the metaphor in order to "explain" the referent, for description and definition are mutually dependent. The line "And yet I quickly might arrive" plays with the ambiguity of the soul's alienation. It is only because of this temporal—and therefore temporary—existence that such union is precluded; the poet might *quickly* arrive at his soul's home if only he weren't *quick*!

The figure of the "Iron wedges" driven by Fate develops the concept of polarity implicit in extension. A wedge forces a breach in a single mass (as in the case of a woodsman's wedge); or it drives apart separate elements which have an affinity for one another. By the act of holding the soul in disparate states, Fate's wedges thereby assure that unity which defines, as it is defined by, polarity. Binding what they separate, Fate's "Iron wedges" are thus analogous to "the great iron nail" driven by Necessity "thorough the axletree of Nature."[28] The necessity which has dominion over heaven and earth is the power that has set them apart: as being is contingent upon separation in the definition of necessity, so, here, is love contingent upon separation in this definition. Fate, as Plato explains, is the daughter of Necessity.

The force that, separating, binds is represented by the line drawn between two fixed points and by the axle that runs from

[27] See Appendix, Note 6: Extension.
[28] See Appendix, Note 7: Fate's "Iron wedges."

pole to pole: extension and polarity are thus analogous terms
for the same concept. Just as extension has a spatial form and
a certain kinetic energy which Marvell adapts for the purposes
of definition, so polarity has obvious visual uses. Stanzas 4, 5,
and 6 develop emblems of polarity, reinforced by sexual
imagery:

> For Fate with jealous Eye does see
> Two perfect Loves; nor lets them close:
> Their union would her ruine be,
> And her Tyrannick pow'r depose.

> And therefore her Decrees of Steel
> Us as the distant Poles have plac'd,
> (Though Loves whole World on us doth wheel)
> Not by themselves to be embrac'd.

> Unless the giddy Heaven fall,
> And Earth some new Convulsion tear;
> And, us to joyn, the World should all
> Be cramp'd into a *Planisphere.*

"Two perfect Loves" is clearly metaphoric, since to assert that
Fate would keep mortal lovers apart because her power de-
pended on that separation would be to forget that Fate, though
seemingly defeated on any one occasion, moves on to further
conquests. These "Two perfect Loves" arouse Fate's jealousy
because their essential unity challenges her own creation.
Therefore rings exultant: the polarity established by Fate's
"Decrees of Steel" is necessary to prevent her very "ruine."
And what would Fate's ruin be? Why, that union in earthly
terms—the embracing of the "Two perfect Loves"—and there-
fore the union of heaven and earth, necessitating the collapse
of the world's poles.[29] The perfection which is essential unity

[29] On logical and syntactical grounds, "World" seems to include
"Heaven" and "Earth," a reading which requires construing "the dis-
tant Poles" as celestial rather than terrestrial. Dean Morgan Schmitter

is, like the secret of time, dependent on polarity, but the union
which is the identification of opposites is that " 'natural impos-
sibility' " (IV, 209) which would be "post-eternal," the counter-
part of the "pre-eternal" Necessity. The threatened identifica-
tion of opposites suggests violence to Marvell's imagination.
This violence may be of a primally grotesque sort, as in "The
Unfortunate Lover," where he who lives outside the timeless
garden of innocent, heavenly love is born into the world of
time amidst confusion suggesting "the Fun'ral of the World";
and sometimes it is described in a comic manner, as here, with
"giddy Heaven" and "new Convulsion" and "cramp'd." The
union of heaven and earth would cramp the world into a
planisphere, the very name a paradox. Most notes on "plani-
sphere," by describing it as a flat projection of the globe,
underwrite the terrestrial reading of "poles." But the term
"planisphere," though it can refer to a stereographic projection
of either the earth or the heavens, also refers to a geographical
astrolabe, an instrument in which a skeletal, planispheric star
chart is superimposed over a planispheric map of earth.[30] The
planisphere is thus an emblem of a union which is the ruining

rejects the celestial identification with the remark that "the idea of
common loves would be embarrassed by a reading that links them
with cosmic values" ("The Cartography of 'The Definition of Love,' "
RES, XII [1961], 49). In my view, it is precisely this correspondence
which is suggested by the "Two perfect Loves." I have found no use
of the term in the terrestrial sense by Marvell.

[30] Donne's compasses are mentioned frequently in commentary on
the imagery of this poem, but the image which is closest in function
(logically and metaphysically defined) to Marvell's planisphere is that
flat map (the simplest type of planisphere) which occurs in a poem
dealing with the fate of the soul:

> I joy, that in these straits, I see my West;
> For, though their currants yeeld returne to none,
> What shall my West hurt me? As West and East
> In all flatt Maps (and I am one) are one,
> So death doth touch the Resurrection.

("Hymne to God my God, in my sicknesse," *The Poems of John Donne*,
ed. Herbert J. C. Grierson [Oxford, 1912], I, 368.)

of the world's polarity. Marvell, with incomparable energy, reverses the grand axiom of the contingency of being upon separation to show the end of being consequent to identification.

The parenthetical line of stanza 5 gives us the poem's master image: "(Though Loves whole World on us doth wheel)." It is a witty *sotto voce*, a riddle which, like the "(My fruits are only Flow'rs)" of "The Coronet," we cannot answer unless we take the metaphor as definition. The definition of love recognizes the sublunary point, the temporal existence that makes possible both earthly love and the love of the heavenly source. The parenthesis is a motto for the emblem of the sphere toward which the entire poem tends, for the sphere is implicit in polarity as polarity is in extension. Extended lines come to circles (III, 146); what are poles and axles for, if not for wheeling? The extended line tends toward the perfection of the sphere: so "Two perfect Loves" in their opposition create "Loves whole World." "Whole" echoes "perfect": the love of the poet, the incarnate soul, for the heavenly source is complete and perfected and necessary.

Stanza 7 returns to geometry:

> As Lines so Loves *oblique* may well
> Themselves in every Angle greet:
> But ours so truly *Paralel*,
> Though infinite can never meet.

The absolute correspondence of the true parallels symbolizes, again, the kind of unity dependent upon opposition. It is not of this world alone. Oblique lines/loves "may well" meet eventually (that is, it is always possible that earthly love can be realized); truly parallel lines/loves can "never meet." Oblique lines imply angles and angles are "imperfections" and thus are symbolic of earthly love; parallel lines suggest the incorruptible.[31] The infinity of these true parallels corresponds

---

[31] With comparable imagery, Marvell in "Eyes and Tears" suggests

to the notion of the immortality of the soul, which depends, of course, on that heavenly place where it is "fixt," in opposition to its temporal state.[32]

The opening stanzas of "The Definition of Love" defined "the soul of the thing" (according to Marvell's definition of definition), a Love born of Despair and Impossibility; intervening stanzas have defined by describing (and have described by defining) the absolute separation of the poet and the "object strange and high"; the concluding stanza completes the definition of this love:

---

that eyes are bound to falsify, whereas tears, the sign of a deeper humanity, are true:

> And, since the Self-deluding Sight,
> In a false Angle takes each hight;
> These Tears which better measure all,
> Like wat'ry Lines and Plummets fall.

[32] Reunion with heaven, after the death of the body, is not precluded by this infinite parallelism. The Drop of Dew thinks on it, but the unity which is Marvell's subject in this poem is the paradoxical unity of the incarnate soul, the "temporizing of essence," as Kenneth Burke has it. (See *A Grammar of Motives* [New York, 1945], pp. 430-40, and *A Rhetoric of Motives* [New York, 1950], pp. 13-15.) Marvell is not speaking of *two souls*, as I implied in an earlier version of this discussion (see note 14, above). My reference to a "heavenly counterpart" misleads since that phrase suggests the part/whole relationship, a concept inadequate for describing the soul's temporal existence. Plotinus, in discussing the relationship of the incarnate soul to the All-Soul, warns of the dangers: "In such questions . . . it is important to clarify the significance of 'part'" (*Enneads* IV. 3, 2. Plotinus is quoted from the translation by Stephen MacKenna, *The Enneads*, rev. B. S. Page [2nd edn.; New York, 1957]). He solves the dilemma by employing various metaphors and, very occasionally, by semantic subterfuges which allow him to discuss, for instance, the divisibility of the indivisible.
Sir Thomas Browne, whose energetic paradoxes solve such enigmas easily, is content sometimes with simple contradictions: "[T]he soule of man may bee in Heaven any where, even within the limits of his owne proper body" (*Religio Medici*, in *The Works of Sir Thomas Browne*, ed. Geoffrey Keynes [3 vols.; Chicago, 1964], I, 60). Somewhere between quibbling and logical contradiction is the rhetorical field where poets sport.

Therefore the Love which us doth bind
But Fate so enviously debarrs,
Is the Conjunction of the Mind,
And Opposition of the Stars.

Both "Conjunction" and "Opposition" are astrological terms
and are generally read in such a way as to provide a simple,
neat antithesis between sublunary lovers' minds in planet-like
conjunction and the malevolent stars in opposition to them.
So read, the lines present a variant of the theme of star-crossed
lovers, fate being accepted with equanimity. But we can ap-
preciate the more profoundly witty relationship that "Con-
junction" and "Opposition" bear to one another if we hear
the voice of allegory. The stars "oppose" man, certainly, but
they do so by their conjunctions as well as by their opposi-
tions.[33] It is not a particular misfortune which the stars have
determined but the condition of existence in time: the opposi-
tion of the stars is the work of jealous fate. Their opposition
has made necessary the "Conjunction of the Mind" which is,
as well, the free act by which the Resolved Soul (the poet)
opposes his fate.

It is enlightening to compare Marvell's concluding stanza
with the following stanza from Cowley's "Impossibilities":

As stars (not powerful else) when they conjoin,
Change, as they please, the Worlds estate;
So thy *Heart* in *Conjunction* with mine,
Shall our own fortunes regulate;
And to our *stars themselves* prescribe a *Fate*.[34]

[33] Sir Thomas Browne speaks of "malignant Aspects, fatall con-
junctions, and Eclipses" (*Religio Medici*, in *Works*, I, 84).
[34] *Abraham Cowley: Poems*, ed. A. R. Waller (Cambridge, 1905),
p. 130. Lovelace's "To his deare brother Colonel F. L." includes a
stanza which is as likely a source as Cowley's poem:

But this way you may gain the field,
Oppose but sorrow and 'twill yield;

Marvell does not promise, as Cowley does, to overthrow fate. Fate has, in effect, created the love Marvell defines: it is the very impossibility of other union which is the ground of the Resolved Soul's response to his fate, his "Opposition of the Stars." The Resolved Soul intends by his opposition not the overthrow of the stars but the transcendence of their power in the celebration of the love which is the creature of their opposition.

That "Conjunction" is both the condition and the result, that "Opposition" is both the challenge and the response, is an irony as intense as that by which is set forth the definition of this Love as the child of Despair and Impossibility. Indeed, the sexual metaphor with which the poem opens and which has been articulated by the figure of the lovers who cannot "by themselves . . . be embrac'd,"[35] sounds at the close. "The Love which us doth bind," since other union is precluded, can only be a "Conjunction" of the mind. (We may remember Sir Thomas Browne's wistful remark: "I would be content that we might procreate like trees, without conjunction. . . .")[36]

Like Love and its parents, conjunction and opposition define one another. Logic, syntax, and imagery distill the central paradox of the unity contingent upon separation; of the freedom that answers necessity; of enabling impossibility and the

---

> One gallant thorough-made Resolve
> Doth starry Influence dissolve.

The cluster of terms is no less striking than the definition of resolute opposition as a means of conquering fate.

[35] It is likely that Marvell, who, as Margoliouth notes, echoes phrases from Carew, has written in "Not by themselves to be embrac'd" a variation on these lines from Carew's "A Rapture":

> And so our soules that cannot be embrac'd
> Shall the embraces of our bodyes taste.

(*The Poems of Thomas Carew*, ed. Rhodes Dunlap [Oxford, 1949], p. 50.)

[36] *Religio Medici*, in *Works*, I, 83.

resolution that springs from the confrontation of fate.[37] "The Definition of Love" ends in quiet exultation which is nonetheless resolute. The concluding stanza has, I think, the same exhilaration as the close of "To His Coy Mistress":

> Thus, though we can not make our Sun
> Stand still, yet we will make him run.

The difference in the argument is the difference between "yet" and "therefore." For the lover of the coy mistress, time is a weapon to be turned against eternity. In "The Definition of Love," the enemy, we might believe, is time itself; but that is not the verdict of the poet who is concerned to define the love that is created by the natural condition of temporal being. If Despair is the sire and Impossibility the dam of this love, they are themselves progenies of Time and Eternity, the generation of the pre-eternal Necessity.

THE LOVE of the incarnate soul for its heavenly life is a philosophic subject. But such philosophic discourse shares the primary poetic mode; that is, it proceeds by metaphor. It is for this reason that reading Plotinus or Plato or Hermes Trismegistus can be instructive in the matter of the logic of Marvell's metaphors. The assumption is not that Marvell was "influenced" by one or another of these philosophers, but that all those who think on the soul's life share a store of symbols.

The mystery of the soul's temporal being is remarked by Sir Thomas Browne throughout *Religio Medici*, especially when, having declared that man is "that great and true *Amphibium*," he turns to a consideration of how the soul joins the body. It must be "transmitted and transfused in the seed of the parents," but still he cannot "peremptorily deny, that the soule in this her sublunary state, is wholly and in all acceptions inorganicall. . . . Thus are we men, and we know

[37] See Appendix, Note 8: Conjunction and Opposition.

not how; there is something in us, that can not be without us, and will be after us, though it is strange that it hath no history, what it was before us, nor can tell how it entered us."[38] Although Sir Thomas Browne here pursues the mystery to an "O altitudo!" he nevertheless shows an interest in those allegorical metaphors by which the life of the soul is conceived and represented. In *The Garden of Cyrus* he cites Plato's use of the decussated circle in his descriptions of the soul. The passage is worth quoting at length because it illustrates so well the radical metaphors of the poet-philosopher:

Of this Figure [the letter χ] *Plato* made choice to illustrate the motion of the soul, both of the world and man; while he delivereth that God divided the whole conjunction lengthwise, according to the figure of a Greek χ, and then turning it about reflected it into a circle; By the circle implying the uniform motion of the first Orb, and by the right lines, the planetical and various motions within it. And this also with application unto the soul of man, which hath a double aspect, one right, whereby it beholdeth the body, and objects without; another, circular and reciprocal, whereby it beholdeth it self. The circle declaring the motion of the indivisible soul, simple, according to the divinity of its nature, and returning into it self; the right lines respecting the motion pertaining unto sense, and vegetation, and the central decussation, the wondrous connexion of the severall faculties conjointly in one substance. And so conjoyned the unity and duality of the soul, and made out the three substances so much considered by him; That is, the invisible or divine, the divisible or corporeal and that third, which was the *Systasis* or harmony of those two, in the mystical decussation.[39]

[38] *Religio Medici*, in *Works*, I, 47.
[39] *The Garden of Cyrus, Works*, I, 220. The reference is to the *Timaeus* 36, 37. Kitty (Scoular) Datta cites another passage from Plato (*Republic* X) in her discussion of the possibility of Marvell's

In Marvell's poem, geometric figures are centrally important to the definition of the soul's temporal being and thereby to the definition of the love of the incarnate soul for its heavenly life. Such figures are the equivalents of all the allegorical metaphors which serve to define what Plotinus calls the "encavernment" of the soul. It is not "allegorization" but a recognition of what we might call the "necessary" character of these metaphors which is at the heart of this passage, for instance: "In the Cavern of Plato and in the Cave of Empedocles, I discern this universe where the breaking of the fetters and the ascent from the depths are figures of the wayfaring towards the Intellectual Realm."[40] Plotinus justifies the metaphor of "encavernment" by adducing the figure of the freed captive and the ascendant, whether bird or air or flame. All these figures are equivalent; each can be seen as necessary if we remember that the problem of representing the soul's temporal being is only the *verso* of the problem of conceiving it.

Of the grand store of equivalent images which define and dramatize the dilemma of a soul in a body, a body inhabited by a soul, the most frequently used is probably the cage or prison. Marvell's "Dialogue Between the Soul and Body" makes traditional use of the prison-body and Marvellian use of a tyrannical soul who, from the body's point of view, is the jailer. Such images function like the geometrical figures; that is, they present pictures which themselves stand for ideas. Marvell uses lines and poles, wedges and planisphere as John Norris uses the prison and the lodestone in a poem called "The Aspiration," quoted below in full:

> How long great God, how long must I
> Immur'd in this dark prison lye!

---

having combined the Platonic spindle and the wedges of the Horatian *Necessitas* ("Marvell's Prose and Poetry: More Notes," *MP*, LXIII [1966], 321).

[40] *Enneads* IV. 8, 1.

Where at the grates and avenues of sense
My soul must watch to have intelligence.
Where but faint gleams of thee salute my sight.
Like doubtful moon-shine in a cloudy night.
    When shall I leave this magic sphere,
    And be all mind, all eye, all ear!

    How cold this clime! and yet my sense
    Perceives even here thy influence.
Even here thy strong magnetic charms I feel,
And pant and tremble like the amorous steel.
To lower good, and beauties less divine
Sometimes my erroneous needle does decline;
    But yet—so strong the sympathy—
    It turns, and points again to thee.

    I long to see this excellence
    Which at such distance strikes my sense.
My impatient soul struggles to disengage
Her wings from the confinement of her cage.
Would'st thou great Love this prisoner once set free,
How would she hasten to be link'd with Thee.
    She'd for no angel's conduct stay,
    But fly, and love on all the way.[41]

The shamed admittance of the charms of earthly life (of "Created Pleasure") is offset by the impassioned declaration of longing for heaven: the "aspiration" is toward death. Heaven's "magnetic charm" may mitigate the pain of temporal existence, but Norris does not make of it the ground of resolution. His theme is not Marvell's, but the emblematic lodestone is comparable to Marvell's geometry in that each figure pictures the lines by which a relationship may be schematically represented. The lodestone's lines of attraction are

[41] *The Poems of John Norris of Bemerton, Miscellanies of The Fuller Worthies Library,* ed. A. B. Grosart (Blackburn, 1871), III, 173.

like Marvell's extended soul and its fixed point; both are representations of that unity-in-separation which defines polarity.

But the further complexity of the figure of the lodestone is made to yield in Crashaw's hands a paradox exactly comparable to that which informs "the Definition of Love":

> . . . yea those dull things,
> Whose wayes have least to doe with wings,
> Make wings at least of their own weight,
> And by their Love controll their Fate.
> So lumpish Steel, untaught to move,
> Learn'd first his Lightnesse by his Love.[42]

It is the very character of "lumpish Steel"—its heaviness—which makes it "light" in the magnetic field of heavenly love. It is by this same reversal that Marvell's Despair creates a Love which by definition is also a denial of despair.

Whereas most Christian poetry on the great theme of the soul's exile stresses the hope of union by way of mystic coalescence or death, Marvell, stressing the very impossibility of union, finds his hope not in faith, not in submission, not in grace, not in death, but in "Magnanimous Despair," which brings him to the resolution to oppose fate by a "Conjunction of the Mind." The soul, aspiring to its heavenly home, is in love, and contemplation of the beloved is the mode of its affection: thus are the complex metaphysics of the soul's earthly existence transmuted, the mind's most profound intuitions given the form of vital human experience.

"To His Coy Mistress"

To turn from the grotesque and melodramatic account of the life and the death and transfiguration of the Unfortunate Lover to the relentless paradoxes of "The Definition of Love"

---

[42] "Against Irresolution and Delay in Matters of Religion," *The Poems English Latin and Greek of Richard Crashaw*, ed. L. C. Martin (Oxford, 1957), p. 349.

and then to the elegant logic and subdued passion of "To His Coy Mistress" is to appreciate at once the range of Marvell's style and the grandeur of his conception of the world of love. Of course, "To His Coy Mistress" is unique among the major poems for the directness of address, for the dramatic tone. Still, it could not be said that a personality or a relationship is discovered or revealed. Leishman feels that we are hearing one half of a dialogue, noting further that "while Donne is . . . primarily concerned with love as an experienced fact, Marvell in this brilliant poem, is primarily concerned with love as a topic."[43] There is little sense of occasion and the dialectic offers no opportunity for response, much less debate. The logical pattern of the argument that a virtual conquest of time is possible in love proceeds with no interruption for the analysis of feeling. Indeed, the most moving lines in the poem are the most chilling, when the burlesque history suddenly stops short:

> But at my back I alwaies hear
> Times winged Charriot hurrying near:
> And yonder all before us lye
> Desarts of vast Eternity.

And yet the tone here and throughout the poem has an immediacy, a nervous intensity which, if it never quite breaks into the dramatic rhythms of actual speech—as, for instance, the Nymph's complaint does—nevertheless brings us close to a man speaking.

With the hortatory close of the poem, the curiously impersonal but nevertheless intense voice becomes prophetic. Here, where we would expect him to be his most direct—after the sardonic homily on what the coy mistress should expect of eternity as she continues so to waste time—the poet seems rather to have his eyes on the horizon:

[43] *The Art of Marvell's Poetry*, pp. 70, 77.

Now therefore, while the youthful hew
Sits on thy skin like morning dew,
And while thy willing Soul transpires
At every pore with instant Fires,
Now let us sport us while we may;
And now, like am'rous birds of prey,
Rather at once our Time devour,
Than languish in his slow-chapt pow'r.
Let us roll all our Strength, and all
Our sweetness, up into one Ball:
And tear our Pleasures with rough strife,
Thorough the Iron gates of Life.
Thus, though we cannot make our Sun
Stand still, yet we will make him run.

The echoing "Now . . . while" conveys an urgency as the
lover sounds the alarm.[44] As the dew is drawn up quickly by
the power of the sun, so "the youthful hew" is transitory, fast
fading. Time is a beast: eat or be eaten. The terse and witty
reversal of time devoured (compare the motif of Cupid pierced
by his own arrows) is preparation for the bravura challenge
to the sun's lead in the race of time. The lover who declares
that they must "tear" their "Pleasures . . . Thorough the Iron
gates of Life" is as clear-sighted as the "Resolved Soul" in
rejecting the feathery ease offered by "Created Pleasure." He
labors under no delusions whatsoever and he offers no blandish-
ments. The "rough strife" promised is a necessary concomitant
of earthly love, but by it are to be won those sweet pleasures
which are the lovers' triumph.

The metaphors of the closing lines are allegorical.[45] They
are neither hyperboles nor simple allusions but images with
the deep resonance which is often a feature of poems taking

[44] H. M. Richmond points out that this rhetorical pattern is a feature
of Ovid's *Ars Amatoria* (III, 57-66), where *nec . . . dum* functions
similarly (*The School of Love* [Princeton, 1964], p. 67).
[45] See Appendix, Note 9: The "Iron gates of Life."

carpe diem as theme. The "Ball" compounded of strength and sweetness represents by its physical shape that same very abstract meaning which the circle bears, or the sphere. Ball, circle, sphere are completed, perfected shapes; like the parallel lines of "The Definition of Love," they become symbols of a conquest of time. Just so, the Drop of Dew

> Round in its self incloses:
> And in its little Globes Extent,
> Frames as it can its native Element.

Marvell's Latin makes explicit the interpendence of opposition and the sweet purity of perfected form:

> Quam bene in aversae modulum contracta figurae
> Oppositum Mundo claudit ubique latus.

The *contracta*, like "Round in its self incloses," and "Every way it turns away," suggests withdrawal in the interest of a fuller being: contraction, withdrawal, but also concentration and therefore strength. Perhaps it could be said that for the lovers, opposition takes the form of imitation, as it does for the Drop of Dew, which by its form imitates its "native Element." For the lovers will create their own time, as the sun does for earth.

But resolution has a cost: love is unifying and beautiful—and it is a fight. The concentration and energy suggested in the lines I have been discussing are called forth by the fact that the gates of life are, like Fate's wedges, iron. That iron, a substance strong and merely strong, the metal of prisons, locks, and chains, should be associated with the fatefulness of life seems an inevitable symbolism. "The Iron gates of Life" suggest, like the Gates of Hercules, the passageway from one world to another; like the "sevenfold yron gates of Hell" of Spenser's "Ruines of Time," they are forbidding, as mortality is forbidding. For just as the gate over which Michael's flaming sword waves, "the gate with dreadful faces thronged," looks out from Eden onto the world, do not these "Iron gates of Life" look out upon the "Desarts of vast Eternity"? From that terrible peaceful kingdom the poet beckons his lady to turn away, having taunted her with descriptions of its emptiness, urging her, instead, to run their "Passions heat." Rounding out the logical form of "Had we . . ./ But I . . ./ Now therefore . . ./ Now let us," the powerful summary underscores the challenge and promises success:

> Thus, though we cannot make our Sun
> Stand still, yet we will make him run.

Exultant resolution is the strong counterpoint to impossibility: "we cannot . . ./ we will." Escape from temporality is precluded by necessity, but the challenge to the sun is the lover's resolute response. Accepting the "natural impossibility" of stopping the sun, the lover chooses to race. He defines the limits of temporality and by opposing ends them: the freedom of the will in the face of necessity is the philosophical conception which underlies the Resolved Soul's opposition to fate, the lover's challenge to time and eternity.

The lesson in love that the poet reads his coy mistress reminds us that resolution can make Bannerets of unfortunate lovers in the sublunary tournaments. Love is like the sun: it has the power to destroy and to fructify; it is strong and it is sweet. Love is the creation of sweetness out of strength and sweetness makes the lover strong. Could not Samson's riddle properly stand as an epigraph for Marvell's poem?

> Out of the eater came forth meat,
> and out of the strong came forth sweetness.

CHAPTER IV

Love, Nature, and Innocence

Pastorals and Semi-Pastorals

F "To His Coy Mistress" is Marvell's greatest love poem, it is very nearly his only love poem. The pastoral mode offers opportunities for the expression of feeling, if not necessarily for the analysis of feeling, but Marvell takes advantage of them only in the Mower poems. There are a variety of pastorals (and "semi-pastorals," as Leishman has it) in which lovers figure, but in none of these poems do we find any interest in the psychological dimension of loving.

There are two courtly lyrics, "The Gallery" and "The Fair Singer," which are exceptional, perhaps. The former is a tour de force, a Marvellian expansion of the convention by which the poet describes the lady engraved in the table of his heart. (Characteristically, Marvell makes his mind and soul the gallery, not his heart.) The pictures are either ethereal or hellish: the mistress is either a Venus, an Aurora, or she is "an Inhumane Murtheress," a malicious "Enchantress" who, having divined how long she shall "continue fair," throws the entrails of the lover to those greedy vultures which ever attend the demise of unfortunate lovers. Close by the entrance to the gallery is the picture he favors, the remembered image of the "tender Shepherdess" "with which I first was took."

"The Fair Singer" is a song whose perfection makes us regret all the more intensely that Henry Purcell, if he saw the 1681 edition of *Miscellaneous Poems by Andrew Marvell, Esq.*, remained uninspired. In this brilliant working of a standard topic, Marvell, with an economy and tact as elegant as any Elizabethan madrigalist could boast, develops a musical-military metaphor, an extension of the "sweet Chordage" pun of

"The Dialogue Between the Resolved Soul and Created Pleasure." It is the Fair Singer's fatal combination of nature ("Eyes") and art ("Voice") that makes the conquest final (italics are mine, added to indicate the fullness of the metaphor):

> To make a final *conquest* of all me,
> Love did *compose* so *sweet* an *Enemy*,
> In whom both Beauties to my *death agree*,
> *Joyning* themselves in *fatal Harmony*;
> That while she with her Eyes my Heart does *bind*,
> She with her Voice might *captivate* my Mind.
>
> I could have *fled* from One but singly fair:
> My *dis-intangled* Soul it self might *save*,
> *Breaking* the curled *trammels* of her hair.
> But how should I avoid to be her *Slave*,
> Whose subtile *Art* invisibly can wreath
> My *Fetters* of the very Air I breath?
>
> It had been easie *fighting* in some *plain*,
> Where *Victory* might hang in equal choice,
> But all *resistance* against her is vain,
> Who has th' *advantage* both of Eyes and Voice,
> And all my *Forces* needs must be *undone*,
> She having *gained* both the *Wind* and *Sun*.

There is an easy spinning out of equivalence with no "prolepsis" or dialectic or any other complication. It is an extended metaphor, but it is not "allegorical." The poem is very close to passages which, though they play a part in a narrative or an argument or in some rhetorical pattern of greater complexity, nevertheless sound in isolation like fragments of a song or madrigal:

> O then let me in time compound
> And parly with those conquering Eyes. . . .

Nature had long a Treasure made
Of all her choisest store;
Fearing, when She should be decay'd,
To beg in vain for more.

Victorious sounds! yet here your Homage do
Unto a gentler Conqueror than you;
Who though He flies the Musick of his praise,
Would with you Heavens Hallelujahs raise.

How safe, methinks, and strong, behind
These Trees have I incamp'd my Mind;
Where Beauty, aiming at the Heart,
Bends in some Tree its useless Dart. . . .

But "The Fair Singer," I would argue, is the one major poem
which is not unmistakably Marvell's, and the reason is that
though Marvell here characteristically speaks of mind and
soul as well as of heart, yet the confrontation is not of fate or
time but only of "fatal Harmony"; and without the grand
Marvellian theme, neither the tone nor the development of
the imagery is typical.

We may well ask what Marvell's aim seems to be in his
love poetry. How does it appear, for instance, in the light of
this description offered by Helen Gardner:

The most serious and impassioned love poetry of the cen-
tury argues, or assumes as a base for argument, that love
is a relation between two persons loving. [Donne's "The An-
niversary," "The Canonization," "The Ecstasy," etc.] have
the right to the title metaphysical in its true sense, since they
raise, even when they do not explicitly discuss, the great
metaphysical question of the relation of the spirit and the
senses. They raise it not as an abstract problem, but in the
effort to make the experience of the union of human powers
in love, and the union of two beings in love, apprehensible.

We never lose our sense of a "little roome" which love has made "an evry where."[1]

Is Marvell, like Donne, concerned to make the experience of loving "apprehensible"? Certainly there are no "little roomes" in his poems and love makes battlefields everywhere—even the garden is not entirely safe. Throughout the pastorals, the themes of "The Unfortunate Lover" continually sound: passionate love is inevitably a tyranny; there is no relief from that tyranny within the bounds of temporal existence. Those "With whom the Infant Love yet playes" are blessed, but when the lover is passionate, when he leaves the chaste garden of green love, it is the Tyrant Love with whom he must do battle. Marvell is concerned not with lovers and their feelings but with love and the plight of the lover; more with metaphysics, less with psychology.

There is, indeed, a psychological interest in his poetry of love, but it derives not from the characters—Daphnis or Celia or Nature—but from the complexities of Marvell's attitudes. There is a fundamental ambivalence in his conception of human love, resulting occasionally not so much in delightful irony as in an unsatisfactorily resolved contradiction.

In "Daphnis and Chloe," for instance, the high-mindedness of Daphnis, who argues that "Gentler times for Love are ment," is revealed as hypocritical and self-serving vengeance. The poem is scarcely "pastoral" except with respect to names, though we might consider the possibility that the Greek romance[2] provided the motif of naïveté alleged of Marvell's Chloe, who "neither knew t'enjoy,/ Nor yet let her Lover go" and of Daphnis, who, though

> . . . well read in all the wayes
> By which men their Siege maintain,

[1] *The Metaphysical Poets* (Baltimore: Penguin, 1957), pp. 24-25.
[2] Legouis, *Andrew Marvell*, p. 29.

> Knew not that the Fort to gain
> Better 'twas the Siege to raise.

Nature connives for her own good reasons, "lay[ing] by her wonted state," to encourage Chloe to yield. As Fate keeps the poet's soul separate from its heavenly home to avoid the world's being "cramp'd into a *Planisphere*," so Nature tries to bring these sublunary lovers together "Lest the World should separate." Coyness is all very well, but chastity would spell *ruin* for Nature, as the poet's essential conjunction with his soul would for Fate.

The situation is established: Chloe yields when she discovers Daphnis is about to leave ("Sudden Parting closer glews"), but Daphnis rejects this last-minute capitulation and in sixteen stanzas rings the changes on the theme of the precious desire which becomes worthless in the circumstances of prescribed enjoyment. He concludes:

> Joy will not with Sorrow weave,
> Nor will I this Grief pollute.
>
> Fate I come, as dark, as sad,
> As thy Malice could desire. . . .

Daphnis goes to his fate and the poem concludes with two stanzas in the poet's voice, first:

> But hence Virgins all beware.
> Last night he with *Phlogis* slept;
> This night for *Dorinda* kept;
> And but rid to take the Air.

The secret is out: Daphnis' fate is named "Dorinda." The "manly stubborness" (line 70) with which he has rejected Chloe's favors is nothing but his revenge for her earlier coyness. This penultimate stanza expresses explicitly that skepticism about the sincerity of lovers which these closing lines of "Mourning" ironically suppress:

I yet my silent Judgment keep,
Disputing not what they believe
But sure as oft as Women weep,
It is to be suppos'd they grieve.

But there is one more stanza in "Daphnis and Chloe":

Yet he does himself excuse;
Nor indeed without a Cause.
For, according to the Lawes,
Why did *Chloe* once refuse?

The final word seems to be that Daphnis' vengeance was jus-
tified. But the sensitive philosopher of love who argues in such
brilliant paradoxes, obedient ever to Nature's laws, is not
consistent with the Don Juan about whom "Virgins all" are
warned, nor is the character of that libertine compatible with
that of the naïve boy who doesn't know when to lift the siege.
What are we to make of these inconsistencies?

Lawrence Hyman concludes that Daphnis is unconvincing
when "he boasts of his promiscuity," that the lover "beneath
the Cavalier cynicism, despises promiscuity." But Professor
Hyman confuses Marvell and Daphnis: it is not Daphnis who
"boasts of his promiscuity" but the poet, who first cuttingly
reveals it and then takes a step toward defending it. "The
assumption implicit in the imagery [is] that sexuality de-
stroys love."[3] Yes, but how does Marvell judge that assump-
tion or conclusion, which is probably indeed his own but is

---

[3] *Andrew Marvell* (New York, 1964), pp. 34-35. Ruth Nevo, one of
few critics who recognize Marvell's narrative powers, solves the prob-
lem of contradictions not by imputing unconscious attitudes to Daphnis
(or Marvell) but by discerning this plot: "That Chloe's imminent con-
sent was not a spiritual embarrassment to a highly-emotional, ardent
if foolish young posturer, but an obstacle to the carefully laid plans of
a blasé young rake, longing to be rid of her comes as an unmitigated
shock" ("Marvell's Songs," p. 17). The high cost of this reading is the
assumption that the interpretive comment in stanzas 5 and 6 is de-
liberately misleading.

certainly not Daphnis'? "Mourning" is simply an exposé of Chloe's fickle nature, Marvell's *così fan tutte*; the form of "Daphnis and Chloe," however, allows for no such easy summary: there is no resolution unless we take either of the two stanzas by itself. The focus is not on Daphnis and Chloe but on the duplicity which Nature's "Lawes" justify, and perhaps require. "Daphnis and Chloe" is less an "elaborately intellectualized description of an encounter"[4] than it is Marvell's inquiry into the claims of love and chastity.

In "Mourning" and "Daphnis and Chloe," the revelation of the meanness and hypocrisy of passion suggests a position which, metaphysically speaking—if not psychologically—we could expect to lead to mysticism. And yet I think there is scarcely a glimmer of mysticism in Marvell's poetry. He is committed to the "rough strife" or to a search for innocence, but not to an escape from temporality, the full implications of which he considers to be not ecstatic but suicidal. In that curious poem "A Dialogue Between Thyrsis and Dorinda," the pastoral figures become so enchanted with thoughts of heaven's endless day that they plan to "steep Poppies" and steal away in sleep to the death which can bring them there. But Thyrsis and Dorinda do not sound like lovers and their innocence has nothing of the poignancy of the Nymph's; nor does it have the prophetic significance of the innocence of Little T. C.

In pursuit of the idea of happy love within the bounds of time, Marvell reveals the consequences of his view that all who leave the garden of the Infant Love are unfortunate lovers. In "Young Love," he sets forth a plan to make "all Rivals vain":

> Come little Infant, Love me now,
>   While thine unsuspected years
> Clear thine aged Fathers brow
>   From cold Jealousie and Fears.

[4] Leishman, *The Art of Marvell's Poetry*, p. 120.

Pretty surely 'twere to see
    By young Love old Time beguil'd:
While our Sportings are as free
    As the Nurses with the Child.

Common Beauties stay fifteen;
    Such as yours should swifter move;
Whose fair Blossoms are too green
    Yet for Lust, but not for Love.

Love as much the snowy Lamb
    Or the wanton Kid does prize,
As the lusty Bull or Ram,
    For his morning Sacrifice.

Now then love me: time may take
    Thee before thy time away:
Of this Need wee'l Virtue make,
    And learn Love before we may.

So we win of doubtful Fate;
    And, if good she to us meant,
We that Good shall antedate,
    Or, if ill, that Ill prevent.

Thus as Kingdomes, frustrating
    Other Titles to their Crown,
In the craddle crown their King,
    So all Forraign Claims to drown,

So, to make all Rivals vain,
    Now I crown thee with my Love:
Crown me with thy Love again,
    And we both shall Monarchs prove.

The rivals are Time and Fate, and they must be beguiled, outmaneuvered, and frustrated. The sense of urgency is expressed almost as a threat: "Now then love me: time may take/ Thee before thy time away." Those "Whose fair Blossoms are too green/ Yet for Lust, but not for Love" can, if they love now, beguile old Time, and those creatures of time, "cold Jealousie and Fears," will be banished. At his "morning Sacrifice," Love can be propitiated by "the snowy Lamb/ Or the wanton Kid." As Marvell distinguishes the "the wanton Love" from the Tyrant Love, he distinguishes the "morning Sacrifice," for which the innocent are appropriate, from the evening's; he distinguishes love from lust. This monarchy of young Love is a morning kingdom where the battle with the tyrant can be delayed.

The explicitly allegorical imagery creates a tone which precludes, surely, any such interpretation as that offered by Professor Legouis, that "Young Love" evokes "des idées de débauche sénile."[5] The poem seems essentially an exhortation closing an unspoken meditation on innocence and fate; indeed, the sober tone is very close to the meditative passages of "Thy Nymph Complaining." And though exultation is not its manner, "Young Love" resembles "To His Coy Mistress" in its tone of urgency, its apprehension of love's fateful confrontation of time. The poem has little to do with the psychology of loving (or aging) and everything to do with the metaphysics of love.

The theme of "doubtful Fate" has a part to play in "The Picture of Little T. C. in a Prospect of Flowers," as it does in "Young Love." But the greater interest of "The Picture of Little T. C." derives not simply from the note of warning sounded in the final stanza, but from the remarkably complex tone of the whole poem, the result of Marvell's combination of the prophetic and the emblematic, presenting both the picture of Little T. C. in the garden and a forecast of the power of the latter-day nymph. The "simplicity" with which

[5] *André Marvell: poète, puritain, patriot, 1621-78* (Paris, 1928), p. 72. Dennis Davison scolds Marvell for writing what he seems to take to be a *Lolita* in rhyme (*The Poetry of Andrew Marvell* [London, 1964], p. 25).

"this Nimph begins her golden daies" is not only subject to "doubtful Fate"—the possibility that Time will take her before her time away—but to the inevitable triumph of "Times winged Charriot." Although simplicity is the best means of combating "The wanton Love" against whom Little T. C. will one day be pitted, simplicity is not given to those who leave the garden. (There seems to be a pun on "simples," i.e., herbs and flowers, whose character, in medieval terms, is "simplicity.") The "plot" of "The Picture of Little T. C." really turns on the fact that Marvell is warning not only of fate and time but of the dangers incurred by innocents who would do battle with love. The double perspective is established in the poem's opening stanzas:

> See with what simplicity
> This Nimph begins her golden daies!
> In the green Grass she loves to lie,
> And there with her fair Aspect tames
> The Wilder flow'rs, and gives them names:
> But only with the Roses playes;
>   And them does tell
> What Colour best becomes them, and what Smell.
>
> Who can foretel for what high cause
> This Darling of the Gods was born!
> Yet this is She whose chaster Laws
> The wanton Love shall one day fear,
> And, under her command severe,
> See his Bow broke and Ensigns torn.
>   Happy, who can
> Appease this virtuous Enemy of Man!

Armed with her chastity, going forth to battle as securely as the "Resolved Soul" meeting "Created Pleasure," this nymph will wage war on "The wanton Love." Given the rigorous necessities of the world Marvell envisions in his poetry of love,

the future is inevitable war when beauty walks abroad, out
of the garden of innocence, for it is the Tyrant Love who
succeeds the Infant Love, and all lovers under his sway are
unfortunate. It would seem, then, that if Little T. C. is to
vanquish love, it will be by defending the garden. In so doing,
she will be the "virtuous Enemy of Man." The nymph's con-
quest over men is represented as the triumph of chastity over
love:

> O then let me in time compound,
> And parly with those conquering Eyes;
> Ere they have try'd their force to wound,
> Ere, with their glancing wheels, they drive
> In Triumph over Hearts that strive,
> And them that yield but more despise.
>   Let me be laid,
> Where I may see thy Glories from some shade.

Since those wheels[6] (eyes) will one day ride in triumph over
hearts that strive (to woo her) and since she will disdain
those who "yield" (to her diffidence, i.e., give her up), it is
prudent to be on her side, to "appease" her so as not to suffer
oneself. It is Marvell's bemused and wry reversal of the oldest
gambit in pastoral. "Then come kiss me sweet and twenty"
becomes an entreaty *not* to love, *not* to win, *not* to charm. He
wants to negotiate his own safety ("to compound and parley"
is a military phrase meaning to treat in the course of warfare),
to become Little T. C.'s ally, even though by the time this child
drives her chariot, he will be dead: "Let me be laid/ Where

---

[6] "Glancing wheels" puns on the Nymph's glance and the murderous
barbs of her chariot's wheels. Cf. Lovelace, "Lucasta paying her
Obsequies" (*Poems*, ed. Wilkinson, p. 77):

> Griefe ne're before did Tyrannize
>   On th' Honour of that brow,
> And at the wheeles of her brave Eyes
>   Was Captive led til now.

I may see thy Glories from some shade." This is prediction and prophecy, not unconscious adumbration.[7] He will witness her glorious triumph from the grave. The tone seems almost a comic version of the chorus in "Dialogue Between the Resolved Soul and Created Pleasure": "Triumph, triumph, victorious Soul." The poet is congratulating in advance.

Meanwhile, nature is itself a kind of "victim," subject to the little nymph's godlike charm, her sovereign power. "Reform the errours of the Spring" recalls the effect of that paragon, Maria Fairfax, seeing whom, "Loose Nature doth itself collect." But perhaps the poet has gone too far in his commendation, for having flatteringly attributed divine character to the child, he now warns that by a reversal of that sympathy she now shares with nature she may anger Flora:

> But O young beauty of the Woods,
> Whom Nature courts with fruits and flow'rs,
> Gather the Flow'rs, but spare the Buds;
> Lest *Flora* angry at thy crime,
> To kill her Infants in their prime,
> Do quickly make th' Example Yours;
>   And, ere we see,
> Nip in the blossome all our hopes and Thee.

The poet who has admitted his own anxiety now feels justified in admonishing the nymph to be fearful herself. Marvell

---

[7] *Pace* Professor Tillyard, who writes that though "*laid* and shade suggest the grave initially, we probably reject this meaning" (*Poetry: Direct and Oblique* [London, 1964], p. 25). The literal and common seventeenth-century meaning of *laid* in the passive is "to be buried." Marvell's stanza, I think, carries the same meaning as the following passage from Vaughan's "Olor Iscanus" (*The Works of Henry Vaughan*, ed. L. C. Martin [Oxford, 1914], I, 39):

> May vocal Groves grow there, and all
> The shades in them Propheticall,
> Where (laid) men shall more faire truths see
> Than fictions were of Thessalie.

plays commendation against rebuke, combining the prophecy of the nymph's tyrannical chastity with this somewhat sardonic warning. It is almost as if the poet seeks to exorcise his apprehensions, so like the "cold Jealousie and Fears" of "old Time," by a cool recognition of that same incontrovertible truth which the coy mistress is urged to confront. As Petrarch's hierarchy of triumphs declares, though Chastity conquers Love, Death conquers Chastity.

The poem combines, I have said, picture and prophecy, each of which is expressed distinctively: there is a smiling regard for the picture, for the present, expressed with an extreme degree of Marvellian whimsicality; for the prophecy, something else. There is an almost fulsome praise for this paragon who will be the "virtuous Enemy of Man." When his attention returns to the little girl (stanza 4), the poet is again delicate and sweet, but with the concluding stanza, there is a sharpness, an edge. The theme of "The Picture of Little T. C." is the inversion of the theme of "Young Love": "Come little infant, love me now before it's dangerous" becomes "Do not make me love you now, because later it would certainly become dangerous." Here, at the close of the poem, that pattern is expanded to include another reversal, of the *carpe florem* implicit in "Young Love" to a Marvellian *noli florem carpere*. The warning is not only an urgent and intense plea for the mollification of "doubtful Fate"; it seems addressed to all those who would choose not to leave the garden. The burden of the warning seems to be not only that death can overtake the virtuous young, but that death conquers chastity. In that recognition there may be, as I have suggested, a measure of comfort for the poet, but as a warning directed to the child it is clearly inappropriate.

The disparity between a warning addressed to a little girl in the hope that she will grow safely to womanhood and that addressed to the "Nimph" who is to ride in triumph over "The wanton Love" seems to me absolute. Compare, for instance, the single-mindedness of Laertes' speech to Ophelia, the imagery and diction of which, incidentally, strikingly resemble those of Marvell's poem:

> . . . keep you in the rear of your affection,
> Out of the shot and danger of desire.
>
> .   .   .   .
>
> Virtue itself 'scapes not calumnious strokes:
> The canker galls the infants of the spring
> Too oft before their buttons be disclosed,
> And in the morn and liquid dew of youth
> Contagious blastments are most imminent.
> Be wary then; best safety lies in fear:
> Youth to itself rebels, though none else near.
>
> (*Hamlet*, I, iii, 34-44)

Ophelia scores the high-mindedness of this address (and, indeed, Laertes is here most his father's son), but Laertes is only asking his sister to bide her time, reminding her that innocence can be a dangerous state. For Marvell's "Nimph," who is to ride in triumph over "The wanton Love," no such limited warning will suffice. She must be called to defend Love's morning kingdom, the green garden of chastity.

Marvell again and again warns, in the allegorical mode, against "Lust"; pities man in his subjection to the tyranny of passion; pleads for innocence. As long as he speaks of "Mankind," his warnings and pleas have an integrity, sustained by the brilliant imagery of garden and battle. But within the frame of his metaphysics, his stance, if he should speak personally—as a moral counselor—would become ambiguous, and inescapably so. This is precisely what happens at the conclusion of this poem, despite the fact that the voice of allegory has sounded from the opening lines. As he moves from the mode of "See how" to the mode of direct address, he issues a warning less appropriate to the "young beauty of the Woods" whom he seemingly addresses than to the tyrannical nymph.[8] For Little T. C., as for Maria Fairfax (and Ophelia), caution is appropriate, not proscription.

Marvell can claim with assurance in "Upon Appleton House" that Fairfax's daughter will wisely and virtuously marry, as he celebrates the heroism of an earlier Fairfax who rescued Isabel Thwaites from the nunnery in order to marry her. But these are occasional verses. Progeny as a means of defeating time; conjugal love as a means of allaying lust; the sacramental marriage of two souls in God; chastity as a symbol of a state of grace: Marvell does not usually write of these. When he salutes the institution of marriage, it is with none but a conventional piety. In short, marriage plays no role in Marvell's metaphysics of love. In his world, the true sacrament is solitude. At the close of "The Picture of Little T. C. in a Prospect of Flowers," he speaks to the little girl, but he addresses himself to the tyrannical nymph. The resultant ambiguity is, I feel, discordant.

There is another way of accounting for what I have been tempted to call the sardonic tone of the concluding stanza. It may be that Marvell is writing in the vein of the epitaphs for the Trotts and Mrs. Oxenbridge, in which poignancy and tough-mindedness are mingled. The little girl is certainly very much in the prospect and there is reason to believe that Marvell indeed meant to focus on her rather than on the prophetic figure of the triumphant nymph. The suggestion has been made[9] that Marvell had in mind an actual child named "Theophila," whose younger sister of the same name had died the second day after birth. The supposition that Marvell, regarding little Theophila Cornewall, pleads with the child not to anger Flora for fear that she might herself become a victim

---

[8] Joseph Summers' reading is: "Man must beware of attempting to anticipate heaven by imposing the ideal, including chastity on earth" ("Marvell's Nature," p. 134n.).

[9] See Margoliouth, "Andrew Marvell: Some Biographical Points," *MLR*, 17 (1922), 359.

makes of the warning a kind of *memento mori* in which the motif of death conquering chastity plays no role. The title does tease us to go "outside" the poem, as perhaps finding a solution to the problem of tonality and continuity of theme requires.

The alternate reading supposes in the concluding stanza a double vision, in which the picture of the little girl and the prophetic figure coalesce: the poet must see, when he regards Little T. C., the figure of Diana as well. But since the burdens of the warnings are incompatible, the result, in my opinion, is a discomforting ambiguity. Whereas the form of "The Nymph Complaining for the Death of Her Fawn" allows for discontinuities and shifts in point of view, the form of "The Picture of Little T. C. in a Prospect of Flowers" seems inadequate to the demands of the allegorical imagination.

As chastity and virtuous youth may inspire vengeance, so the promise of fame may cause a fearful jealousy, as Marvell suggests in an early poem commemorating the death of Lord Hastings, that young hero of such promise and achievement who had died in his nineteenth year:

> Alas, his *Vertues* did his *Death* presage:
> Needs must he die, that doth out-run his *Age*.
> The Phlegmatick and Slowe prolongs his day,
> And on Times Wheel sticks like a *Remora*.
> What man is he, that hath not *Heaven* beguil'd
> And is not thence mistaken for a *Childe?*
> While those of growth more sudden and more bold,
> Are hurried hence, as if already old.
> For, there above, They number not as here,
> But weigh to Man the *Geometrick* yeer.

Man perhaps can beguile a jealous heaven and by a mystical mathematics so calculate his virtue that it not outweigh his age. But it is Eternity alone who rides in triumph over Time.

In tokens of eternity, then, man may find ways to stay the force of time.

In "The Match," Marvell turns to the imagery of warfare to suggest the plight of lovers. The poet declares to Celia: "we . . . have within our Selves possesst/ All Love's and Nature's store." This store has been laid up to defeat time.

> Nature had long a Treasure made
>   Of all her choisest store;
> Fearing, when She should be decay'd,
>   To beg in vain for more.
>
>   .   .   .   .
>
> Love wisely had of long fore-seen
>   That he must once grow old;
> And therefore stor'd a Magazine,
>   To save him from the cold.

Love's burning powders have been stored in the poet; all Nature's beauty has been gathered in Celia. Love's fire could inflame all creation and one grain of Nature's beauty could repair the world. But despite the fortification of Love's magazine, that store of "all that burns the Mind," dangerously compressed, caught fire:

> Thus all his fewel did unite
>   To make one fire high:
> None ever burn'd so hot, so bright;
>   And *Celia* that am I.

A "match" was a wick used to explode a charge, before the widespread introduction of flint and steel: Celia is the "match" whose beauty has ignited Love's powder magazine. The "match" refers to the poet and Celia too, of course, with the emphasis on the physical (compare *Measure for Measure*, V, i, 204-7). Indeed, the concluding stanza suggests not an entreaty but a celebration:

So we alone the happy rest,
  Whilst all the World is poor,
And have within our Selves possesst
  All Love's and Nature's store.

Love and Nature had sought to build a fortified defense against Time. But their deputies, the poet and Celia, have no use for the strategy of retreat (successful only when it is solitary) and so have converted the defense against time to a "match."

The morning kingdom of young love and the simplicity of "golden daies" in the garden are stays against the "rough strife," but they can only be temporary. The best way to conquer "The wanton Love" may be to refuse combat, though on all who attempt such an escape, nature may be expected to wreak revenge. Once out of the garden, the lover is engaged in an unending battle in which the only conquest is in the "story" he creates, that "red rose 'round the briar" which "all true lovers can admire," and in that race which is run to the death. All lovers are unfortunate, as souls who are born into time are all subject to fate's "Decrees of Steel." They have only their resolution, these unfortunate souls, these resolved lovers. But resolution is enough. In one of the grandest passages of "Upon Appleton House," Marvell foretells that the aged trees—symbols of eternity—"as they Natures Cradle deckt/ Will in green Age her Hearse expect." Green age; strength and sweetness; fire and beauty: it is the very life of nature which attends the Resolved Soul in his battle, in his race.

The Mower Poems

Damon the Mower seeks freedom not from time but from love, for it is love which has destroyed the ground of his being, his life in nature. As "green Age" is tolerant of time, so Damon's world can and does accommodate death itself. But

in the order of nature as Damon has known it, human passion
is an intrusion:

> How happy might I still have mow'd,
> Had not Love here his Thistles sow'd!

The "fable" of the Mower poems is the loss of that innocence
in which man and nature are one. That is a state contingent
upon solitude. Damon discovers what it is given to Marvell's
heroes to know, that there is no escape from love's tyranny
within the bounds of time. Unwilling and unprepared for the
"rough strife," he looks to death as the only release.

Like all pastoral figures, Damon is a metaphor. Though we
may distinguish the mower and the philosopher, the com-
plexity of the figure is inherent and intentional. There is no
point in separating out a voice which is supposedly Marvell's
own, assigning the rest to the persona. Nor is it possible to
settle for the "real" Damon, discounting all bits that do not
somehow substantiate the figure we have defined. By the
economy of allegory, he is both mower and philosopher-poet,
just as the Nymph who complains for the death of her fawn
is at once innocent and wise.[10] Like the Nymph, the Mower
mediates between the two worlds of innocence and experience.
Such antitheses are the defining characteristics of the pastoral
form: work and play, town and country, joy and sorrow, past
and present, love's labors won and lost. And the pastoral
figure himself incorporates these contrasts to one degree or
another. Though only an authentic countryman could cite the
real joys of country life, only a poet would be free to express
the joy. The pastoral hero is always a countryman and always

---

[10] Barbara Everett, in a lively and perceptive essay on "The Mower's
Song," writes: "We are never certain . . . whether we are seeing a
child with the eye of an adult, or a courtier with the eye of a grass-
hopper" ("Marvell's 'The Mower's Song,'" *The Critical Quarterly*, III
[1962], 220). A further comment suggests a rationale for the radical
irony of pastoral: "Perhaps a society uses pastoral to ask itself precisely
these questions to which there is no conclusive answer."

a poet, a singer, not by formal necessity only, as an operatic hero *is* a tenor, but because the art of song has traditionally been conceived of as part of his life. Singing contests, Hesiod's happy kind of strife, are as central to the pastoral life (as represented in pastoral poetry) as the care of sheep. If the crook is emblematic, so is the oaten reed.

As a poet naturally would, the pastoral hero gives form to desires and fears and dreams. He imagines himself to be master and city man; bird, star, stream; god, satyr, immortal: he fancies life in all its forms and can see himself in any role. Thus Marvell does not say or imply that Damon is Death; *Damon* says that he is like Death, or, rather, that Death is like him. And of course Damon the poet plays with language:

> My Mind was once the true survey
> Of all these Medows fresh and gay;
> And in the greenness of the Grass
> Did see its Hopes as in a Glass. . . .

If one misses the wit of "Hopes" being meant literally, then of course "greenness of the Grass" can be taken symbolically and the poem can be construed as a treatise on the redemption of nature, "the Body of Hope."[11] But hope of that kind is supererogatory in paradise, and, until Juliana comes, that is Damon's home. Damon's hope has been not the lover's dream or the Christian's faith but the farmer's expectation.

The logic of such metaphors is determined by the dramatic voice, sounding not only in the single poem but in the group of poems in which Damon is figured. "Damon" is not like "Menalcus" of Virgil's *Eclogues*, a name given to different persons. (The shepherd in "Clorinda and Damon" is, of course, not the Mower.) There is a consistency in the figure who presents to us many faces in turn: naïve countryman,

[11] Hartman writes: "Marvell shows hope [for redemption] in Nature frustrated by love or by the very strength of hope" ("Marvell, St. Paul, and the Body of Hope," p. 191).

pageant figure, even "Economic Man." Consistency is, of course, to be expected in a pastoral figure. As convention requires and the history of usage assures that no stream runs clear or muddy without significance, so each figure has his own character magically circumscribed by a certain range of interest. Each is assigned, as it were, a frequency of temperament. Though profound religious feeling may be expressed and nuances of social attitudes explored with the full resources of ironic wit, psychological subtlety is not, generally speaking, characteristic of the pastoral mode. The price of consistency is usually a loss of depth. The remarkable point about Marvell's Damon is that in him a surprisingly original and fresh particularity of feature consorts with the general and universal attributes of the poet-countryman, creating a character of some complexity.[12] The details of his life, beginning with the fact that he works, that he is an active farmer rather than a contemplative shepherd, give Damon a presence more distinctive than that of the usual Renaissance shepherd. His kinship is rather with the hard-working herdsmen of Virgil's *Eclogues*, and the Marvellian impress can best be appreciated in the context of those poems.[13]

In "Damon the Mower," especially, the use Marvell has made of the formal character of figure and landscape can be seen.[14] Here, as in the Second Eclogue, the scene is the im-

[12] Hartman believes that the mower is "almost completely Marvell's new emblem" (*ibid.*, p. 190n.). Kermode, on the other hand, sets Damon firmly in the French tradition: "Like some of the French poets whom he obviously knew so well, Marvell makes his pastoral commentator a mower rather than a shepherd" ("Two Notes on Marvell," *N&Q*, CXCVII [1952], 136-37).

[13] It is not only in the matter of properties and trappings that the Mower poems have a classical ambience. Eleanor Winsor Leach's study, "Nature and Art in Vergil's Second Eclogue," *American Journal of Philology*, LXXXVII [1966], 427-45, is suggestive of the kinds of conventions which Marvell might be said to have imitated, including the critical use of the pastoral mode itself.

[14] With its emphasis on the obvious beneficence of cool shade, this

mediate subject and Marvell interprets it in terms of his hero's experience. If there is a single defining characteristic of pastoral, it is not to be found, I think, in one particular pair of supposed opposites—e.g., art and nature, lords and swains—but in the theme of the correspondence of man and nature. Pride in husbandry is as important as artfulness in song. Dream and visions are set in contrast to the joys and cares of country life which are, in varying degrees, present and relevant. The touching actuality of a countryman's life in combination with a troubled search for permanence and security is the classical ambience of Marvell's pastoral.

He regards his models ironically, even to the point of parody. Damon's boast that he is, after all, presentable—"Nor am I so deform'd to sight,/ If in my Sithe I looked right"—is a charming rehabilitation of Corydon's boast.[15] The "harmless Snake" that Damon presents to Juliana parodies all the natural, innocent baubles—the coral and amber, the reed baskets and flutes—with which shepherds ply their maids.[16] Along with the iridescent chameleon (momentarily, it seems that Damon intends to make use of the enmity between Eve and the serpent to get Juliana out of his fields!), the Mower brings as a

---

poem can serve to remind us that the landscape of pastoral, like the figures, is literary. Cool caves, and gelid fountains (Cf. "gelidi fontes," Tenth Eclogue) have the same meaning in the Mediterranean that the Sweetwater River in Wyoming had for pioneers emerging from the plains, but an English herdsman or harvester would more likely seek the sun. Curtius remarks that "olive trees were extraordinarily abundant in the medieval North" and that "French epic swarms with lions" (*European Literature in the Latin Middle Ages*, trans. Willard R. Trask [New York, 1953], p. 184).

[15] Second Eclogue, ll. 25-26. Legouis, citing this example, calls "Damon the Mower" "a (characteristically free) imitation of Virgil's 'Alexis'" (*Andrew Marvell*, p. 26n.).

[16] Is this the withered skin shed in the cool shade by the snake who "glitters in its second skin"? A snake burst by incantation is mentioned in Virgil's *Eclogues*; perhaps Marvell has amused himself with this mild extirpation of a vulgar error. He has certainly given new life to a conventional property.

present "Oak leaves tipt with hony due." These come straight from the forests of the Golden Age—and from Damon's fields, which are of this world. They are leaves and they are metaphor, a token of paradise, which Damon considers his fields to be.[17] The honeyed oak leaves provide a context in which "the harmless Snake . . . disarmed of its teeth and sting" seems Damon's version of the rose without a thorn. Marvell parodies, but it is clear that in Damon's eyes these presents are beautiful and valuable.

In this paradise he has lived like the lord of creation. In the next stanza he blithely presents himself as might a meadow god:

> I am the Mower *Damon*, known
> Through all the Meadows I have mown.
> On me the Morn her dew distills
> Before her darling Daffadils.
> And, if at Noon my toil me heat,
> The Sun himself licks off my Sweat.
> While, going home, the Ev'ning sweet
> In cowslip-water bathes my feet.

In Marvell's pastoral world, the hard work of country life is not the counterbalance to sweet delights of pastoral existence: the work of harvesting, the tending of sweet fields is itself the joyous life. Nymphs and fairies, the gods themselves attend the Mower. Entirely at home in a beneficent world, no wonder he speaks so easily and with such assurance! The next stanza is a bit of braggadocio which, though it echoes Corydon

[17] Cf. Fourth Eclogue, l. 30: "et durae quercus sudabunt roscida mella." The motif has a long history. Leishman cites it as a typical item in the classical "catalog of impossibilities" and it is a feature of many an earthly paradise. As my friend Eleanor Leach has observed, oak leaves do indeed exude a sticky substance one year or another, so that it can be claimed that there is an actual base for the mythical image. Marvell the poet would certainly delight in having Damon the poet smuggle these oak leaves across the semantic border into the real worlds of his fields.

(Second Eclogue, lines 19-22), makes Damon sound like a figure in a pageant or a folk play:

> This Sithe of mine discovers wide
> More ground then all his Sheep do hide.
>
> .   .   .   .
>
> And though in Wooll more poor then they,
> Yet am I richer far in Hay.

The four stanzas addressed to the shepherdess end with the image of the Mower protected by a magic ring formed by the "deathless Fairyes."[18] The picture recalls the poet of the woods at Appleton House, encamped behind the trees. For Damon is not courting Juliana; the gifts are really only symbols of his station and prowess. No other favor than recognition is asked. He would prefer to stay out of "the shot and danger of desire," but it is too late: the meteors have fallen. As the Unfortunate Lover is shipwrecked into passion, so is the Mower lost. Distracted, he cuts his ankle with his own scythe. This is what happens when the countryman fails to attend his business. So Corydon realizes with sudden fury and self-disgust that in the course of his pleading to cruel Alexis (no more present than Juliana is), the winds have shaken his flowers and the boars have muddied his crystal streams.

> And there among the Grass fell down,
> By his own Sythe, the Mower mown.

[18] C. S. Lewis' analysis of the "complexity of the tradition [of "Fairies"] which the Middle Ages had bequeathed to [Milton] and his public" (*The Discarded Image* [Cambridge, Eng., 1964], p. 123) suggests that Marvell's "deathless Fairyes" should not, perhaps, be taken as mere whimsy, though they seem to me, juxtaposed as they are with the Virgilian allusion, rather like the "Shepherds-purse" and "Clowns-all-heal," a bit of folklore. The rings of deeper green in the grass of a meadow which result from a fungus whose spores nourish the grass roots are called, even now, "fairy rings." It seems likely that Marvell here is showing that customary delight in moving back and forth between the phenomenal and the figurative.

This bleeding can be staunched by herbs and flowers, but the wounds of love are closed only in death. The sweet address— "For Death thou art a Mower too"—is delivered as if to a brother. It is the only consolation left him, the thought of the sympathy Death will someday show, a sympathy like that shown by the Sun himself in greener days.

Without passion, man can be free to oppose time as best he can, by the contemplation of heaven or by identification with nature in its simplicity. "The Mower's Song" explores the full significance of the closing couplet of "The Mower to the Glowworms":

> For She my Mind hath so displac'd
> That I shall never find my home.

The correspondence has been broken because love has no place in the scheme of that paradise. Juliana makes nonsense of innocence, destroys solitude and happiness. The theme of "The Mower's Song" is envy for the continuing life of nature. If we wonder how anything could be sadder than nature's seeming to answer to the lover's condition—"wither'd like his Hopes the Grass"—it is that there is sometimes no such sympathy at all.[19] Damon is lost and withered, but the meadows flourish:

> Unthankful Medows, could you so
> A fellowship so true forego,
> And in your gawdy May-games meet,
> While I lay trodden under feet?

If he must be cut down by Juliana, then the grass must fall too, in sympathy. The compassion so hopefully sought in "Damon the Mower" is not forthcoming and so the Mower must take his revenge:

[19] "Damon the Mower" and "The Mower's Song" form a diptych in which a theme is presented and then reversed. "Young Love" and "The Picture of Little T. C. in a Prospect of Flowers" are similarly matched.

> But what you in Compassion ought,
> Shall now by my Revenge be wrought:
> And Flow'rs, and Grass, and I and all,
> Will in one common Ruine fall.
> For *Juliana* comes, and She
> What I do to the Grass, does to my Thoughts and Me.

How will this revenge restore correspondence? By means of
metaphor. Damon has thought himself back into the scheme
of things by identifying himself with the fallen grass. In the
imagination of death, he becomes part of the natural cycle,
rejoining the fellowship.[20] The grass of the meadows

> Shall now the Heraldry become
> With which I shall adorn my Tomb. . . .

But of course it is a dream of escape. Damon the poet dreams
of dying and finds a comfort in that dream as the Nymph
does in her vision of the statue. And this is the only banneret
that ever love created yet, the lover who dies into the story of
his strife.[21]

It is Damon's continuing discovery, expressed with bitter-
ness and surprise, with innocent dismay and angry regret, that
although man can recreate paradise in nature, it is, like young
love, only temporary and safe only if it is solitary. But artful-
ness is as grave a danger as woman. "The Mower Against Gar-
dens" stands apart from the other Mower poems because

[20] Corydon, looking back at the natural scene from his corner of
anguish, longs to be a part of the scheme (Second Eclogue, ll. 65-68):

> . . . trahit sua quemque voluptas.
> aspice, aratra iugo referunt suspensa iuvenci,
> et sol crescentis decedens duplicat umbras:
> me tamen urit amor; quis enim modus adsit amori?

[21] Miss Everett makes Juliana the agency of his transfiguration: "as
he turns the grass into a perpetual blazon, she perpetuates and im-
mortalizes him. He becomes himself an Unfortunate Lover, perpetuated
by her into an heraldic device—in this case, a poem" ("Marvell's 'The
Mower's Song,'" p. 223).

Juliana is not involved, but for Damon, the gardens of "Luxurious Man" are as destructive of his paradise as love's thistles. His disaffection is not with man's attempt to create order but with the excessive zeal expended in the attempt to control nature on his own terms.[22]

> Luxurious Man, to bring his Vice in use,
>> Did after him the World seduce:
> And from the fields the Flow'rs and Plants allure,
>> Where Nature was most plain and pure.

The catalogue of horticultural experiments is a testimony to man's ingenuity, to his pride. It is comic, this marvelous list, but there is an edge to it. "Man, that sov'raign thing and proud" has expended his ingenuity needlessly, for all the while "willing Nature does to all dispence/ A wild and fragrant Innocence." Why be proud of statues of gods in the garden, when in the meadow "The *Gods* themselves with us do dwell."[23]

Pastoral is that "region in the mind"[24] where Marvell found once more those radical metaphors which had served so long to figure forth man's apprehension of his life in nature; he was the last poet so to use pastoral. We are familiar enough with the concept of the *voices* of a poet, of the man and his *masks*. The poet and his muse long ago came to be, Roger Hinks has pointed out in a discussion of the *daemonic* function, "an allegory of the intellectual life."[25] In comparable

[22] The old analogy between gardening and poetry is excuse enough for using as a gloss for this poem Marvell's "To his Worthy Friend Doctor Witty upon the Translation of the Popular Errors." There is the same emphasis put upon the purity of an original.

[23] It is Corydon's argument too: let them who wish live in cities and in villas; "habitarunt di quoque silvas."

[24] C. S. Lewis wrote that pastoral symbolizes "a region in the mind which should be visited more often" (*The Allegory of Love*, p. 352). (He clearly did not mean to characterize it as a picnic ground, as one critic implies.)

[25] *Myth and Allegory*, p. 98.

fashion, the figures of pastoral "stand in" for the poet, or they are there for him to contemplate. There are the unfortunate lovers who are willing to enter the "rough strife" and to run their "Passions heat"; there are those who seek to recover the lost dimension of timelessness—for a while. With the fresh-gained knowledge that she can dream of the life to come, Dorinda cries,

> Oh sweet! oh sweet! How I my future state
> By silent thinking, Antidate.

But the dream of Elysium is only one way for the Resolved Soul to recreate heaven: in his pastorals, Marvell sings of solitude, of green age, of young love, celebrating the vanished past and the imaginable future in the eternal now.

CHAPTER V

The "active Minde"

N HIS poetry of love, Marvell continually returns to the thought of an escape from the world of passion, but since passionate love and temporal being are virtually coextensive, the contemplation of escape engenders radical paradoxes. It does not, however, issue in mysticism. The alternative to the battle which is sublunary love is the garden, but that green world does not for Marvell provide the setting for mystical experience. Solitude in the garden, no matter how suffused with religious or philosophic significance it might be said to be, becomes the occasion not for ecstasy, but for the contemplation of time's course, for celebrating and lamenting the soul's temporal life.

Time is man's fate, the dimension in which he suffers his being. Young love, green age, solitude—all offer means of opposing his fate, but the absolute conquest of time has no earthly relevance. Time conquered by Eternity is not only the last of the Petrarchan triumphs but also the most hollow: so the poet would remind his coy mistress. The escape from temporality, like stopping the sun or creating a new one, is a "natural impossibility." The seasonless, static landscape of the Golden Age, mystic transport, the permanence represented in myth: Marvell treats them all ironically, recognizing the profound contradictions of the soul's temporal life. Marvell's poetry is witness to the terror and beauty of the paradox that time is both creator and destroyer, the source of joy as well as the cause of suffering. Time is therefore not to be banished or ignored merely; the true conquest is that resolute opposition which takes the forms of love, heroic action, and contemplation.

To the contemplation of the life of nature, Marvell devoted

in both "The Garden" and "Upon Appleton House" his genius
for natural description, his witty command of language, and
his special talent for recreating landscapes. For Marvell, as for
Herbert and Traherne, contemplation is not a passive state
but an active search. In neither poem is the role of the poet
that of the bystander or of the painter of pictures or of the dis-
interested moral counselor. As in "To His Coy Mistress" and
"The Definition of Love," the speaker is the poet and in both
poems he is involved not only as a narrator but also as an
actor: in "Upon Appleton House," the poet is given to ex-
planation and comment in an essentially public manner; in
"The Garden," to exclamation and implicit exhortation. In
both poems, the focus is on the recreating of what Marvell
once called the "active Minde."¹ The act of contemplation in-
volves far more than the expression of momentary states of
feeling.² "Upon Appleton House" is organized as the peripa-
tetic poet's daylong exploration, the day in the country be-
coming a celebration of man's place in nature; "The Garden"
is the poet's definition of "sweet and wholsome Hours." As the
"active Minde" moves through time, discovering and creating,
temporality—the very passage of time—becomes a theme itself.

The poet is at the center of each poem. His purpose is clear:
to consider the uses of time and solitude, to sing the corre-
spondence of earth and heaven. In the woods section of "Upon
Appleton House" (stanzas 71-74), Marvell has written a de-
fense of poetry based not on the quasiholy powers of the poet
who supposedly reads the secret of the universe in scattered
leaves but upon the wit by which he conceives of himself as
a natural cipher and of nature as a masque. Boccaccio in refut-

¹ In Marvell's early poem "Upon the Death of the Lord Hastings,"
the young hero is the captive ally of jealous heaven, having been, as it
were, saved by death from the distractions of life: "So he, not banisht
hence, but there confin'd,/ There better recreates his active Minde."
² I have used "contemplation" simply to mean imaginative consid-
eration or, as Dorinda says, "silent thinking." I have not set it over
against "meditation," nor do I mean to suggest by it a mystic tran-
scendence of any sort.

ing the notion that poetry is the ape of philosophy suggests that poets are, indeed, the apes of nature.[3] This familiar notion is treated ironically by Marvell, for in his view the poet imitates the order of heaven not by mystically meditating on the "creatures" or by reading a pattern of signs in the book of nature but by his simultaneous annihilation and re-creation of the forms of nature. Celebrating the life of nature is indeed contingent on the discovery of the correspondence between the two realms of being, but that imagination of order springs from the contemplation of time's course.

"The Garden"

As conceived by the allegorical imagination, the English garden becomes the equivalent of the mythical scene of the creation, and the herbs and flowers, emblems of this paradise regained. The poem follows the course of the "active Minde." Though it is not a "narrative" in the sense that "The Nymph Complaining for the Death of Her Fawn" and "The Unfortunate Lover" are, it nevertheless develops and unfolds. The "argument" of "The Garden," in contrast to those of "To His Coy Mistress" and "The Definition of Love," does not have an explicit form, but it is nonetheless dialectical, proceeding by antithesis and hyperbole to paradox and definition. The emphasis on justification gives the poem a "rational" air, even when it is most lyrical. Marvell plays the "How vainly" of the opening stanza against the "How well" of the concluding stanza[4]; "that happy Garden-state" against "this Dial new"; the body's delight against the mind's happiness; and so forth. The rationale for retreat is offered in the first four stanzas with a humor deriving from the ironic logic by which the amorous,

[3] *Boccaccio on Poetry, being the preface and fourteenth and fifteenth books of Boccaccio's Genealogia Deorum Gentilium* . . . , ed. Charles G. Osgood (Princeton, 1930), pp. 78-80.

[4] A point made by Paola Colaiacomo in her excellent discussion of the poem in "Alcuni Aspetti della Poesia di Andrew Marvell," *English Miscellany*, II (1960), 75-111.

lovely green is shown to be superior to the usual white and red; and from a Marvellian game of wit played with the symbols of civic and artistic glory whose beauty and value is challenged by the garden's plants. The humor is sustained throughout the poem since it is the consequence, as well, of a profound—and therefore gay—understanding of the limitations of temporal life. The reversals and surprises continue until in the penultimate stanza we find that paradise and solitude can be seen as equivalents because Adam's paradise was secure when he was yet alone. If one is alone, therefore, this earth, this demiparadise is, Marvell's syllogism has it, two paradises in one. The concluding stanza declares that this world of time can, after all, be man's paradise, if only, *and only if*, he be content with sweet and wholesome hours, the only kind that can be measured by herbs and flowers. The poet regains that paradise which is the condition and the effect of innocence.

Seeking in this green world an escape from the maze of life, he finds Solitude and that Innocence which is sister to "Fair quiet." These three graces offer higher pleasures than does the pursuit of honor and glory. Further, in this happy state, the poet can escape the anguish of passion, for here the object of passion is transmuted. Marvell juxtaposes the "am'rous . . . lovely green" of the trees with the heraldic colors of love (white and red) and by playing on the ancient association of *amor* and *amoenus*[5] concludes that trees, not nymphs, are choice. The gods themselves knew the truth of this judgment:

> *Apollo* hunted *Daphne* so,
> Only that She might Laurel grow.
> And *Pan* did after *Syrinx* speed,
> Not as a Nymph, but for a Reed.

Marvell is, of course, not claiming poetry and music as the benefits accruing to those who forsake love, but only char-

[5] See Curtius, *European Literature*, p. 95.

acteristically, by prolepsis, converting myths to literal truths.

But as long as the body is still fully alive to sensuous pleasure, the further benefits of solitude, quiet, and innocence cannot be enjoyed. There must be a metamorphosis not of the object only but of passion itself, and to that end the body must first be brought low by a surfeit of delight: if this is the fall, it is into the Land of Cockaigne:[6]

> What wond'rous Life is[7] this I lead!
> Ripe Apples drop about my head;
> The Luscious Clusters of the Vine
> Upon my Mouth do crush their Wine;
> The Nectaren, and curious Peach,
> Into my hands themselves do reach;
> Stumbling on Melons, as I pass,
> Insnar'd with Flow'rs, I fall on Grass.

The poet supine, his senses stupefied: does he not call to mind the scribe sprawled under the trees in Brueghel's painting? Marvell's "curious Peach" is the English equivalent of those pies which are ready to slide into the open mouth of Brueghel's knight; the grapes which crush their wine for the poet are like the egg offering itself and the pig crying to be bacon. The personification of nature is, of course, the central motif of pastoral. By elaborating in his characteristic manner upon the notion expressed in such a phrase as William Lawson's "Now begin Summer Fruits to ripe, and crave your hand to pick them," Marvell recreates the garden, briefly, as the antitype of paradise.

The comic aspect has been there from the first: Virgil's Fourth Eclogue, chief source of the Golden Age topos, de-

---

[6] Empson based his allegorization of the stanza as a parody of the fall on a reading of "melons" as a covert reference to the apple. But this garden's melons are probably what John Evelyn says melons are: "Cucumbers, cabbages, beetes."

[7] See Leishman, *The Art of Marvell's Poetry*, p. 295n., for an explanation of the confusion over "in" and "is" in this line.

scribes a world where goats "uncalled . . . shall bring home their udders swollen with milk . . . the stubborn oak shall distil dewy honey . . . wool shall no longer learn to counterfeit varied hues, but of himself the ram in the meadow shall change his fleece, now to sweetly blushing purple, now to a saffron yellow; of its own will shall scarlet clothe the grazing lambs. . . ."[8] We cannot enjoy Marvell's picture if his comic prosopopoeia is construed as the bearer of dark and complex significance. There is here that same delight in the notion of a double metamorphosis—nature becoming mindful, man insensate—which is a feature of the woods section of "Upon Appleton House," where the poet speculates on his conversion to a natural thing. Misreadings of stanza 5 have led to a sexualization of solitude which may produce a more complicated, more "interesting" sense, but the arcane has its price: in this case, it renders meaningless the joyous innocence and solitude which Marvell is describing as essential in the celebration of the rites of contemplation.

The poet escapes Nature by first succumbing to her delights. The metamorphosis of passion can now be accomplished; with the body held in fee by sensuous delight, the "active Minde" begins its recreating. Stanza 6 is pivotal:

> Mean while the Mind, from pleasure less,
> Withdraws into its happiness:
> The Mind, that Ocean where each kind
> Does streight its own resemblance find;
> Yet it creates, transcending these,
> Far other Worlds, and other Seas;
> Annihilating all that's made
> To a green Thought in a green Shade.

As the poet has withdrawn from the maze of life to the gar-

---

[8] *Virgil* I, trans. H. Rushton Fairclough (rev. edn.; London and Cambridge, Mass., 1960), pp. 31, 33.

den, so the mind withdraws from the direct and sensible experience of nature to the contemplation of nature, that is, to its own creations. Nature is less a pleasure to the mind than its own thoughts, but these thoughts are, nonetheless, *natural*. The opening lines of stanza 6 present a metaphor of the correspondence of mind and nature, a notion which is pursued to the point of identity: "a green Thought in a green Shade." The notion of correspondence is supported too, I think, by the term "streight." Though of course it can be read to mean "straightaway," "in the proper order" seems as likely a meaning when we consider Marvell's praise of Maria Fairfax.[9]

The mind's happiness lies in the contemplation of forms which the mind creates. The poet enjoys not created pleasure, but the pleasures of creation, for which Marvell's term is "annihilation." This teasing definition is the motive of the stanza. Annihilation is, of course, the logical opposite of creation (just as "shade" is the opposite of substance) and is appropriate to an agency which is set over against the creation, as the mind is here set against nature. The annihilation of creation by the "active Minde" is itself the condition of a new creation which is thought: "annihilation" here is hyperbole for that metamorphosis of nature which the mind works.[10]

---

[9] *She* streightness on the Woods bestows;

.   .   .   .

She yet more Pure, Sweet, Streight, and Fair,
Than Gardens, Woods, Meads, Rivers are.

"Streight" seems to have connoted for Marvell both the creative ordering of the mind and the generative power of feeling. In a passage of his prose (IV, 49) the term clearly indicates a paradigm, a template, as it were, of man's faith.

[10] Margoliouth notes that annihilation can mean "either 'reducing the whole material world to nothing material' . . . or 'considering the whole material world as of no value compared to a green thought.'" But the double sense of annihilating is ironic, not ambiguous. Margoliouth's "either/or" ignores the paradox whereby creation is defined

The concept of annihilation offered for seventeenth-century philosophers a test of their concepts of mind. Could we imagine space without bodies? Could we imagine bodies if they were all annihilated? Philosophers as different as Hobbes and Henry More pose the question of how the mind could conceive of extension if all substance were annihilated. The wit that plays with the notion of extension (as in "my extended soul is fixt" in "The Definition of Love") and with *horror vacui* in the "Horatian Ode," the wit that creates the ingenious and comic paradoxes of the "Dialogue Between the Soul and Body" is apparently at work in conceiving of the *annihilation* of *all that's made*.

The transcendence of the natural world of creation; the creation of "far other Worlds, and other Seas"; the annihilation that precedes thought or is its concomitant: *contemplation takes time*. The temporal dimension of the mind's creating and the soul's freedom, the sequences of transformation, are essential to the poem's structure. To read the "am'rous green" as a symbol of heavenly hope is therefore not only to

---

as the function of ruin, an expression of the metaphysical truth that a death is precursor to life and, as well, of the psychological truth that the mind "dissolves, creates and rears," in that order. (The nature of that sequence is one of the chief insights of the Romantic philosophy of the imagination and it has not been superseded.)

Daniel Stempel, in a brilliant reading of stanza 6, has discussed the philosophical implications of these lines: "Although the two realms (mind and matter) are separate, they confront each other in the human brain; the code of the material world, transmitted through the senses as a mixture of noise and information, is immediately, but not simultaneously (the occasionalist theory), translated into a mental analogue which is part of an already existent parallel language. This, then, is how each kind finds its own resemblance" (" 'The Garden': Marvell's Cartesian Ecstasy," *JHI*, XXVIII [1967], 99-114). Stempel's interesting conjecture is that "annihilation" can mean essentializing, isolating into essential categories. "The annihilation of 'all that's made' can also mean the reduction of all creation to the two basic substances, thought and extension. This, of course, was precisely what Descartes did when he created his hypothetical world. He did not reduce the material world to 'nothing'; he reduced it to the ultimate 'something.' "

misapprehend the tone of these stanzas,[11] but also to ignore the dramatic course of the poet's discoveries of the power and joy of the mind's creations; for annihilation is accomplished not in favor of the direct revelation of heaven but of green thoughts. Marvell does not give voice to mystic ecstasy: he celebrates the vital mediation of the recreating mind.

One green thought is that at moments such as these, with the body sated and the mind active, the soul may find the paradigm of its final freedom:

> Here at the Fountains sliding foot,
> Or at some Fruit-trees mossy root,
> Casting the Bodies Vest aside,
> My Soul into the boughs does glide:
> There like a Bird, it sits, and sings,
> Then whets, and combs its silver Wings;
> And, till prepar'd for longer flight,
> Waves in its Plumes the various Light.

This stanza has been taken as a description of ecstasy, either "spiritual" or "sensuous"; but certainly there is no ecstatic expression here or in any other part of the poem. There is neither an agonizing, near-wordless wonderment nor that tumultuous, "baroque" outpouring of metaphor energetically expressing an intense desire to communicate what is by definition inexpressible. Rather, the poet coolly considers the temporary departure of his soul from the body: it is a very Marvellian ecstasy indeed, this emblematic transfiguration of the word *ekstasis*.

The bird, with its plumes and silver wings, is an exotic fancy, one of the mind's transcendent creations, an *avis allegorica*, not some thrush which in a moment of rapture is endowed with symbolic significance. The brilliant figure of "the various Light" has proved irresistibly attractive to his-

---

[11] For a good-humored analysis of the identification of green as a color of hope and heavenly love, see Frank Kermode, "Two Notes on Marvell," pp. 136-38.

torians of ideas seeking to assign to it one or another particular ambience. But the mythic quality of this allegorical metaphor, more than its literary heritage or its philosophical forebears, is responsible for the resonance which shapes the ideas of multiplicity, the mutability of natural forms, the moving serenity of the temporal world. Although—or, remembering the logic of polarity, *because*—it is opposed to the single sun of heaven, "the various Light" is an incarnation, as it were, of the sun's power and glory.[12] This world of time is indeed the map of paradise. Thus the "longer flight" which will in time take the poet's soul to its source is "prepar'd for" in those momentary flights provided by green thoughts in the garden's green shade.

The assumption that stanzas 6 and 7 describe a mystic ecstasy has led frequently to readings which reverse Marvell's emphasis. The mind transcends, but as the soul glides to an earthly tree, so these garden thoughts are green. The denial of temporality is nothing to Marvell's purpose. The bird waving its plumes in "the various Light" is analogous, it seems to me, to that other famous bird which "once out of nature" is "set upon a golden bough" only to sing "of what is past, or passing, or to come." Mysticism is a denial of mediation, and the *immediate* finds no place in Marvell's poetry, which celebrates, rather, those paradoxical acts, green and temporal, by which the Resolved Soul solves the ambiguities of time.[13]

As the providential hero ruins "the great Work of Time," creating anew; as the lovers "devour" time to defeat it; so

---

[12] The relationship between the diffuse light of the earth and heavenly splendor is figured forth by the imagery of the colloquy in which "Created Pleasure" promises a very Helen:

> All this fair, and soft, and sweet,
>   Which scatteringly doth shine,
> Shall within one Beauty meet,
>   And she be only thine.

To which the "Resolved Soul" replies: "If things of Sight such Heavens be,/ What Heavens are those we cannot see?"

[13] See Appendix, Note 10: Marvell and Cusanus.

the poet annihilates "all that's made" as he recreates a world in the image of Eden. Love, heroic action, contemplation: each transforms the various, the mutable, the impermanent to an image of time-defying perfection. Those images define in terms of distillation, compounding, fusion; they are to be found in Marvell's major poems, generally at the close, where the unity of opposites is a new and felicitous creation: "Let us roll all our Strength, and all/ Our sweetness, up into one Ball"; "Musick, the Mosaique of the Air . . . gain'd the Empire of the Ear"; "In a Field *Sable* a Lover *Gules*"; "the Love which us doth bind . . . Is the Conjunction of the Mind/ And Opposition of the Stars." The close of "The Garden" shows the same faithfulness to order in diversity, unity in multiplicity, for the *poet* (not his body, not his mind, not his soul), renewed and enlivened by his contemplations, alive to beauty and awake to meaning, celebrates time's course in the single, quiet figure of the dial:

> How well the skilful Gardner drew
> Of flow'rs and herbes this Dial new;
> Where from above the milder Sun
> Does through a fragrant Zodiack run;
> And, as it works, th' industrious Bee
> Computes its time as well as we.
> How could such sweet and wholsome Hours
> Be reckon'd but with herbs and flow'rs!

Admired and beloved, the poet's garden has become the emblem of the garden which is the earth. Close as it is to "that happy Garden-state," this earthly garden—this garden, this earth—is nevertheless a dial by which the bee, as he goes about his work, and the poet, as he goes about his recreating, must reckon time. They cannot do otherwise, for they have inherited the earth. All life, action, knowledge is subject to time. Though the sun is milder here than in the heavens, his fierce power mitigated by the garden, by the beauties of the earth which the herbs and flowers represent, still he *runs*; the poet no more than the lover can make him stand still, but he opposes him as he can.

"Of flow'rs and herbes . . . with herbs and flow'rs": with this delicate circling, Marvell ends the poem. It is as if his heart is too full to attempt a grandiose summary in the manner of the close of "Upon Appleton House," where he hails the incomparable beauty and sweetness of gardens and fields in these words:

> *You Heaven's Center, Nature's Lap*
> *And Paradice's only Map.*

Sequent to the garden's metamorphoses is the dial's evocation of the garden's simplest, purest form. Still, as the Drop of Dew represents in itself the theme of that poem, herbs and flowers are emblematic of the garden and of the poet's discoveries there.

ALTHOUGH there are reverberations in "The Garden" of a dozen grand themes and although the imagery inevitably recalls major poems from all of European literature, classical and modern, Marvell's garden is his own. The reciprocity of poet and garden, each the other's creature, provides the safeguards against fanciful readings as those which have followed Empson's explication. At every stage of discovery, the garden is what the poet makes of it: a quiet retreat; a lover's delight; the paradise of the temporally bound soul; man's earthly heaven, his second Eden.

Marvell's garden shares as many features of the sweet fields and the woods as a garden decently can. The poem opens with a pun—"How vainly men themselves amaze"—which is a clue to the notion of the formal garden as a symbol of man's artfulness, his social instincts, his self-defeating pride. A "maze" is the network of grassy paths in a "labyrinth," a puzzle

formed by hedges or berry bushes; it is a common feature of
the kind of garden Damon decries:

> 'Tis all enforc'd; the Fountain and the Grot;
>   While the sweet Fields do lye forgot:
> Where willing Nature does to all dispence
>   A wild and fragrant Innocence.

The poet's garden is closer to the Mower's "sweet Fields" than
it is to the corrupt world "within the Gardens Square"; other-
wise, it could neither provide for the active, recreating mind
nor effect the freedom of the soul. The Mower derides the
garden which is a seduction of the earth by "Luxurious Man,"
but the poet's garden is, like nature and unlike the society of
men, "pure and sweet," and the seduction it accomplishes is
beneficent.

Certainly it is fair to argue that there is a consistency in
Marvell's views about gardens. It is often held that the Mower's
complaint is only an exercise in dramatic expression; or that
a wide range of attitudes should be allowed a man of sophisti-
cation who might at one moment long for the gardens of Italy
and the next condemn anything but a simple English meadow.
But each kind of landscape becomes for Marvell, it seems to
me, representative and important.

There is in Renaissance aesthetics a moral justification for
the modification of nature, for "Art playing second Nature's
part," in Spenser's words. But for Marvell, such artfulness is
associated with ostentation, and, indeed, with the corruption
of nature.[14] Nunappleton is characterized, for instance, as fol-
lows:

> But Nature here hath been so free
> As if she said leave this to me.
> Art would more neatly have defac'd

[14] On this point, see Marcia E. Allentuck's interesting note, "Mar-
vell's 'Pool of Air,' " *MLN*, LXXIV (1959), 587-89.

What she had laid so sweetly wast;
In fragrant Gardens, shaddy Woods,
Deep Meadows, and transparent Floods.

(ll. 75-80)

Nature has laid waste: so it would seem to an eye hungry for "enforc'd" order. But to the poet, it is "sweetly" done. This is the pleasant irony at the heart of "The Garden": in the rejection of passion, as in the preference for nature "pure and plain," something is of course sacrificed, but what is won is like unto heaven.

We cannot be sure, of course, that the details set forth in "The Garden" derive from any one actual place: it should not matter and it does not matter. But at the same time that we dismiss as finally irrelevant the question of actual location, we should be careful to entertain no unquestioned assumptions about the *kind* of garden to which the poem refers. "Upon Appleton House" is topical and allusive; the tendency is to assume that "The Garden," which in all probability also dates from the Yorkshire years, when Marvell was living with the Fairfaxes, likewise bears reference to a particular garden associated with the manor house at Nunappleton. "The Garden," that is to say, is often read in the context provided by the formal garden at Nunappleton (described in stanzas 36 through 40). But Lord Fairfax, who had some reputation in the arts of husbandry and gardening,[15] was surely as adept at designing the grounds of his manor house as he was in planning and executing the flower-fort which overlooks, as a bastion should, the lower grounds, the meadows of the River Wharfe at the south of the manor. Clearly, there is more to the gardens of Appleton House than this studied and completely artificial garden, a *jeu d'esprit* of the retired commander, to be admired and enjoyed in a public fashion. Mixed polity was becoming the ideal of government by the middle of the seven-

---

[15] Miles Hatfield, *Gardening in Britain* (London, 1960), p. 91.

teenth century; we might say that a comparable ideal held in garden design and that Lord Fairfax's Nunappleton was probably exemplary.

My assumption concerning the scene of "The Garden" is that it is the kind of garden to be found in a less open location, at the side of the house, for instance—a kitchen garden, or what John Evelyn calls a "fountain garden," for which he prescribes fruit trees.[16] Instead of artful parterres and the other floral displays of the formal garden, the keynote here is simplicity. The point is not at all to decide where Lord Fairfax's kitchen garden was, if he had one, but only to clarify that Marvell's meditations assume a certain informality of setting, even as his descriptions suggest it, if we read them afresh, unencumbered by a prejudice in favor of knots and topiary.

The garden is discovered to be an analogue of Eden, but it is first and always the earthly scene of the poet's contemplation.[17] It is the allegorical imagination that discovers the correspondence of earth and heaven by the contemplation of nature and time's course. The notion that Marvell's garden is a late-blooming version of the medieval *hortus conclusus* seems to me at odds with the tone, the temper, and the manner of the poet, and certainly at odds with his theme. For it is not the values of civilization and art or of piety which are represented here but the values of nature, and these are simplicity and plenitude, innocence and ease. If it is to be defined in topological terms, Marvell's garden is a *locus amoenus*, that ideal landscape whose provenance so many scholars have lovingly traced.[18] The details of this *locus amoenus* are few: grass,

---

[16] *Directions for the Gardiner at Says-Court* (1687).

[17] M. C. Bradbrook hits exactly the right note: "Earth is never lost to sight: nothing is omitted as the merely personal omits or as the merely contemplative omits" ("Marvell and the Concept of Metamorphosis," *Criterion*, XVIII [1938], 243).

[18] See J.A.W. Bennett's discussion in *The Parlement of Fowles* (Oxford, 1957), Chap. II. "Park of Paradise and Garden of Love." See also Curtius, *European Literature*, pp. 192ff.

green shade, fruit trees, herbs and flowers, and a fountain. The Mower names the fountain, with the grot, as an example of "enforc'd" order; but in "The Garden" the fountain is juxtaposed with the fruit tree, from which it is hardly differentiated: the detail of the "sliding foot" suggests that the fountain has become a part of nature, scarcely different in kind from the trees, the fruits, the flowers and herbs, the grass of the garden.

And what of the dial? How are we to read these lines:

> How well the skilful Gardner drew
> Of flow'rs and herbes this Dial new. . . .

There are three possible interpretations: the gardener and the dial are mundane and there are no wider references; an actual gardener (Fairfax?) and a particular floral dial are symbolic of God and the beauties of nature; "Gardner" and "Dial" are allegorical metaphors expressing the conception of this garden as a symbol of the earth, that garden given to man in recompense for the loss of "the eternal Spring . . . standing serenity and perpetual sunshine" (III, 368) which characterized "that happy Garden-state."

To construe "this Dial new" simply as a floral sundial (and, as I remarked in Chapter I, all editors have so construed it since Charles Lamb wrote fancifully of it) deprives us of a figure of much more serious wit. There is neither historical nor stylistic reason for insisting on an actual planting in the shape of a dial to account for "this Dial new"; furthermore, the clock of flowers envisaged by literalists of the dial, though possibly more amusing, is (exactly) too clever, too particular a figure to support the meaning toward which the poem tends. The supposition that Marvell is describing a formal garden in which such a planting would be appropriate (if somewhat anachronistic) is, it seems to me, far more difficult to justify than the assumption that for any poet the metaphoric resources of a garden are there to be exploited; that for a poet writing of gardens in mid-seventeenth-century England the resonant notes would not be those of the *hortus conclusus* or *hortis mentis* or of the garden of an androgynous Adam but of the garden that is the earth; and, finally, that Andrew Marvell, for whom the passage of time, the weighing of years, the course of history were the most compelling themes, would find the garden itself a dial by which to compute these "sweet and wholesome Hours."[19]

Presumably, the expectation of a Donne-like image is in part responsible for the failure to consider that "herbs and flowers" refers, simply, to that part of the green out-of-doors which is not subsumed under "trees."[20] As the trees of Nunappleton are said to outlast nature (stanza 62), so the growth and decline and fall of herbs and flowers is a dramatic register of change. Sir Thomas Browne remarks in *The Garden of Cyrus* that the willow's leaves do indeed turn to follow the sun's course and that the flower of the convolvulus turns equinoctially, the stalk twisting "according to the annual conversion."[21] But his real interest—passionate as always—is in the marvelous variety of ways in which all "plantations" respond generally, as a matter of course, to weather and season, ways that may be studied in "the great volume of Nature." Marvell's interest, too, is in the response of the earthly garden to the influence of the heavens: the botanical fact provides the ground of metaphor. The substance of the metaphoric equivalence is not, I think, "This floral dial which the gardener skillfully drew is like God's creation," but, rather, "God created the earth as a gardener would draw a dial." The figure is comparable to that with which Marvell concludes "The Unfortunate Lover" and it is one of his most characteristic inventions. There, the heraldic

[19] See Appendix, Note II: "Of flow'rs and herbes this Dial new."
[20] So Traherne in the "Second Century," §22: "The Sun and Moon and Stars shine, and by shining minister influences to Herbs and flowers." And Cowley in "The Change": "So the Earths face, Trees, Herbs and Flowers do dress."
[21] *Garden of Cyrus, Works,* I, 211-12. Marvell notes a comparable phenomenon in "Upon Appleton House," stanza 40.

banner depicts the heroic battle; it is an emblem that gives visual form to the subject of the poem, just as the narrative of the Lover's battle has given it historical form. We do not conclude that Marvell is indicating such a device on the wall of a gallery. No more than "Fair quiet" and her sister are the "Dial" and the "Gardner" present and actual. Like the bird with silver wings, they are the mind's transcendent creations, each "a green Thought in a green Shade."

Since paradise is a garden, it is a commonplace that God is a gardener. "Paradise itself," John Evelyn writes in *Sylva*, "was but a kind of Nemerous Temple or sacred *Grove*, Planted by God himself, and given to *Man*."[22] By using the term "skill," Marvell substantiates the metaphor. (William Lawson speaks of "the painful plowman" and the "skillful" gardener and we remember that the Shepherd of "The Coronet" has worked "skillfully" with flowers.) As the "Resolved Soul" claims that "When the Creator's skill is priz'd/ The rest is all but Earth disguis'd," so the happy poet of the garden admires God's "skill," a term which, like "glide," mediates between the particular example and the general conception.

The close of Marvell's "Hortus" is the one place where there is a similarity in tone as well as substance to that generally quite different poem, "The Garden." It is therefore worth noting that Marvell writes "Opifex horti." "Opifex" is Cicero's translation of the word "Demiourgos" as found in the *Timaeus*, literally, "a worker for the people, a craftsman," and by extension, "creator." Ovid in his account of creation writes, "ille opifex rerum, mundi melioris origo."[23] We can assume that Marvell, of all poets, would hear the resonance of this word. But, as relevant as the literary ancestry of the word may be,

---

[22] *Sylva, or a discourse of Forest Trees, and the propagation of Timber* . . . (1670), pp. 228-29.

[23] Milton, too, in *Prolusion VII* (from which I have taken a famous passage, in translation, as an epigraph for this book), refers to God as "magnum mundi opificum."

the important point is that the metaphor is rooted in language itself. Like all allegorical images at their core, "opifex" is a mythic metaphor: it is the indispensable figure of thought by which mortal man conceives of his Maker.

The conceptions we entertain of time are likewise mythic at their core. As man conceives of his Maker anthropomorphically, so he conceives of time spatially. Roger Hinks in his searching analysis of classical conceptions of time has pointed out that in mythic formulation it is "the repetition of a fixed point in space, not the duration of an infinitely subdivisable process in time, which constitutes a temporal event. It is therefore the completion of the given cycle which is regarded as significant, not the chronometry of this process. Consequently, *hora* may mean 'hour' or 'season,' *annus* 'year' or that period of time during which the constellations return to the same place."[24] Read in this light, Marvell's Latin encourages the reading of "Dial" and "Gardner" allegorically:

Nec tu, Opifex horti, grato sine carmine abibis:
Qui brevibus plantis, & laeto flore, notasti
Crescentes horas, atque intervalla diei.

The metaphoric substitution of space for time is a primary act of imagination, a point of departure for the "active Minde" which creates in its image of the garden as a zodiacal dial—a *space* in which *time* can be computed—a vision of order. Marvell's poem celebrates the correspondence of earth and heaven by naming the garden a second paradise: only if we read "Gardner" and "Dial" as allegorical metaphors can we satisfactorily account for "new," a term which is important, exact, resonant.[25] Life in time becomes for this Resolved Soul a second paradise because he contents himself with these "sweet and wholsome Hours."

[24] *Myth and Allegory*, pp. 42-43.
[25] Marvell does not lard his verses, except with expletives, as Legouis (*André Marvell*) and Leishman (*The Art of Marvell's Poetry*) amply demonstrate.

The tutelary spirits of Marvell's garden are innocence and ease and solitude: what of plenitude, so often associated with the earthly paradise? It is represented here only by the willing fruits of the garden; the usual conies and multitudinous birds are missing, for Marvell does not sing the praises of that love by whose means nature replenishes the earth. The innocence of nature and the emptiness of paradise seem reciprocal terms in Marvell's metaphysics. But though it is a somber notion, this emptiness of paradise, it is not merely a Marvellian fancy: "The gardens of Adonis were so emptie that they afforded proverbial expression, and the principal part thereof was empty spaces, with herbs and flowers in pots."[26]

"The Garden" ends with the contemplation of time's course. The quiet stability of the place allows for the discovery of that dimension of time represented by Spenser's Adonis, who

> All be he subject to mortalitie,
>
> Yet is eterne in mutabilitie,
>
> And by succession made perpetuall,
>
> Transformed oft and chaunged diverslie. . . .
>
> (*Faerie Queene*, III. vi. 47)

[26] Sir Thomas Browne, *The Garden of Cyrus, Works*, I, 227, J. W. Bennett in two lengthy discussions of Spenser's Garden of Adonis has described the paradisiacal aspects of this place "remote from the everyday world" ("Spenser's Garden of Adonis," *PMLA*, XLVII [1932], 46) and has sketched the history of the image: "The original 'Gardens of Adonis' were pots of quick-growing herbs, which were carried at the spring festival of Adonis. His death was celebrated at mid-summer, and the gardens came to be proverbial for the shortness of life. But as the emblems of the sun god it cannot be doubted that they were originally symbols of the power of the sun on seeds, which, with the aid of moisture and earth, or matter, produces the living plant" ("The Gardens of Adonis," *JEGP*, 41 [1942], 70).

I am suggesting not that Marvell's garden is the Garden of Adonis but that the phrase "herbs and flowers" has its own mythic associations and that the ambience of the image of the dial of herbs and flowers is not merely local and personal—that it is an allegorical metaphor, not simply a literal description.

The eternal dimension of time is known to man in mutable form; it is discovered in temporality (succession) itself. In Marvell's poem, even the bird of the soul sits in an earthly tree.

The whole of creation responding to the Creator is the theme of the chorus that ends "Clorinda and Damon":

> *Of* Pan *the flowry Pastures sing,*
> *Caves eccho, and the Fountains ring.*
> *Sing then while he doth us inspire;*
> *For all the World is our* Pan's *Quire.*

Though the final stanza of "The Garden" is not exultant in the manner of this *Jubilate Deo,* the dial because of its temporality shares the dynamic character of "Pan's *Quire*" and like it declares the living correspondence of earth and heaven. That is a grand theme, but Marvell's particular examples give the general notion a vivid and poignant presence, whether in the pastoral landscape of "Pastures, Caves, and Springs" or in the garden's green shade. As the dramatic sense of a man speaking lends urgency and intensity to the poet's argument in "To His Coy Mistress," so here the figure of the bemused solitary counterbalances the grave abstractions of the "Gardner" and his "Dial." The poet remains the man in the garden, alone with his thoughts and the bee.

"Upon Appleton House": The Masque of Nature

The contemplation of time has a moral and psychological character in "The Garden," which is a profoundly private poem. In "Upon Appleton House" the emphasis is on the aesthetic and political aspects of the soul's temporal life, on man's social existence. Even solitude is celebrated theatrically in this essentially public poem which defines virtue rather than happiness.

There is such an obvious variety of manner and matter in

"Upon Appleton House" that defining the unity of the poem is the tack we should expect criticism to take. But the question of the poem's unity has been raised only recently, because it is only recently that the poem has been read as a whole. For readers who saw Marvell as the garden poet, "Upon Appleton House" was not choice, for the taste that favors sweet or luxurious imagery does not generally honor longer poems with the attention necessary for their enjoyment. Instead, the poem was mined for gems and abandoned. But now the mine has been reopened and a search instituted for richer political and philosophic ores. Definition of the poem's unity in terms of political or philosophical theme has generally been no more successful than definition by genre, for the practice has been to read all themes and images in the context provided by two or three passages. Unity at this price comes dear.[27]

[27] D. C. Allen has read the poem as a political allegory characterized by subtlety and secrecy, a habit of mind which later victims of Marvell's satires would surely have wished that he had retained (*Image and Meaning*, pp. 115-53). Claiming that even the wide-flung net of Allen's allegory cannot provide a rationale for the total design of the poem, Maren-Sofie Røstvig proffers the thesis that "Upon Appleton House" is based upon "a theological or religious concept . . . the contrast between innocence and corruption" ("'Upon Appleton House' and the Universal History of Man," *ES*, XLIII [1961], 337). By adducing very abstract theory from images that she interprets in the light of medieval treatises, she sees the poem as representing a universal history of man. It is amusing to consider Marvell's scornful regard for writers who would choose a lesser form than epic for such a subject, as expressed in these lines from "On Mr. Milton's *Paradise Lost*":

> Jealous I was that some less skilful hand
>
> .   .   .   .
>
> Might hence presume the whole Creations day
> To change in Scenes, and show it in a Play.

Miss Røstvig and many others who have asserted that the poem has a thematic unity deriving from one or another arcanum have assumed that Fairfax, who was translating the hermetic books at the time Marvell was a member of his household, was on intimate terms with his daughter's tutor, that they enjoyed one another's company, that their temperaments must have been congenial, and so on. As for

Although "Upon Appleton House" is the fruit of Marvell's retirement to Yorkshire in the first years of the Commonwealth and though it is dedicated to "my Lord Fairfax," the poem's unity does not derive from a political theme nor from Marvell's keeping a steady eye only upon General Fairfax. "Upon Appleton House" is indeed a philosophical poem in many respects; but while it is rich in allusions to the Bible and folk wisdom and to popular philosophical notions, the unity of the poem is not to be found in a complex conceptual scheme. In discussing the poem I will stress one or another aspect of its unity, but my principal contention is that "Upon Appleton House" can best be considered as a masque of nature presented as a tribute to a public figure whom Marvell seeks to honor as a man of virtue. As such, it is unified by theme and purpose, by voice and manner, and by time itself and place.

To take the last-mentioned first: the "unities" are strict. The action takes place in a single afternoon during which the peripatetic poet makes his way about the grounds of Appleton House. Though the poem is continuous, with no marked divisions, it clearly falls into six parts, each determined by the setting. The poem assumes a certain familiarity with the place —which is, as it were, being offered to Fairfax anew—but the descriptions do more than simply depict charming scenes; they also recreate the landscape in a celebratory act. The topography and the buildings not only provide the setting, but also are themselves thematic. For the poem presents a continued metaphor of the correspondence of heaven and earth: Nunappleton is *"Paradice's only Map."* Thus the woods and

---

most phases of Marvell's life, documentation is slim indeed and thus reliance on "must have" is hard to resist. The status of the tutor in seventeenth-century households was not very high and if Marvell's position had been exceptional, should we not expect some acknowledgment of the debt Fairfax owed the young scholar in his will? But that prolix document, which Markham prints along with a sample of Fairfax's poetry, makes no mention whatever of Andrew Marvell.

meadows, the gardens and the manor house, indeed, every aspect of Nunappleton serves to figure forth the grand and simple theme of correspondence. Vivid country scenes are recreated as images of heavenly beauty by the celebrating poet. The unity of the poem derives from the unity of time, the unity of place, and the sustained theme of correspondence; they are all interdependent because they have been so conceived by the allegorical imagination of the poet, who celebrates the creative powers of virtue in the character of Fairfax and his daughter. In the course of his afternoon's exploration, he discovers in his contemplations of the scene and of the passage of time the virtue of the landscape. And this transforming power of the "active Minde" is a virtue comparable to that of character and soul: the meadow, the woods, and the riverbank which so challenge the poet's imagination are as much the scenes of virtuous action as the house itself and the allegorical garden, the creations of the hero and emblematic of his virtue. The "active Minde" discovers that "all things are composed here/ Like Nature, orderly and near." It is an order Marvell associates with heroism and greatness of soul, and, indeed, with the creations of the moral imagination.

But this order is associated, too, with delight and pleasure. Precisely because the correspondence of image and scene or act with moral qualities is certain, felt, real, the poet can afford to follow his fancy in expressing his apprehension of it. His attitude is voiced for the most part in tones of amusement, modulating now and then to a related key of quiet melancholy. Marvell has no need to convince himself of the truth of the correspondence of countryman and countryside, of house and master, and so the figures, extravagant as they are, arise spontaneously from his affectionate regard. They are fanciful and comic because Marvell can afford the comic: love and truth licence wit. It is a wit born of the knowledge of the discrepancy between heaven and any equivalent in earthly form; no expression of that correspondence can ever escape the inherent irony of matter's limiting spirit. And it is the wit of this poem which so often is "mistook," as Marvell says of nature's book. But if the poem is to be read and enjoyed as a whole, the role of witty metaphor must be understood; otherwise we will mistake the tone of the telling.

The poet's voice, like the varying scenes of his contemplations, enlivens and sustains the unifying theme of correspondence. The mode of his discourse changes as he moves from one scene and subject to another. I have schematized the poem as a guide to the discussion that follows:

			Scene and Subject	Mode
I.	ll.	1-80	House and Garden and Fairfax	Treatise
II.*		81-280	Isabel and the Nuns	Historical narrative
III.		281-368	The Formal Gardens and Fairfax	Allegory
IV.		369-480	The Harvest; the Water-Meadow	Masque
V.		481-616	The Woods	Masque; Homily
VI.		617-776	The River and Maria	Masque

* Discussion of Part II is reserved until p. 193.

Part I is a treatise on that virtue of humility shared by house and master. The pattern for the imagery is to be found in "Upon the Hill and Grove at Bill-borow," Marvell's five-finger exercise for the 776 lines of "Upon Appleton House." There the correspondence of the sacred shade and the hill with the genius of the house (the hero Fairfax and his family) is rather simple, the only elaboration coming in puns and conventional comparisons. Between the place and the hero there is a mutual regard: Marvell sees to it that the trees speak feelingly. The symmetry and order of the hill, the "soft access and wide" by which it is approached and the ease with which it can be climbed, all represent in the form of a natural monument that heroic virtue of humility Marvell most admired.

> See then how courteous it ascends,
> And all the way it rises bends;
> Nor for it self the height does gain,
> But only strives to raise the Plain.

The estate at Nunappleton shares this character. The account of the nuns' intrigue (Part II), which elaborates so many negative analogies for the subjects of the poem, ends with these lines:

> Though many a *Nun* there made her Vow,
> 'Twas no *Religious House* till now.

Appleton House is a "*Religious House*" because it is the house of a hero of great moral stature, and its architecture represents that character. As nests are "equal" to birds, so the house is "equal" to such a man as Fairfax. The principle of correspondence is a civilized version of sympathetic magic: if Fairfax is virtuous and the house imitates him, then the house will be virtuous. This is the reverse of the relation between nature and Cromwell that Marvell defined in the "Horatian Ode": because Cromwell acts like a natural force, he must therefore *be* a natural force, sanctified by heaven. In its sobriety, which it shares with Fairfax, the house provides a model for the gate of heaven. Because of its lack of pretension, it is a mark of "Grace," an "Inn" for the soul on its way heavenward. Appleton House is religious because it is natural and natural because it is religious; this circular causality is the logic from which the imagery stems.

The "sober Frame" of this English house displays none of the overwrought, pretentious, wasteful character associated with the designs of a "Forrain *Architect*" who builds too high. Nor is Appleton House too wide, in the manner of those new Babels in breadth which man, "sov'raign thing and proud," as

Damon calls him, is tempted to construct. There is nothing prideful here:

> *Humility* alone designs
> Those short but admirable Lines,
> By which, ungirt and unconstrain'd,
> Things greater are in less contain'd.
> Let others vainly strive t'immure
> The *Circle* in the *Quadrature*!
> These *holy Mathematicks* can
> In ev'ry Figure equal Man.

The grand alliance of nature, hero, and heaven which is represented in the house is represented a fortiori by the rest of the estate:

> Him *Bishops-Hill,* or *Denton* may,
> Or *Bilbrough,* better hold than they:
> But Nature here hath been so free
> As if she said leave this to me.
> Art would more neatly have defac'd
> What she had laid so sweetly wast;
> In fragrant Gardens, shaddy Woods,
> Deep Meadows, and transparent Floods.

"Leave this to me": Bilbrough and Fairfax's other country estates may offer elegance and show and formality (all that "Art" means in this context), but Appleton House will be as close to nature as architecture and a civilized landscape can be. Legouis has noted that the claim Marvell makes in this stanza is hardly in accord with "Fairfax's horticultural amusements."[28] But the formal garden, artfully "laid out in sport," is not, any more than the house, "superfluously spread": "In the just Figure of a Fort," the garden is architecture at a single remove and like the house it corresponds to its master.

The metaphor of soldiery is continued, the description serv-

[28] Legouis, *Andrew Marvell,* p. 46.

ing to develop variations on the subject of the soldier-gardener and the garden-fort. The state of England at the time of Fairfax's retirement gives to the description of the garden a certain sobriety. Thus Marvell easily moves from the bee-sentinels and the flower-regiments to the hymn to the garden of the world. And the garden, no matter how fanciful it momentarily seems, is also an emblem of that England which is itself an image of lost paradise.[29]

The lines concerning the gardener-soldier—

> Who, had it pleased him and *God*,
> Might once have made our Gardens spring
> Fresh as his own and flourishing—

are poignant if we have in mind Marvell's lines about that other soldier-gardener who left his garden plot, called by heaven "to ruine the great Work of Time." Though Fairfax too does the work of heaven, his reward is not earthly glory but the peace of retirement. The difference in tone between the "Horatian Ode" and "Upon Appleton House" reflects the difference between Cromwell and Fairfax; it is not a question of shifting loyalties. Yet one could perhaps say ("perhaps" because it means hypothesizing about the secret ways of the imagination, ever a hazardous undertaking) that as Marvell turns from this saintly man of good conscience to a long last look at the flower-fort, he is troubled and even bitter. For does not the description of the batteries of sight aimed from the garden at the deserted seat of a onetime neighbor, the Archbishop of York, suggest a waste of spirit, an irrelevance? The dispossessed Anglicans, after all, are not now the dangerous antagonist.

Marvell does not return to the theme of the soldier's retirement. His purpose is neither to justify nor, of course, to

[29] The identification of England and Eden was a commonplace. For instance, the fifth edition (1660) of Sir Hugh Platt's *The Paradise of Flora* (1600) was entitled *The Garden of Eden, or an accurate description of all Flowers and Fruits now growing in England.*

question explicitly his employer's choice, but to describe the circumstances of its enactment and its moral consequences. Ironic speculation about the safety of retreat, the loss of heroic leadership and the chance of earthly glory—this is nothing to Marvell's larger purpose. He honors the private person, whose choice he does not question. And he makes a good case because he is not making a case at all but following the course of his deepest sympathies. The sympathy is there because Marvell, more than most men, knew the cost of the choice involved.

The stanza closes abruptly, returning to the "artillery of sight":

> But ore the Meads below it plays
> Or innocently seems to gaze.

Marvell so far has but celebrated that which the heroic character of the Fairfaxes has created. The poem now develops to include those correspondences discovered by the transforming power of the "active Minde." As architecture is the parent metaphor in Parts I and III, so the masque is central to Parts IV, V, and VI. Ben Jonson wrote of a certain device in a masque, "Upon this hinge, the whole invention moved."[30] In the harvest, water-meadow, woods, and river sections of Marvell's poem, the masque is itself that "hinge." The scenes he describes are set forth as if they were in a masque. The mowers, the salmon-fishers, and finally Maria enter as onto a stage, a grassy, out-of-doors stage; appearances change; prospects shift; the poet himself, as privileged spectators will, joins in at times and in the woods becomes the chief masquer. What we are watching is the masque of nature as it is enacted in the theater of Marvell's imagination.[31] Part IV opens thus:

[30] Quoted in Enid Welsford, *The Court Masque* (Cambridge, Eng., 1927), p. 256.
[31] Rosemond Tuve remarks: "The reasons for the affinity between masque device and pastoral imagery are not alone those of literary history, date, fashion, fitness for 'scene' and production, common clas-

And now to the Abbyss I pass
Of that unfathomable Grass,
Where Men like Grashoppers appear,
But Grashoppers are Gyants there:
They, in there squeking Laugh, contemn
Us as we walk more low then them:
And, from the Precipices tall
Of the green spir's, to us do call.

The peripatetic poet joins the harvesters momentarily and there is the laughter of surprise in every line. Men are made small by the tall grass they walk in; grasshoppers perched high on "the Precipices tall" are like giants. A. Alvarez has suggested that this passage was written to amuse Maria Fairfax, much as Lewis Carroll wrote to amuse his precocious young friends.[32] The archness of *Alice* may be worlds apart from Marvell's wit, and yet the instinct for delight is shared and I think Alvarez is closer to the mark than those who read the grass as history, the rail as Christ/Charles, the grasshoppers as clergymen, the mowers as the New Model Army, and so on.

For this is not religious or political allegory but a description of the harvest, which we are watching as if it were a masque:

No Scene that turns with Engines strange
Does oftner then these Meadows change.

The description is sustained by the idiom of mock epic played off against precise observation. The scenic illusion is of a sea

sical origin. They are alike with respect to their metaphorical base" (*Images and Themes*, p. 124). Of the characteristics of the masque as they are defined in the course of her essay on "Comus," the following I find relevant to "Upon Appleton House": the masque is understood via the eye; it is "inescapably symbolical"; it is not primarily dramatic, but proceeds by presenting oppositions; design rather than plot is paramount; actors are themselves spectators; and, finally, the masque celebrates someone (pp. 113, 115, 119, 143, 154).
[32] *The School of Donne* (London, 1961), p. 111.

of grass. Marvell's imagination of space is the "engine" by which it is effected.[33]

> To see Men through this Meadow Dive,
> We wonder how they rise alive.
> As, under Water, none does know
> Whether he fall through it or go.
> But, as the Marriners that sound
> And show upon their Lead the Ground,
> They bring up Flow'rs so to be seen,
> And prove they've at the Bottom been.

These "Marriners" recall the "*Indian* Slaves" of "Mourning" who "sink for Pearl through Seas profound." First cultivator-divers; then mower-Israelites, "walking on foot through a green Sea":

> To them the Grassy Deeps divide,
> And crowd a Lane on either Side.
>
> With whistling Sithe, and Elbow strong,
> These Massacre the Grass along.

To the visual brilliance of the scene is added a dramatic, kinetic imagery which fills out the picture in such a way as to suggest, again, a painting of Brueghel's: the harvest scene entitled *Autumn*, where the pictorial effect of such details as the flowers that can be seen through the grain is strengthened by the presence of figures against whom the deep meadow and the tall grass can be measured. The vigorous action of the mowers and the effect of their mowing is as dramatically realized in Marvell's picture as in Brueghel's. His descriptions are visually accurate and dramatically alive, but in the theater of Marvell's imagination, the language of description itself creates drama. The witty development of the conventional metaphor

[33] The forcefulness of this imagination is remarked by Geoffrey Walton in his discerning essay on Marvell in *Metaphysical to Augustan* (London, 1955), p. 131.

of the sea of grass has given us divers and mariners and Israelites and their (green) sea. "Massacre" succeeds the image of the divided sea as the controlling figure and we may think that we have therefore left the Israelites behind; but they take on a life of their own and their history, especially the scene of their escape out of Egypt, suggests further images for the harvested field and the flooded meadow.

The unexpected death of the rail—the sudden, dramatic intrusion of discord is a characteristic development in pastoral and the masque—quickly becomes a comic interlude.

> While one, unknowing, carves the *Rail*,
> Whose yet unfeather'd Quils her fail.
> The Edge all bloody from its Breast
> He draws, and does his stroke detest;
> Fearing the Flesh untimely mow'd
> To him a Fate as black forebode.

Speculation on the fearful significance of this untimely death is cut short by the appearance of "bloody *Thestylis*," who

> . . . cryes, he call'd us *Israelites*;
> But now, to make his saying true,
> Rails rain for Quails, for Manna Dew.[34]

This astonishing trick of having a metaphor come to life is comparable to having a figure unmask. Marvell picks up "carves" (line 395) and follows it with the appearance of the mowers' cook, who trusses the one bird and seizes another. To have the Virgilian figure ("Thestylis" pounds garlic for

[34] The Israelites, *in extremis*, have provided Marvell with another allusion:

> And I parting should appear
> Like the Gourmand *Hebrew* dead
> While the Quailes and *Manna* fed
> He does through the Desert err.
>   ("Daphnis and Chloe," ll. 77-80)

the weary classical mowers) answer to the Biblical epithet creates as complex a "prolepsis" as can be found in Marvell's poems.

The Lovelace-like quibbling—"Rails rain for Quails, for Manna Dew"—is followed by a contemplation of the death of the rail which keeps the sentiment ironic (in a manner recalling Burns) by a slightly sardonic warning tone. The episode of the bird mistakenly killed is abruptly ended:

> Or sooner hatch or higher build:
> The Mower now commands the Field.

The second illusion is that what we are witnessing is a scene of battle. It is described by one critic thus: "The scene is one of nightmarish discord, of pastoral idealism distorted by violence."[35] A harvest does indeed present a varied scene. The actions are rapid and confusing, senseless until they are recognized as parts of a whole. But whatever violence there is in Marvell's scene is the "violence" of a vigorous imitation of a battle, not of a mob free-for-all. The spectator may be at a loss unless he finds a form in what he sees: Marvell is making sense out of what is proceeding in front of us by means of the radical metaphor of war as a harvest, characteristically reversing the image and referent: the mown grass is like men cut down in battle. The best argument against the labored allegorization of the harvest/battle is that we do not need it and that, if allowed, it disrupts the poem. The abyss of grass, the green sea, the masquelike spectacle of the mowers prepare us for this "battle" as another illusion, not as a picture-history of an idea.

Following the battle scene, there is a dance of celebration. If we think of opera—the closest thing we have to masque—how expectable it is!

[35] Toliver, *Marvell's Ironic Vision*, p. 117.

And now the careless Victors play,
Dancing the Triumphs of the Hay;

    .   .   .   .

When at their Dances End they kiss,
Their new-made Hay not sweeter is.

Those who read the harvest as an allegory of war do not ex-
plain how such a sweet and charming scene is congruent with
the "massacre," nor how the "dangerous amazons" who in
their "aggressive heterosexuality" have been so violently threat-
ening above can be so friendly here. This stanza seems to me
to be in the same key as "Ametas and Thestylis Making Hay-
Ropes," which may indeed have been an offshoot of this
passage. Marvell, perhaps, was loath to leave the scene.

The meadow changes again, and now, with the hay "pil'd
in Cocks," is "like a calm Sea [that] shews the Rocks."

We wondring in the River near
How Boats among them safely steer.

Does the poet become part of the scene he describes, as is the
case with the mowers? Legouis remarks of the syntax of this
stanza (stanza 55) that "though the grammarian cavils, who
runs may read."[36] I am tempted to read "wondring in the
River" as referring to "we," to consider that the poet surveys
from a punt as he steers among the "rocks" (haycocks) in this
"sea" (river-laced meadow), that he wonders as he wanders.
However, the illusion here and in the stanzas that follow
directly does seem to depend on distance: the changing scene
is presented as a panorama, considered from, say, a hillside
beneath the garden parapet. The second analogy of the plain
describes the prospect in terms of "the *Desert Memphis Sand*":
the Israelites are with us still.

This *Scene* again withdrawing brings
A new and empty Face of things.

[36] Legouis, *Andrew Marvell*, p. 66.

176

The pictures of the shorn field are extravagant and showy, as a masque's should be, and of course Marvell does not miss the chance for brilliant portraiture of this "empty Face." None of the pictures is more "symbolic" than the others. Thus, "this naked equal Flat/ Which *Levellers* take Pattern at" has its place in the catalogue along with "Clothes for *Lilly*" (canvas stretched for the painter Peter Lely), "a Table rase and pure," "the Toril . . . at Madrid," and so on. Like the Israelites who come to life, the "equal Flat" is caught between the literal and the figurative: the topographical feature shares its name with Lilburne's faction; but the Levellers are metaphorically named after such phenomena as the field before us. It is that circular logic by which Marvell's wit operates, producing concepts out of words and words out of images and images out of conventional figures.

Next, the villagers are allowed to let in their cows to glean. They appear to the poet like "th' Universal Heard" in a "painted World." Marvell returns to the notion of the "Face of things" and in the next stanza expresses the wonder and delight inspired by the grand distances of the English countryside. The "Looking-Glass" and "Multiplying Glasses" are guises of the eye of imagination by which the poet, in his perception of the landscape, sees the very idea of space. The harvest in, the battle over, the spectacle's meaning is now in the design it makes, in what it appears to be, as, for instance, in this description of the cattle grazing:

> They feed so wide, so slowly move,
> As *Constellations* do above.

The lines echo, again, "How wide they dream!" Like the figures of the "Marriners" and the "Israelites," these starry cattle suggest a dreamlike dimension of time and space. The poet's themes coalesce, the correspondence of earthly beauty and goodness with heaven merging with the transforming power of eye and mind. For indeed, the masque of the harvest is visionary. The clarity of the scene as perceived by the poet's eye becomes symbolic of precious serenity, of beauty, of timeless order. And these are heavenly virtues.

Another metaphor comes to life next, as the meadow is flooded. This phenomenon—agronomic, not seasonal—[37] is described as a transformation scene, a favorite masquing device:

> Then, to conclude these pleasant Acts,
> *Denton* sets ope its *Cataracts*;
> And makes the Meadow truly be
> (What it but seem'd before) a Sea.[38]

There is another fireworks display, a burst of fancifulness as the character and appearance of the flooded meadow is described in one marvelous topsy-turvy image after another, figures which play on the ambiguity of a water-meadow. To read this concluding stanza (stanza 60) as a prophecy in the manner of Nostradamus, teeming with political implications, is to miss a fine exhibition of Marvell's wit. In its ludicrous extension of figures of speech, in the literalization of rhetoric, the stanza recalls a poem that amused even Carlyle,[39] Marvell's salute to the giant water-meadow that is Holland, where

[37] The reference is not to the flood season but to the deliberate and temporary flooding of the low-lying meadows flanking the river: a "cataract" is a floodgate. Eric Kerridge, who gives a description of the methods of floating a meadow, notes that "by 1657 the system was normal amongst gentlemen farmers and cultivating landowners" (*The Agricultural Revolution* [London, 1967], pp. 255ff.). The misreading of "*Denton* sets ope its *Cataracts*" as a natural occurrence provides the basis for assuming a seasonal time-scheme in this poem. Following the references to the sun's course, from the time of the mowing until the final stanza, is a sure guide through the poem's long day.

[38] Would Marvell refer to a somber allegory of the Civil War as "these pleasant Acts"? A. B. Chambers, having accepted the allegorization of the mowing scene, is bound to call this "ironic" ("'I was But an Inverted Tree': Notes towards the History of an Idea," *Studies in the Renaissance*, 8 [1961], 291).

[39] Legouis, *Andrew Marvell*, p. 237.

The Earth and Water play at *Level-coyl*;
The Fish oft-times the Burger dispossest,
And sat not as a Meat but as a Guest.
("The Character of Holland," ll. 28-30)

The poet as spectator of the harvest and flood has gloried in
the imagery of show on a panoramic scale. Having enjoyed
the pleasures of inventing metaphors for the amazing plain,
the poet now gives himself over to the delight of close ob-
servation. In the woods section which follows the descriptions
of the water-meadows, the theme of the transforming powers
of the "active Minde" is further developed in these three sub-
jects: the solitary retreat into the dark and secret woods; the
poetic identification with nature; and the interpretation of
nature.

This section of "Upon Appleton House" features passages
which have served in various stylistic analyses as examples of
the Hermetic or Platonic modes or of the manner of the
precieux and the libertine poets. Also, critics who have allego-
rized the harvest and the flood have found themselves bound
to allegorize the retreat as well, finding Marvell's interpre-
tation of history figured there, his judgment of the state of
England after the civil war, and so forth. The tone of the
woods section has again and again been misapprehended.
Stanza 61 begins the section:

> But I, retiring from the Flood,
> Take Sanctuary in the Wood;
> And, while it lasts, my self imbark
> In this yet green, yet growing Ark;
> Where the first Carpenter might best
> Fit Timber for his Keel have Prest.
> And where all Creatures might have shares,
> Although in Armies, not in Paires.

Certainly there is a retreat to quiet and delightful meditation,
but this is not to say that "Ark" signals a sober, mystic tonal-

ity.[40] I think it possible that Marvell may have used "Ark" not only to introduce the ideas of safety and plenitude but also to suggest the curious and fantastic nature of the woods and its creatures. "Ark" to this day carries with it connotations of the extraordinary. (The Tradescants—nurserymen, gardeners royal, antiquarians—collected "what is rare in land, in seas, in air" and offered it for the public's delight. Their museum, which was fated to become the Ashmolean Museum, was called "Tradescant's Ark.")[41] At any rate, Marvell is a sort of cicerone in this "green Ark," ready and willing to explicate the meaning of nature and to describe its joys.

"Imbark," a neat pun involving boat and tree and the notion of a beginning of an exploration, designates another stage in the identification of the poet and nature which the imagination pursues and expresses here in hyperboles that recall the celebrated correspondence of Appleton House and its master. Architecture as a figure is never far off in "Upon Appleton House," here providing image rather than referent; the woods themselves are described as the poet's habitation. Marvell's masque calls for a "Temple green," an "Ark," a "Sanctuary" which is another "Religious House," its "columns" and "arches" expressing the order of nature. "Yet green, yet growing Ark" names the wondrous energy and power, all the virtues that *green* signifies for Marvell, of creation. The "Creatures"—exclusively birds and a caterpillar or two, for all the talk of "Armies"—and the trees: with these the poet will "confer" and as an equal, discoursing on their significance.

It is characteristic of the woods section to be intensely visual and explicitly symbolic, and for the symbols to depend upon

[40] Marvell uses the image of the ark in *The Growth of Popery* when he mockingly considers "the defection of considerable persons both male and female to the Popish religion, as if they entered by couples clean and unclean into the ark of that church, not more in order to their salvation, than for their temporal safety" (IV, 412).

[41] See G. W. Johnson's *History of English Gardening* (London, 1829), pp. 99ff., for a brief account.

visual images. Symbol here is in the service of moral insight and the celebration of virtue, in contrast to the symbolic description of the harvest, which serves chiefly to define the rhythms and hidden order of a splendid human activity. The stanzas describing the "double Wood" (stanzas 62 and 63) are typical of the poet's descriptive discourse. The observation that many trees have been sacrificed in war is from the point of view of agronomy a quite pertinent one[42] and the description of the planting and its effect is as precise as it is amusing: the identification of the "double Wood" as a *Fifth Element*— i.e.,"Wood" is added to the other four[43]—suggests that this wall of green is a pole hedge, close-planted trees clipped to present a flat surface. Later references to the lane between "the double Wood" (the hedges) and to the "Labyrinths" (line 622) fill out the picture of this grove as part of the garden complex. But by identifying "the double Wood of ancient Stocks" with the founding families of Fairfax and Vere, Marvell punningly moves beyond description to celebrate the continuing life of heroes, as of trees:

> Of whom though many fell in War,
> Yet more to Heaven shooting are:
> And, as they Natures Cradle deckt,
> Will in green Age her Hearse expect.

The tone of the stanza about the "double Wood" is courtly, like the end of Part II (stanzas 31 and 36), where Marvell is also saluting his patron's family. But for the rest of the woods

[42] That is, they have been used for shipbuilding, not destroyed in the course of carrying out a scorched earth policy, as one critic avers. John Evelyn was concerned in *Sylva* to prove the need for systematic reforestation with an eye to future naval needs.

[43] Kitty Scoular believes that "the woods hold up the crystalline heavens, the 'Fifth Element,' and within is the vastness of the night skies." (*Natural Magic: Studies in the Presentation of Nature in English Poetry from Spenser to Marvell* [Oxford, 1964], p. 182). I read "Fifth Element" in apposition with "the huge Bulk," and take "thrust up," like "shooting" (l. 494), to mean "growing up."

section, the tone is homely and amused (the bird stanzas) and then, I think, mocking and ironic.

The birds are introduced thus:

> And underneath the winged Quires
> Echo about their tuned Fires.

The flamboyance of this couplet is not sustained and the birds with medieval pedigree, the nightingale and the heron, take second place to native stock doves and the woodpecker. In the three stanzas devoted to the "*Hewel's* wonders," precise observation is juxtaposed with allegorizing in a sophisticated way, though the lesson itself is as homely as the bird. The delight in the economy of nature is as strong as the delight in moral significance, for the traitor-wormlings feed the hewel's young, and the oak, once satisfied that treason is punished, will serve as the house of the hewel-scourge.

The "imbarked" poet continues to undergo a transformation into what he studies, for he speaks the birds' "most learned Original" and, given wings, could fly away; and he is already a tree of sorts:

> Thus I, *easie Philosopher,*
> Among the *Birds* and *Trees* confer:
> And little now to make me, wants
> Or of the *Fowles,* or of the *Plants.*
> Give me but Wings as they, and I
> Streight floting on the Air shall fly:
> Or turn me but, and you shall see
> I was but an inverted Tree.

It is a Marvellian description of the power hailed by Sidney as distinctively that of the poet who, "lifted up with the vigor of his own invention, doth grow into an other nature. . . ."[44] In the character of the "*easie Philosopher*" Marvell has offered his own "Defence of Poesie," and it is based not upon any

[44] *Defence,* in *Works,* III, 8.

profoundly serious view of the poet's vatic function but upon the powers of his "active Minde."[45] The *"easie Philosopher"* boasts that

> No Leaf does tremble in the Wind
> Which I returning cannot find.

> Out of these scatter'd *Sibyls* Leaves
> Strange *Prophecies* my Phancy weaves:
> And in one History consumes,
> Like *Mexique Paintings*, all the *Plumes*.
> What *Rome, Greece, Palestine*, ere said
> I in this light *Mosaick* read.
> Thrice happy he who, not mistook,
> Hath read in *Natures mystick Book*.

The leaves of the trees reveal all the world's wisdom, accounting for everything: after all, if the trees are to outlive nature (lines 495-96) they of course antedate history.

How are we meant to take all this? Is the poet, for all his self-amused irony, nevertheless as serious as Vaughan and Traherne?[46] Even the diction, it seems to me, warns us away from gravity, and the imagery is nowhere in the poem more lighthearted. It features Marvell's favorite device of converting a symbol (the sibylline leaves) into its phenomenal form and then reconstituting it metaphorically. The whole passage seems to have grown from the metaphor of nature's book. The poet claims to see all, know all "in this light *Mosaick*," a triple pun if there ever was one. In "Thrice happy he who, not mistook,/ Hath read in *Natures mystick Book*," a pleasant boast has been delightfully downgraded, as the sly condition surely indicates.

The role of the poet is to exercise his imagination in the exploration and contemplation of nature, not to indulge in somber theorizing, as dull and irrelevant as those empty cere-

---

[45] See Appendix, Note 12: The *"easie Philosopher."*
[46] Toliver, *Marvell's Ironic Vision*, p. 123.

monies that Marvell once derided as "Mosaical rubbish" (III, 379). The *"easie Philosopher"* is only the poet. When he reads the homily on the hewel from *"Natures mystick Book,"* he displays his understanding of the "poetic of correspondences."[47] It is an understanding that also informs "On a Drop of Dew." But how different in tone is the homily! It is surely unimaginable, for instance, that Marvell at the close of "On a Drop of Dew" would have turned to a self-amused consideration of his own interpretive powers or that the *"easie Philosopher"* could have ended his discourse with an exaltation of the wood-pecker.

There will be time for lofty celebration in the final hymn to Nunappleton and Maria, the genius of the place; but for now, the poet moves quickly to avoid solemnity:

> And see how Chance's better Wit
> Could with a Mask my studies hit!
> The Oak-Leaves me embroyder all,
> Between which Caterpillars crawl:
> And Ivy, with familiar trails,
> Me licks, and clasps, and curles, and hales.
> Under this *antick Cope* I move
> Like some great *Prelate of the Grove.*

The *sortes Virgilianae*, the "chanceable hitting upon any [of such] verses"[48] which Sidney chose as a symbol of poetic power and a sign of the esteem in which poets were anciently held, becomes for Marvell the subject of parody. "Chance's better Wit" is the handmaiden of the "active Minde"; it is associated not with the allegorizing of the hewel homily but with the enjoyment of the self as a natural cipher. Of course it takes "Phancy" to discern and construe that costume and char-

---

[47] See Joseph A. Mazzeo's two articles, "A Critique of Some Modern Theories of Metaphysical Poetry," *MP*, L (1952), 88-96, and "Metaphysical Poetry and the Poetic of Correspondence," *JHI*, XIV (1953), 221-34.
[48] *Defence*, in *Works*, III, 6.

acter devised by shadow and shade, bugs and plants, there in the green woods, but there is more show, more spontaneity, more display than there is deliberation; and the comic transformation to the "great *Prelate*," an out-and-out masque figure, seems happily made.

Invention and masquing, moralizing and celebrating are all pleasant enough, but in the woods at Nunappleton, it is the mind's creation which becomes a "pleasure less." "Languishing with ease," the poet falls on grass and yields next to purely sensuous pleasure. This is the "wond'rous Life" of "The Garden," but it is sequel to the mind's ardent labors, not the condition of its creating.

The poet seems to have anticipated that nature's "loose" order will finally lead to this luxuriant, thoughtless ease, for he seems to give himself to it with abandon. We are brought up short, however. If these are not "sweet and wholsome Hours," neither are they given over to a voluptuary's dream.

> How safe, methinks, and strong, behind
> These Trees have I incamp'd my Mind;
> Where Beauty, aiming at the Heart,
> Bends in some Tree its useless Dart;
> And where the World no certain Shot
> Can make, or[49] me it toucheth not.
> But I on it securely play,
> And gaul its Horsemen all the Day.

It is a far bolder plan than that set forth in "The Picture of Little T.C.": "Let me be laid,/ Where I may see thy Glories from some shade." Where there is melancholy and fear in "The Picture of Little T.C.," there is in "Upon Appleton House" vigor and a disdain which leads directly to a parody

---

[49] Margoliouth did not find this odd. It seems to make better sense if read "on."

of[50] all those lyrics in which the lover begs his mistress to bind and secure him, to take him, to make him her captive:

> Bind me ye *Woodbines* in your 'twines,
> Curle me about ye gadding *Vines,*
> And Oh so close your Circles lace,
> That I may never leave this Place:
> But, lest your Fetters prove too weak,
> Ere I your Silken Bondage break,
> Do you, O *Brambles,* chain me too,
> And courteous *Briars* nail me through.

Bind, curl; chain me, nail me. From woodbine and ivy (which clasps the *"Prelate,"* in stanza 74) to brambles and briars: it seems an inevitable sequence, given the logic of oxymoron, the same by which a slightly distraught lady might say "Force brandy down my throat!" Tie me in the labyrinth for the day; stake me by the river at dusk. It recalls "Insnar'd with Flow'rs"; it is Damon's pleasant manner as he addresses the glowworms and sings of the services done him by dew and sun. The exuberance of "Bind me ye *Woodbines*" and the disdain of the preceding stanza on the encampment of the mind are ironic counterparts. That solitude afforded by the green world which alone can offer security from the dangers of sexual passion always elicits Marvell's imaginative energy. Here, it is all very lighthearted. Nevertheless, critics in single-minded pursuit of the ambiguities of the theme of retirement have been unable to resist the connotations of *"Briars"* and, disregarding decorum, to say nothing of Marvell's wit, have found here somber significance of sacrifice.[51] But briars, until

---

[50] Miss Bradbrook makes the point in "Marvell and the Poetry of Rural Solitude," *RES,* XVII (1941), 39.

[51] Empson led the way with this comment in his famous essay in *Some Versions of Pastoral:* "The masculine energy of [ll. 607-08] is balanced immediately by an acceptance of Nature more masochistic than passive, in which he becomes Christ with both the nails and the thorns" (p. 123). Hartman spoils the game by commenting that in *"Briars"* and "nail" there is "a hint of the redemptive relation of poet and

they are woven into that crown which is one of the Instruments of the Passion, are only sharp and uncomfortable and useful for snaring a nature-lover. The woodbine becomes the emblem of the love Marvell imputes to the lovely green; the briars and brambles (which surely must prove embarrassing to anyone attempting allegorization) are but hyperbolical cousins of the willing fruits of "The Garden."

THE transition from the woods section to the poem's concluding section is neatly made by an indication of change both in time and place:

> But, where the Floods did lately drown,
> There at the Ev'ning stake me down.
>
> For now the Waves are fal'n and dry'd,
> And now the Meadows fresher dy'd;
> Whose Grass, with moister colour dasht,
> Seems as green Silks but newly washt.
> No *Serpent* new nor *Crocodile*
> Remains behind our little *Nile*;
> Unless it self you will mistake,
> Among these Meads the only Snake.

The woods have provided an "Ark" during the "Flood"; now that the waters have subsided, the *"easie Philosopher"* finds a fresh world. After Marvell's flood, there is "no *Serpent* new" other than the river which holds the meadow in its "wanton harmless folds." Grosart notes an implicit contrast with the *old* Serpent; it is a pertinent reminder that after the Flood there was a new dispensation. And indeed, does not Marvell's picture of the serene and "newly washt" green world ("fresher dy'd ... moister colour ... newly washt" are caught up again in the homely image of lines 657-60, where nature, collecting

---

Nature" ("Marvell, St. Paul, and the Body of Hope, p. 108n.). If martyrdom and redemption rather than the captivity of love provide the context, then those words are more than a "hint."

itself, appears "whist and fine") remind us of "this Dial new" by which can be counted "sweet and wholsome Hours"? As the day ends the poet proceeds to the riverbank, another "captivating" place, to enjoy yet further the innocent pleasures nature affords. Happiness awaits the fisherman at the river's edge. As he has been embarked in the "yet green, yet growing Ark," so now he is "stretcht as a Bank unto the Tide"; he again identifies himself with a tree.[52] And then, like the evening, Maria comes.

As THE masque has provided imagery for Marvell in his description of actors and scenes, appearances and panoramas, so now it suggests a way for the poem to end: Marvell compliments his patron by praising his daughter. Indeed he renders homage. But what has been deemed tasteless or irrational flattery is best understood as the kind of tribute paid in a court masque when a nobleman is identified as the symbol of some virtue or other. Maria is the genius of the place and is described in terms appropriate to that identification. An illuminating contrast may be found in Part II, where the "Suttle Nunn" flatters Isabel in an idolatrous fashion, stressing the beauty of her person rather than the symbolic character of her presence and being.

Appleton House took as a model nature itself; with the conclusion of the poem we learn that nature found its prototype in Maria, "Pure, Sweet, Streight, and Fair." Again, Marvell salutes that magical, creative virtue which is the feature of the poem's opening. The genius of the place from whom nature itself learns, by whom nature is given direction and purpose: this is Marvell's subject.

[52] Kitty Scoular considers that he becomes identified with the river too: "The poet becomes a river-god, with a posture reminiscent of Renaissance statuary and illustrations. Yet he is closer to the natural state than to myth. His side is 'a Bank unto the Tide,' and the 'glissant pas' of poetic tradition becomes 'my sliding foot'" (*Natural Magic*, p. 171).

> See how loose Nature, in respect
> To her, it self doth recollect;
> And every thing so whisht and fine,
> Starts forth with to its *Bonne Mine*.[53]

There is a playfulness that does not condescend, an apprecia-
tion of the beauty of wisdom and virtue that exalts and does
not merely flatter. Clearly, Maria is a sweet child; she is, as
well, the one to carry on the line of heroic Fairfax, and she
figures forth the beauty of virtue. The imagery continually
bespeaks the coalescence of all these aspects of her character.

Marvell's favorite image of the heavenly comet follows the
elegant circling imagery of stanza 85, which describes the
halcyon's flight across the river:

> The viscous Air, wheres'ere She fly,
> Follows and sucks her Azure dy;
> The gellying Stream compacts below,
> If it might fix her shadow so;
> The stupid Fishes hang, as plain
> As *Flies* in *Chrystal* overt'ane;
> And Men the silent *Scene* assist,
> Charm'd with the *Saphir-winged Mist*.
>
> *Maria* such, and so doth hush
> The *World*, and through the *Ev'ning* rush.
> No new-born *Comet* such a Train
> Draws through the Skie, nor Star new-slain.
> For streight those giddy Rockets fail,
> Which from the putrid Earth exhale,
> But by her *Flames*, in *Heaven* try'd,
> Nature is wholly *vitrifi'd*.[54]

[53] Nature is the child, Maria the nurse: Is this another proleptic joke
whereby Plato's metaphor of matter as the nurse of spirit is reversed?
See Appendix, Note 5.
[54] Sir Thomas Browne notes in *The Garden of Cyrus* that "provi-
dence hath arched and paved the great house of the world, with colors
of mediocrity, that is blew and green" (I, 176). Kitty Scoular in an

The glasslike clarity of the scene—its "standing serenity"—be-speaks a form beyond change; nature is emblematic of heaven's order. Between day and night, "the silent *Scene*" in its serenity and innocence is, like the "newly washt" world of the meadows, transcendently beautiful. Marvell displays for our enjoyment and wonderment this transfiguration scene which, as it were, holds the stage during the ten stanzas that bring the masque of nature to a close.

The mutuality of the beauties of Nunappleton and the beauties, physical and moral, of Maria is the theme of the next pair of stanzas:

> 'Tis *She* that to these Gardens gave
> That wondrous Beauty which they have;
>
> .   .   .   .
>
> Therefore what first *She* on them spent
> They gratefully again present.

This hymn to the correspondence of nature and nature's heroine is interrupted for five stanzas (stanzas 89 to 93) in which Marvell foresees the escape of this "*Blest Nymph*" from

interesting discussion of these stanzas elucidates the notion of medi-ocrity: "Maria resembles some of the most mysterious creatures in her own landscape. Her affinities are with the halcyon and the comet, be-longing to the middle regions, participating both in earth and in heaven" (*Natural Magic*, p. 174). She explains the odd diction thus: "The adjective 'viscous,' the verb 'to suck' was used technically in descriptions of magnetism: the spirit of iron was thought to be sucked by the loadstone. So the air attracted the colour of the halcyon to itself" (*ibid.*, p. 175). It is possible to speculate that the key image of the comet might have given rise to the image of the "gellying Stream" which, though it of course has its own rationale, might also be said to represent a stage in the process by which nature will be vitrified. C. H. Wilkinson notes of these lines from a sonnet by Lovelace, "by the glorious Light/ Of both those Stars, of which (their Spheres be-reft)/ Only the Gellie's left," that the allusion is "to the belief that shooting stars became jellies on falling to the earth" (p. 265).

190

the "*Ambush*" of love, safe and chaste for marriage. Maria is "a sprig of Misleto" growing on "the Fairfacian Oak":

> Whence, for some universal good,
> The *Priest* shall cut the sacred Bud;
> While her *glad Parents* most rejoice,
> And make their *Destiny* their *Choice*.

By example, precept, and "Discipline severe," Maria has been reared in such a way as to be graced with knowledge and virtue. This acclamation is followed by an odd injunction to those who scorn such education (stanza 92), a miniature sermon on vanity. The entire passage is rather strained; Marvell seems much more at ease when his terms are grand and impersonal again. He urges the "Fields, Springs, Bushes, Flow'rs" to take themselves as models forever: do not decay, do not change, for perfection is here.

> 'Tis not, what once it was, the *World*;
> But a rude heap together hurl'd;
> All negligently overthrown,
> Gulfes, Deserts, Precipices, Stone.
> Your lesser *World* contains the same.
> But in more decent Order tame.

Margoliouth's reading—"The world is no longer the world; since you created a new standard, it becomes by comparison a rude heap"—loses an important emphasis. The lines suggest a ratio: just as "loose Nature, in respect,/ To her [Maria] it self doth recollect," so the world to which men have given some degree of order, should, in respect to Nunappleton, recollect itself. Chaos has indeed been modified; civil and moral and topographical orders have, since the fall, given form to the world. But, in comparison, the order of Appleton House is "more decent"; the grammatical emphasis should not be overlooked. The sequence—chaos, the world's order, the order of Appleton House—is of a gradual ordering which finally creates a form fit to correspond to heaven itself. It is a sequence that Marvell describes in "Music's Empire": "First was the World as one great Cymbal made"; then "*Jubal* first made the wilder Notes agree." A further ordering wedded "Virgin Trebles" to "the manly Base"; from this,

> Then Musick, the Mosaique of the Air,
> Did of all these a solemn noise prepare:
> With which She gain'd the Empire of the Ear,
> Including all between the Earth and Sphear.
>
> Victorious sounds! yet here your Homage do
> Unto a gentler Conqueror than you;
> Who though He flies the Musick of his praise,
> Would with you Heavens Hallelujahs raise.

"Music's Empire" is a grand and measured articulation of the single, majestic theme of order which is beautiful to the sense and filled, too, with the beauty of holiness because it is in the service of heaven. At the close of "Upon Appleton House," Marvell is declaring that although the world, like Jubal, has achieved some order, Appleton House is like music, where more than simply the "wilder Notes" agree; and, as it takes Maria for its guide, Appleton House is "*Heavens Center, Nature's Lap/ And Paradice's only Map.*"

But the poet who has enjoyed himself so much chooses to end not with pious exaltation but with a final comic transformation, a brilliant retreat from sonority. Such a deliberate change of pace and hence of tone is as much Marvell's manner as the choice of grand themes and the playing with metaphor. The final stanza, so often derided, should be acclaimed for its grace and propriety, for it sounds once again the themes of the poem, the correspondence of heaven and earth and the transforming power of the "active Minde," in the poem's major key of affectionate wonder and witty delight. It also confirms the unity of time and place by first reminding us that we are by the river, the scene of the glassy transformation of nature, and then inviting us "in"—into the manor house, that is, where the poem began.[55] The sun, which was high for the harvest and which "*Narcissus* like" enjoyed its reflection in the river, once the mud had settled after the flood, was retiring when Maria came on the scene; and now the shadows which had crept out from the banks onto the river have lengthened into night. The pantomime of the fishermen ("And Men the silent *Scene* assist,/ Charm'd with the *Saphir-winged Mist*") is now the focus:

> But now the *Salmon-Fishers* moist
> Their *Leathern Boats* begin to hoist;
> And, like *Antipodes* in Shoes,
> Have shod their *Heads* in their *Canoos.*
> How *Tortoise like*, but not so slow,
> These rational *Amphibii* go?
> Let's in: for the dark *Hemisphere*
> Does now like one of them appear.

Like the starry cattle and the halcyon-Maria, like the square grown spherical and the river-snake, the great prelate of the grove and the mariners of the hayfields, like all the masquers of this afternoon's pageant, these fishermen are caught in a metamorphosis which is the creation of the transforming eye of imagination. The visionary poet sees in the picture of a salmon-fisher with his boat over his head an image of the earth and its heaven: the correspondence excites amusement and wonder and delight because it is beautiful and true.

LIKE AN enchanter's magic visions, Marvell's changing scenes— from house to garden, from meadow to wood and to river— are pictures of hypnotic beauty. They are also scenes of such virtuous action as can transform the life of nature. What is

---

[55] See Curtius, *European Literature*, on the "concluding topos . . . 'we must stop because night is coming on'" (p. 90). Probably the best known example in English is the close of Sir Thomas Browne's *The Garden of Cyrus.*

lost and what is gained, what is changed and what is created: this is the poem's dialectic. We are persuaded by pictures and by lyrical praise; *argument* is heard only from the devil's advocate. In Part II, one of the "Suttle Nunns" tells the "Virgin Thwates":

> "These Walls restrain the World without
> But hedge our Liberty about."

The Nun's argument is presented in such a way that "Liberty" seems larger than what is given up, and indeed it is a subtle case. Just so, "Created Pleasure" tempts the "Resolved Soul" at first with an appeal based on spiritual aspects of beauty, stressing "the Souls of fruits and flow'rs." The Nun wants Isabel to know that the inmates of her convent gain more than they give up. They enjoy, for instance, in the absence of men, sexual pleasure and chastity at the same time, by the economy of a love which she describes as one more sensuous delight, beautiful and sinless. Throughout her argument, the Nun stresses the spiritual value of the enjoyment of the sensuous: "Here Pleasure Piety doth meet." And of course she claims a mutual influence. But the image of transformation, though superficially comparable to *"Nature vitrifi'd,"* is very different in what it suggests:

> "So through the mortal fruit we boyl
> The Sugars uncorrupting Oyl:
> And that which perisht while we pull,
> Is thus preserved clear and full."

Is there any stronger evidence that Marvell knew the charge and shape a metaphor imparts to what it defines than the fact that he gives to Maria the power to turn nature to glass and to the Nun the power to make jam of souls?

Young Fairfax is deeply offended by all that the nuns stand for and argue from:

"For like themselves they alter all
And vice infects the very Wall."

Although this passionate denunciation is directed against the
same target as the Mower's tirade, the *alteration* of nature and
life, it is not tempered by irony as the Mower's words are,
perhaps because Fairfax is not denouncing fallen man and
his ways but only Roman Catholics and theirs.[56]

The iron gates are closed to the world, but the "innocent,"
"holy" leisure which the Nun tries to justify is really given
over to idolatry and "art" which throughout Part II, even more
strongly than in Part I, denotes everything that is hypocritical,
unworthy, unnatural, and destructive of virtue. As Young
Fairfax asks, " 'Is this that *Sanctity* so great/ An Art by which
you finly'r cheat?' " Marvell lets the Nun damn the uses to
which this leisure is put in everything she says to Isabel, from
her description of their reading of the "holy Legend" (instead
of "holy Writ") and their praying by beads down to her
summarizing description of activities in the nunnery, a couplet
with overtones as sardonic as anything to be found in his
satires:

"For such indeed are all our Arts;
Still handling Natures finest Parts."

But it is not only the points of emphasis and the tone that
give away the Nun's argument; Marvell's narrative provides a
critique. For young Fairfax knows that the nuns are scheming

---

[56] Though it will be twenty-five years until the Act of Supremacy
and the subsequent ruination of these cloisters, a Protestant horror in-
forms such lines as: "I know what Fruit their Gardens yield/ 'When
they it think by Night conceal'd.' " Fairfax's sinister charge could stand
as epigraph to those later testimonials (such as *The Awful Disclosures
of Maria Monk*) attacking the hypocrisy and secret sins of Papists.
The Protestant horror may well have been Marvell's own: about
thirteen years earlier, shortly after he had taken his degree, he had
himself been "seduced" by Jesuits. See Margoliouth, "Andrew Marvell:
Some Biographical Points."

for control of Isabel's property; he also has the legal right to hold Isabel to the marriage contract. And so he leaps over the wall and, disregarding wooden saints, holy water, beads, incantations, and *"Relicks false,"* all meant to thwart his virtuous assault, rescues "truly bright and holy *Thwaites*/ That weeping at the *Altar* waites." (She is about to become the bride of Christ.) The happy ending of this melodrama includes the demise of the wicked building:

> Thenceforth (as when th' Inchantment ends
> The Castle vanishes or rends)
> The wasting Cloister with the rest
> Was in one instant dispossest.

This lively story does not set "action" over against "retirement" any more than "The Coronet" opposes art to religion. The nuns' "holy leisure" is fraudulent, as the Shepherd's aims are prideful. The nuns' piety is false, their thoughts of heaven materialistic, their worship idolatrous, their devotions impure. Because it is vain, their "sanctity" is no virtue, but a sin. The beauty of life in the nunnery is not the beauty of holiness and innocence. The life of nature cannot be transformed in such circumstances.[57]

Healthy, virtuous change, then, is not the "altering" of a vainglorious false piety, any more than it is that neat defacement of artfulness which Marvell derides in Part I. Nor is it that "use" of nature which the poem's opening stanza describes as wanton destruction. Nor, of course, is superficial change to be mistaken for it: "your own Face shall at you grin/ Thorough the Black-bag of your Skin" (lines 733-34).[58] Virtuous transformation is both necessary and natural. As it is the fate of stone to become masonry, so the Body in the "Dialogue

---

[57] Between the nuns' retirement and Lord Fairfax's there is nothing in common; it seems to me a preposterous misreading to align them.

[58] Margoliouth's note explains: "It will be still your own face mocking the efforts which have in fact spoiled your complexion. *Black-bag*: mask."

Between the Soul and Body" bravely admits that its fate is to be trained and mastered by the Soul: "So Architects do square and hew,/ Green Trees that in the Forest grew." The cost of order is a price the man of virtue is willing to pay, as the godly hero is willing to assume the burden of lawful duty, if he is free thereby to do the will of heaven. Marvell held that man's greatest virtue is to make his destiny his choice. This is a political theme which is served by his moral imagination, in "Upon Appleton House" as well as in the Cromwell poems. Thus, as the "active Minde" recreates the life of nature, the great themes of correspondence and transformation are resonant with the idea of freedom. In "Upon Appleton House" Marvell has celebrated a landscape bearing the shape and form of a virtuous man's will, a civilized landscape in which the felt correspondence of man's life and heaven's order has commanded his purpose: in his masque of nature, Marvell declares the equivalence of peace and the countryside, of the moral order and the green world.

APPENDIX

NOTE 1

"Prolepsis" and the Allegorical Imagination

ROSEMOND TUVE's discussions of the interpenetration of image and statement and the balance struck between sensuousness and significance support the judgment that Marvell draws his metaphors through the stages of a witty development radically characteristic of all figures which serve to body forth the complexly conceptual (*Elizabethan and Metaphysical Imagery* [Chicago, 1947], pp. 95, 102, 105, 163, 222). Frank Kermode remarks that Marvell's characteristic metaphor is simply "a typical 'metaphysical' use of the figure called by Puttenham the Disabler" ("The Argument of Marvell's 'Garden,'" *Essays in Criticism*, II [1952], 233). But Puttenham's "Disabler" is *meiosis* (a form of *litotes*), which belittles by diminishing; that is, it allows us to judge an act or circumstance, person, or phenomenon only as less than it is, not as other than it is. Furthermore, the term in no way suggests the shifting roles of tenor and vehicle. Although the character of Marvell's metaphors is rather more complex than the term "proleptic" ("the saving shore" is a prolepsis) at first suggests, Professor Hartman explains that he means to indicate by it something more than the merely anticipative character of the figure, noting that he uses the term "heuristically to indicate figures that would include 'inversion' and 'reversal.' The wittiest mottos of the emblem books were generally conversions in this sense . . ." ("Marvell, St. Paul, and the Body of Hope," p. 188n.). I will follow Hartman in his use of the term.

By helping to define the anticipative and generative character of Marvell's metaphors, the notion of prolepsis may serve to emphasize that the allegorical imagination proceeds from general to particular quite as easily as it develops idea from picture. It is only dull habit (or an inadequate aesthetics) which leads us to assume that the particular "comes first" and it is a limitation of taste and judgment to *prefer* that the idea arise from the object which the poet "sees" as a symbol. So it may, but, as often, he "sees" in the language or in the idea, an image. This two-way street which meaning travels in allegorical formulation is an indication of mythic heritage, for in mythic ideation symbol and conception are mutually dependent; the study of the kinds of equivalences which develop from that profound identity is necessary to stylistic analysis. The fondness for proleptic metaphor is in part a matter of temperament, but temperament has more than a psychological dimension. As long as the discovery—or recovery—of Marvell's themes constitutes a critical problem; as long as metaphors which he took seriously are read as hyperboles, unrecognized as constituting theme; as long as the tone of descriptions is misconstrued, so long will it be necessary to consider style as something more than the expression of personality. The *circulus methodicus* by which stylistic analysis proceeds—the expectation of matter being determined by an appreciation of manner, the manner judged in the light of what we take to be the matter—requires an attention not only to personality and the history of taste but to the philosophical implications of a characteristic use of language.

The proleptical metaphor is favored by poets responsive equally to the reality of abstractions and to the exemplary nature of experience. A mind actively moving from general to particular and back, deducing as easily as it induces, harboring no suspicions of the theoretical, seeks forms which can express this dynamic sense of the sources of truth. In the seventeenth century, the allegorical imagination and the scientific imagination both display this dialectical skill, the capacity to proceed as easily from the general to the particular as to "ascend," to use Bacon's terminology, from experience to general laws.

It is one of the fine ironies of intellectual history that the critical impetus to the growth of scientific thought came not from the man who considered himself its chief exponent but from men who conceived of themselves as guardians of the spirit. For it was not Bacon but the Cambridge Platonists whose doctrines of knowledge were of "decisive influence" on Descartes and Newton (Ernst Cassirer, *The Platonic Renaissance in England* [Austin, 1953], trans. James P. Pettegrove, p. 148).

In his analysis of the epistemology of the Cambridge Platonists, Cassirer lays great stress on the generative power of the concept as being central to their approach. His discussion is illuminating in regard to the proleptical character of knowledge in Cudworth's theory: "The chief weakness of the empirical doctrine of knowledge, according to Cudworth, is that it starts from an analysis of sense-perception instead of from an analysis of judgment. . . . If judgment is to be possible, and therewith the beginning and seed of all knowledge, then a sensible object must always be connected in this way with a conceptual predicate, the particular with the general, and the perceived or imagined with the purely abstract. The image of 'phantasm' is meaningless without the idea or 'noema' by which it is determined and given significance. . . . It is not the general that always follows the particular, but the particular that follows and is implied in the general. Genuine knowledge does not proceed by imitation, but by anticipation; it is not a copy of the given, but 'prolepticall.' The main object of Cudworth's doctrine of knowledge is to reinstate this significance and force of 'prolepsis,' and safeguard against the attacks which Bacon had levelled against 'anticipationes mentis'" (pp. 56ff.).

The seventeenth century saw the development of new conceptions of mind, of mental operations, of the limits of knowing. These new conceptions are, I am suggesting, discernible not only in the scientific and philosophic discourses of the time but in such lively explorations of the relationship of ideas and language as those to which the creations of Marvell's allegorical imagination attest.

NOTE 2

The Providential Hero

J OSEPH M AZZEO contends that "the universe of the 'Horatian Ode' lacks the providential dimension in any religious sense," urging that we consider "Heaven . . . fate . . . fortune . . . mutually convertible terms" ("Cromwell as Machiavellian Prince in Marvell's 'An Horatian Ode,' " *JHI*, 21 [1960], 1-17). But we need not read "Heaven" in a "pious sense" in order to perceive "the providential dimension" of Marvell's poem. Mazzeo holds that only "in the last poem on Cromwell" will we find "the Machiavellian moment subsumed into a providential conception of his role as Davidic King, as instrument of the God of the Bible and history" (p. 12). But the Cromwell of the "Horatian Ode" "does both act and know" and, as Ruth Nevo comments, "it is . . . the hero's knowledge of the meaning and direction of emergent history which turns a random, classical *virtu* into a messianic election" (*The Dial of Virtue* [Princeton, 1963], p. 102). Professor Nevo studies the poem in the context of "contemporary panegyric and the contemporary preoccupation with the problem of history and the hero" (p. 98). Her judgment of Marvell's contribution to the genre is based on this contention: "There is, in Marvell . . . the beginning of a dialectical determinism which, through a new analysis of the nature and function of the republican leader, of authority vested not alone in personal power but in a collective public body, can reconcile the hero's significance and value with his historical instrumentality" (p. 77).

There has been considerable discussion of Marvell's attitudes toward Cromwell since the Brooks-Bush controversy over alleged ambiguities in the "Horatian Ode" fifteen years ago. Referring to what Brooks called the "tension" of the poem, Mazzeo remarks that it "has far less to do with a conflict of

feeling in the poet . . . than with the poet's deliberately main-
tained attitude to historical and political events which tran-
scends questions of personal commitment and reveals his full
awareness of the ethically irrational and problematic character
of human experience." John M. Wallace has concentrated not
on Marvell's supposed Machiavellian ethics but on the chosen
means of justifying certain judgments ("Marvell's 'Horatian
Ode,'" *PMLA*, 77 [1962], 33-45). His rhetorical analysis
answers many questions falsely raised by those committed to
one or another view of Marvell's politics. John S. Coolidge
disagrees that there has been a "setting aside of personal ideas
of right and wrong in order to celebrate an accomplished fact"
("Marvell and Horace," *MP*, LXIII [1965], 111-20). This in-
terpretation of Wallace's argument seems faulty, since the
conception of the *dux bellorum*, which Wallace considers one
of the guiding principles of Marvell's portrayal of Cromwell,
precisely justifies the appeal to necessity by translating ideas of
righteousness to the public sphere, not quite the same thing as
"setting aside." Coolidge's own study of the poem is a fascinat-
ing demonstration of how Marvell has rehabilitated classical
idiom in the climate of seventeenth-century politics.

The figure of the hero who "does both act and know" is an
archetype of the moral and political imagination. The contro-
versy over the alleged Machiavellianism in the "Horatian Ode"
is, it seems to me, irrelevant insofar as Marvell's fundamental
interest in the dialectic of power is neglected. Defining such
"Machiavellian" concepts as expediency and self-interest is
only a point of departure in the perennial search for an un-
derstanding of power. The conception of the hero held in any
age is but an expression of the current understanding of the
problem of freedom and necessity.

Christopher Hill's comment on the "Horatian Ode" properly
emphasizes the nature of those profound principles which
alone could have given Marvell the support his dangerous life
required: "Marvell is clearly aware of a fusion of opposites:

the life of the community demands the death of the individual, rest is obtained only through and by means of effort, eternal vigilance is the price of liberty, freedom is the knowledge of necessity" (*Puritanism and Revolution*, p. 362). These themes are brilliantly illuminated in Professor Wallace's recent study of Marvell's prose and the political poems, *Destiny His Choice: The Loyalism of Andrew Marvell* (Cambridge, Eng., 1968).

NOTE 3

"Still keep thy Sword erect"

THE UPRIGHT sword of the closing lines of the "Horatian Ode" has excited speculation. Interpretation of the image depends on how the tone is understood and that, in turn, is a matter of construing attitude. Margoliouth surmised that the lines describe a sword held by the blade: "the cross-hilt of the sword would avert the *Spirits of the shady Night*." That Marvell would choose to associate with the soldier whose armor was prayer such an outrageously popish device would seem to argue a degree of malice beyond that which most of those readers alleging ambivalence on Marvell's part could defend. For many critics, Marvell's attitude toward Cromwell is one of suspicion at best. Thus E. E. Duncan-Jones sees in the closing lines a version of what Clarendon cites as a "common old adage" in his comment on Cromwell's career: "He who hath drawn the sword against his prince, ought to throw away the scabbard, never to think of sheathing it again" ("Notes on Marvell," *N&Q*, CXCVIII [1953], 431). Clarendon interprets it thus: "They who enter upon unwarrantable enterprises, must pursue many unwarrantable ways to preserve themselves from the penalty of the first guilt" (*Selections from Clarendon*, ed. G. Huehns [London, 1955], p. 305). If in accepting the adage as the motto for Marvell's emblem we are accepting Clarendon's interpretation, that is more than the poem warrants. Wallace offers a third explanation: "not only is it the sword of war which Cromwell holds of necessity, but the sword of justice; if Cromwell were to sheath it, the dark spirits of anarchy would once again unleash their fury on England" ("Marvell's 'Horatian Ode,'" *PMLA*, 77 [1962], 44). It is questionable that Marvell would claim that anarchy could be forestalled by the power of justice, but the interpretation of "the Spirits of the shady Night" as "forces of anarchy" is, I think, more satisfactory than that suggested by Mrs. Duncan-Jones, namely, that they are "the spirits of the dead . . . Cromwell must keep his sword erect to govern the living: it will also serve a purpose in warding off the dead" ("The Erect Sword in Marvell's 'Horatian Ode,'" *Études anglaises*, 15 [1962], 173-74). Mrs. Duncan-Jones seems to admit at the back door the notion of a superstitious use of the sword-hilt, which earlier she had been arguing against. I think it is possible that "the Spirits of the shady Night" could be a jab at sanctimonious republicans, the "Emulous" against whom Marvell has already shown Cromwell acting (ll. 14-16). Throughout the Cromwell poems, the figure of the providential hero is set over against not only the ruined work of time but also against those bloody-handed, divisive men who have been part of the venture. The reference to Cromwell's artful use of "crossest Spirits" in the "First Anniversary" lends weight to this suggested reading. Cromwell, associated throughout with air, flame, heaven, burning, lightning (as in the other poems he is the equivalent of the sun) is by definition opposed to "shady Night" and all its progeny of evil.

Those who find ambivalence (conscious or not) or veiled cynicism in the "Horatian Ode" consider that this poem stands in marked contrast to others that follow. Mrs. Duncan-Jones argues, for instance, that Marvell's view of Cromwell in "A Poem upon the Death of O. C." as the one who "first put Armes into *Religions* hand" marks a departure from the opinion he held at the time he wrote the "Horatian Ode" because in that poem he has Cromwell destroying "Temples." But "Temples," like "Pallaces," with which it is paired, surely carries the suggestion of the pagan, of the corrupt power of priests (bishops!) and tyrants. Jesus himself scourged the Temples.

Professor Legouis finds no contradictions within the "Horatian Ode" itself, declaring that the real puzzle is the composition in the same year of "Tom May's Death," a poem in which Marvell is contemptuous of the man who has turned "Chronicler to Spartacus" (*Andrew Marvell*, pp. 91-94). There is no puzzle for Margoliouth, who in his notes on "Tom May's Death" says flatly of the supposed incompatibility of views expressed in the two poems: "Marvell, although he was coming to admire and fix his hopes on Cromwell, was still a royalist in the first place. . . ." Professor Coolidge confronts squarely "the apparent contradiction . . . [which] should make us look all the more carefully for an underlying consistency between them." It is a question of what attitude is appropriate in peace: "The Horatian art of time-serving, to give it a name acknowledging its moral dangers, calls for a kind of mental poise among the changing possibilities and impossibilities of life" ("Marvell and Horace," pp. 116, 118).

In a sense, this problem is only a straw man, the creation of literary critics who, though they know that political passions are not susceptible of rational analysis, try nevertheless to make syllogisms out of supposed political positions. Thus R. H. Syfret argues: "Would Marvell have so bitterly denounced May for deserting the *ancient rights* if this is just what he had been doing?" ("Marvell's 'Horatian Ode,'" *RES*, 12 [1961], 167). The answer is, I think, "very likely," particularly if he considered that he had himself made a careful case which might be confused with a merely opportunistic stand because of superficial similarities. Marvell is as scornful of insolent supporters of a cause he himself championed as he was, later, of those who had never faced the choice. The fear of association with those whose views are superficially his own drives him to sharper and sharper distinctions. Marvell is never more fierce than when a hit is close, than when a contention seems reasonable and high-principled. He will meet it head on and then show how inadequate the argument is, giving ground at first in order later to regain it and more. The following stands as a memorable example: "if to murther the King be, as it certainly is, a fact so horrid, how much more hainous is it to assassinate the Kingdom? and as none will deny, that to alter our Monarchy into a Commonwealth were treason, so by the same fundamental rule the crime is no less to make that Monarchy absolute" (IV, 261).

The " 'natural and politique capacity' "

THE differentiation of the " 'natural and politique capacity' "
is for Marvell at once a political necessity and a religious tenet.
The conclusion to be drawn from the doctrine that "men are
all infirm and indisposed in their spiritual condition" (IV,
81-82) is that government must assure liberty of conscience,
the essential link with God. Civil order is to stay against chaos
in society, but the condition of man's soul is not a social con-
cern. Since "all laws . . . are but probationers of Time" (III,
401), Divine Providence, not man's order, is the court of ap-
peal for the soul. Nor is God's grace assured by the institutions
of religion: "The soul is too precious to be let out at interest
upon any humane security, that does or may fail; but it is only
safe when under God's custody, in its own cabinet" (IV, 127).
It is only Divine Providence which, as a modern theologian
crisply puts it, "overcomes and heals man's moral and natural
necessities."

Although the government has a duty to the soul, that obli-
gation does not imply divine sanction: "As it is unlawful to
palliate with God, and enervate His laws into an humane only
and politick consideration; so it is, on the other side, unlawful
and unnecessary to give to common and civil constitutions a
divine sanction; and it is so far from an owning of God's
jurisdiction, that it is an invasion upon it" (III, 403).

Neither earthly governments nor heavenly decrees relieve
man of the burden of his freedom. In the "Defense of John
Howe," Marvell establishes the relationship of the "naturally
impossible"—that which is necessary—and the freedom of the
will: "From Mr. Howe's having said, 'Nothing is more ap-
parently a simple and most strictly natural impossibility, than
to do an action whereto the agent is determined by an infinite

power.' It [the discourse Marvell is attacking] hath the ridiculous grossness to charge Mr. Howe with there affirming that predetermination forces the will; as if nothing could make a thing naturally impossible to a man but force. He cannot make a new sun; but what force hinders him?" (IV, 209-10).

Marvell is no Calvinist. He rejects the doctrine of predestination by which men have sought to rationalize the operation of God's foreknowledge, arguing that it is better to tolerate mystery than to seek such dangerous rationalizations as "reducing grace, and making it a meer FABLE, of which [we are given] the MORAL" (III, 225). He quotes John Howe approvingly: "'It cannot . . . be so affrightful a thing to suppose God's foreknowledge of the most contingent future actions, well to consist with our ignorance how He foreknows them, as that we should think it necessary to overturn and mingle heaven and earth rather than admit it'" (IV, 203-4). There are limits to man's will, but these limits are the natural impossibilities ordained by the pre-eternal necessity.

NOTE 5

Shipwreck, Storm, and the Birth Into Time

THE Unfortunate Lover's birth/shipwreck is accompanied by just such upheavals as are threatened by the union of "Two perfect Loves" in "The Definition of Love." And in a passage I have cited earlier (p. 71), Marvell sets the natural life of man over against the "eternal Spring," "standing serenity," and "perpetual sunshine" of paradise, describing it in the imagery of natural cataclysm: man is subjected to "the dismal influence of comets from above, to thunder, and its lightning, and tempests from the middle region, and from the lower surface to the raging of the seas and the tottering of earthquakes." The contrast echoes that drawn between the garden where the infant Love plays and the raging sea where the Unfortunate Lover is shipwrecked. The association of storm and shipwreck is an obvious one and the association of both with the imagery of birth is logical, given the primal metaphor of the voyage of life.

In interpreting Marvell's particular concatenation of storm, shipwreck, violent birth, and meteors it is useful to have in mind the close of Plato's *Republic*, where, in the tale of Er whose soul had enjoyed a miraculous sojourn in the other world, it is told how souls are born into temporal life. Having chosen their destinies and having crossed the plain of Forgetfulness, they encamp by the river of Unmindfulness: "Now after they had gone to rest, about the middle of the night there was a thunderstorm and earthquake, and then in an instant they were driven upwards in all manner of ways to their birth, like stars shooting" (*Republic* X, 621).

In his figure of the Unfortunate Lover, Marvell has combined the figures of the shipwreck and the infant, emblematic derivatives of the mythic metaphors of journey and birth, commonplaces of classical literature. Professor Coolidge has suggested to me that Marvell would certainly have been familiar, for instance, with Lucretius' comparison of the new-born infant and the shipwrecked sailor tossed up on shore (*De rerum natura* V, 222-27). Though he depends generally on metaphors of flight and extension, Plotinus also uses the figure of the Soul "embarking in the skiff of the universe," Necessity assigning its "seat for the voyage" (*Enneads* III. 4, 6. Plotinus is quoted from the translation by Stephen MacKenna as revised by B. S. Page). In discussing the effects of the stars on human destiny, he remarks that "their symbolic power extends to the entire realm of sense, their efficacy only to what they patently do. For our part nature keeps us upon the work of the Soul as long as we are not wrecked in the multiplicity of the Universe" (*Enneads* II. 3, 8). "Would it," he asks, "be sound to define Time as the Life of the Soul in movement from one stage of act or experience to another?" He answers, "Yes" (*Enneads* III. 7, 11).

The sea-torn and shipwrecked soul is a familiar figure, from Plato down to Blake and Whitman. Marvell's triumph in this poem, I think, is to have constructed a new mosaic, to tell the myth as if it were his own legend. It is his narrative skill that makes of "The Unfortunate Lover" a poem of greater interest than, say, Quarles's emblematic sketch (*Emblems, Divine and Moral*, III, viii) depicting the soul's journey. He moves rather automatically from eyes to tears to drops to seas in a storm of sighs

> . . . wherein
> This lab'ring vessel, laden with her sin,
> Might suffer sudden shipwreck and be split
> Upon that rock, where my drench'd soul may sit
> O'rewhelmed with plenteous passion.

Just so, Marvell's brilliant use of emblem contrasts with the treatment Matthew Arnold gives images which are strikingly close to Marvell's:

> A wanderer is man from his birth.
> He was born in a ship
> On the breast of the river of Time;
> Brimming with wonder and joy
> He spreads out his arms to the light,
> Rivets his gaze on the banks of the stream.

(Quoted from Matthew Arnold, "The Future" in Herbert J. C. Grierson, *Cross Currents in Seventeenth Century English Literature* [London, 1929], p. 47.)

The figure of the "*Cesarian Section*" is, of course, another unique contribution to the story of the shipwrecked soul. It is, as I have remarked, a linguistic trick, there being no dramatic role for a mother to play in Marvell's poem. It is worth noting, however, that the figure of the mother is a very common metaphor for the material aspect of life. Plotinus comments that Plato's "appellation 'Recipient and Nurse' [for matter] is the better description," since matter "has no begetting power" (*Enneads* III. 6, 19). His discussion of "the impassivity of the unembodied" provides an interesting gloss for Marvell's curious description of the inert Lover "floting" in the "Shipwrack" before he is "brought forth."

NOTE 6

Extension

IN HIS witty geometry of the soul, Marvell has recreated solid and linear forms as emblems, delighting in the proleptic puzzles which develop. It is their allegorical character which is so often ignored when these images are scrutinized. Thus L. N. Wall ("Some Notes on Marvell's Sources," p. 172), considering the image of the "precipice" which the "Body" becomes by virtue of the "stretching" of the soul without attending to the logic of Marvell's metaphor, compares it to the straightforward simile in Lovelace's "Aramantha" ("Fond man thus to a precipice/ Aspires, till at the top his eyes/ Have lost the safety of the plain").

Emblems deriving from the concept of extension serve Marvell, in prose as well as poetry, when he undertakes to define the relationship of the two orders of reality. He typically develops the spatial and implicitly dynamic character of geometrical images, as in the description of the dewdrop: "Moving but on a point below/ It all about does upward bend." As the perfect sphere answers to purity of soul, so the kinetic energy of "Moving" and "bend" expresses temporality. The same kind of imagination is at work when Traherne writes in the "Fourth Century," §66 that the soul of love is like the sun whose beams extend equal to all: "in Length it is infinit as well as in Bredth, being equally vigorous at the utmost Bound to which it can extend as here, and as wholly their as here and wholly evry where" (*Centuries, Poems, Thanksgivings*, ed. H. M. Margoliouth [Oxford, 1958], p. 203).

The metaphysical relationship defined by the allegorical metaphor of the place "where my extended soul is fixt" is illuminated by the imagery of extension in the following passage in which Marvell berates Mr. Necessity Bayes: "You would do well and wisely not to stretch, gold-beat and wier-draw humane laws thus to heaven; lest they grow thereby too slender to hold, and lose in strength what they gain by extension and rarefaction" (III, 408). This passage is followed by the observation that "Reverend Mr. Hooker ought to have serv'd you for a better example, who, though he was willing to drive this nail [binding church and state] as far as it would go, yet, having spent his whole eighth book in sifting the obligation of humane laws, concludes his whole Ecclesiastical Politie with these words. . . ." And Marvell goes on to demonstrate how far short Hooker comes of promulgating the doctrine Parker is setting forth. That Marvell found himself in sympathy with Hooker on the matter of the relationship of church and state is certainly of interest in any assessment of this Puritan's political views. The reference to the eighth book of *The Laws of Ecclesiastical Polity* is especially interesting in light of Hardin Craig's comment: "Hooker's explanation of human law as the outcome of the social contract was not acceptable to the dominant political theorists of the reigns of James I or Charles I, a circumstance which possibly caused the later books of *The Laws of Ecclesiastical Polity* to be withheld from publication during their author's life and, in turn, brought about their publication at the time of the Great Rebellion and the Commonwealth" (*The Enchanted Glass* [New York, 1936], p. 28).

NOTE 7

Fate's "Iron wedges"

IT IS the binding power of the wedge that Isabel G. Mac-Caffrey has discussed in her very suggestive analysis of the passage ("Some Notes on Marvell's Poetry, Suggested by a Reading of His Prose," *MP*, LXI [1964], 265). Citing Marvell's definition of necessity, she suggests that a wedge does indeed serve the same function as a "nail, i.e. an axle." Professor MacCaffrey finds support for "this merging of prose 'nail' and poetic 'wedge'" in Chaucer's Astrolabe "where 'a litel wegge' is said to hold together all parts of the instrument." But Chaucer's "wegge" seems to affect directly only the "pyn" as a kind of adjustment screw—rather a minor role for necessity. Nevertheless, the action of holding together while separating is shared by wedge and nail.

This point is given further support by Kitty Datta, who suggests that Marvell followed a commentary on an ode by Horace addressed to the goddess Fortuna ("Marvell's Prose and Poetry: More Notes," *MP*, LXIII [1966], 319-21). (Bradbrook and Lloyd Thomas first noted [*Andrew Marvell*, p. 45n.] that wedges are the attributes of Necessity as she appears in this poem, *Carmina* I, 35.) The commentary stresses the binding power of wedges "by the insertion of which, things are not only separated but also joined together" (Mrs. Datta's translation). Citing a further reference to Necessity in *Carmina* III, 24, she offers this interpretation of Marvell's image of Fate's wedges: "Fate in her binding together of the universe both joins the lovers by the invisible axletree, the great iron nail running from pole to pole, and at the same time sets them irrevocably apart." Marvell does not endorse this identification of axle and axletree, but Mrs. Datta's emphasis on the paradox of separation which assures unity further illuminates the poem's design, for that paradox is sounded later in the "Conjunction" which is an "Opposition," as it is sounded, of course, in the opening stanzas.

John S. Coolidge suggests that Necessity's "ambiguous emblems" are associated with both the art of building and torture, and that Marvell's prose shows evidence that he "understands those emblems . . . to be instruments of cruelty" ("Marvell and Horace" (*MP*, LXIII [1965], III, 20). Such essential ambiguity is found in figures at whose center is a mythic metaphor which, in the service of allegory, can become the fulcrum of paradox. Thus in the passage cited by Coolidge (III, 366) Marvell's emphasis, I think, is not on torture or punishment, but on the action of separation by which unity is effected, an action set over against the use of wedges only to join (*clavi figenda causa*). It is not violence that Marvell stresses in his attributes of Necessity, but only the paradoxical character of the necessary conditions of life. Violence is associated, rather, with that union which is the ruination of polarity: the identification of opposites.

NOTE 8

Conjunction and Opposition

"There is, strictly speaking, no proper opposition but be-
tween the two polar forces of one and the same power."
—S. T. Coleridge

THE CIRCULAR logic which underlies the imagery of the last
stanza depends, of course, on the syntax. And any syntactical
construction has a metaphysical rationale, ultimately, though
to explain how is to risk becoming ensnared in what Marvell
scorned as a "university quibble." As I read the concluding
stanza, each of the definitions of love conditions and supports
the other. Rather than there being three defining characteristics
of love, with the "cause" of love more or less tacked on, it
seems to me reasonable that there are, indeed, four character-
istics being defined and that they are all mutually defining:
love binds (but) it is debarred; love is a conjunction (and) it
is an opposition. Marvell's definition of this kind of love, im-
plying as it does the metaphysical interdependence of conjunc-
tion and opposition, would seem to require that the logical
relationship each of these predicate nouns bears to "love" be
the same. I contend that the verb "is"—which "Conjunction"
and "Opposition" share—has the force of "results in" as well
as "results from." Both nouns are subject to the logical require-
ments of "therefore"; i.e., each should be expected to express re-
sult. Here the result is a cause. As despair is the result of a condi-
tion which is the cause of love, so conjunction is determined by
fate or necessity and is itself an expression of that opposition
created by Fate. Opposition belongs to the stars—it is a
"cause"—but it is, as well, a result. "Of" (which has the
most complex history of all the English prepositions) can ex-
press the relation of the objective genitive after a noun of
action, which *opposition* certainly is. The *OED* lists as the

seventeenth-century example of this usage a phrase from Marvell's prose, "Obstruction of the publick justice," which seems to me precisely analogous to one of the meanings intended by the phrase "Opposition of the Stars."

The astrological imagery is as symmetrical and logically rigorous as the syntax and it does more than establish the rather vague antithesis of a heavenly opposition and an earthly conjunction. Like the imagery of love, it defines a dialectical relationship. "Conjunction" defines the meeting or passing of two celestial bodies in the same degree of the zodiac; thus the sublunary soul can enjoy such proximity to its heavenly home only by the power of mind. "Opposition" defines a position in which one celestial body is as far from another as it can be; thus "Opposition" is yet another figuring forth of the separation of earth and heaven.

The "Iron gates of Life"

No ONE passage in Marvell's poetry has been subjected to so many rackings as the conclusion of "To His Coy Mistress." (It is the "here/ Buckle! AND the fire that breaks from thee then" of seventeenth-century poetry.) The critical problem is the definition of the relationship between the images. Surely they do not follow one another in a smooth narrative sequence, but neither are they logically or rhetorically discontinuous. For one thing, the boldly kinetic character of the images is unifying: "roll," "tear," making the sun "run"—each metaphor describes an action that supports and answers the others. And the commands are accumulative, intensifying the urgency: *now let us sport us as we may; now* let us *at once our time devour;* now *let* us *roll up into one ball our strength and sweetness;* now *let* us *tear our pleasures with rough strife thorough the iron gates of life;* now let us *run* a race with the sun. No single phrase can be read out of the context which the entire passage creates. Thus, when "Ball" is torn from the dramatic fragment to which it logically and grammatically belongs (a phrase which, in turn, belongs rhetorically and logically with what comes before and after), when it is denied its passionate abstraction and assigned a significance on the basis of a particularity which is not there, the way is open for drawing up a catalogue of interpretations limited only by the ingenuity of readers. Margoliouth's pomander (an orange stuck full of cloves) heads such a list and there are many other items, including the ashes gathered by the phoenix "into a compact mass" and a cannonball. A case could be made, I suppose, for its being a *pellet* ("a little ball, esp. of food which a bird of prey devours").

The same fate has befallen that superb allegorical metaphor, "the Iron gates of Life." Margoliouth, with an uncharacteristic burst of enthusiasm for the concept of ambiguity, perpetuates an absurd reading in a note to the poem in his second edition: "In the third image 'the gates of Life' where the sexual strife is waged, suggest the well-known reach of the Danube." Such a concatenation of physiology and geography is appropriate to Anna Livia Plurabelle, but there is no rhetorical support for such a reading of Marvell's figure. Nor is the stanza from Lovelace's "Lucasta taking the waters at Tunbridge," cited by Dennis Davison ("Notes on Marvell's 'To His Coy Mistress,'" N&Q, 5 [1958], 521) analogous. Even Tennyson, who expressed the wish that Marvell had written "grates," is more faithful to the ambience of the image than industrious Freudians have been. The commonplace metaphor of the body/prison makes "gates" or "grates" standard figures for the portals of the body from which the soul can or can not issue, as in these execrable lines from "To His Mistress for her True Picture," by Lord Herbert of Cherbury: "Hear, from my bodies prison, this my Call,/ Who from my mouth-grate, and eye-window bawl." (See, also, "The Aspiration," quoted on pp. 108-9). The emphasis is generally on imprisonment, not simply on entrance/exit. "The Iron gates of Life" has the same kind of complexity as the "prison of the body" because it is, likewise, an allegorical metaphor. When we consider that the last defile of the Danube in its southeasterly course is so called and that Marvell on his trek to Russia (or in his reading of ancient history) may well have learned the name of this strait, the figure of "the Iron gates of Life" may grow more and more attractive in its particularity, if this is what we prize. But the particularity which is actually there is the particularity of mythic metaphor, not of historical or geographical or physiological allusion. We could as easily assume, for instance, that since "iron gates" is a technical garden term the metaphor has reference to an ornamental fence separating the garden of life from the vast park of eternity. That reading is as justifiable (and as irrelevant) as the one a recent editor offers us when he remarks that the line "certainly refers to the act of defloration."

In the concluding couplet, Marvell plays off world and time against one another as brilliantly as in the opening hyperboles. I have cited the passage in his prose where Marvell defines a "natural impossibility" by giving the example of stopping the sun; here, that impossibility, that recognition of the pre-eternal necessity, is transcended by the resolve to create world enough and time, not by denying time, but by living so that time does not matter. Walter A. Sedlow, Jr. suggests the pertinence of the bridegroom/sun metaphor of Psalm 19:4-6 in a reading which explains the logic of the imagery successfully: "With a sufficient intensity of loving in a brief time, the equivalent in experience can be achieved of slow-paced loving over a vast eternity. . . . If the Sun (who creates time . . .), a powerful runner, would have to run hard, then he must create a vast amount of time and a vast amount of world indeed. . . . If he won't be made to stand still (i.e. to create an infinity of time), this powerful runner will be 'made to run' . . . (i.e. to create a vast, if finite time and world), and that is all that was asked for any way: 'world enough and time,' not infinity and eternity" ("Marvell's 'To His Coy Mistress,'" *MLN*, LXXI [1956], 7).

Marvell and Cusanus

MARVELL's contemplations have over and over again been described as "mystical," despite the fact that neither mystical motive nor ecstatic tone can be successfully identified and despite the fact that such "mysticism" would run counter to every other aspect of his mind and art. Mysticism, like its sister literalism, dispenses with mediation, but every aspect of Marvell's style suggests not a mystic transcendence but a profound contemplation of time and place, the resolute acceptance of the conditions of being. If we should consider Marvell's contemplations without any preconceptions regarding their "mysticism," we might discover a pertinent analogue not in the visions of Richard of St. Victor but in the *visio intellectualis* of Nicholas of Cusa, "the famous and learned C. Cusanus" whose *Idiota* was translated into English and published in London in 1650.* (His *De Docta Ignorantia* is mentioned by Marvell [III, 314], as Bonaventura, I think, is not.) Both metaphysically and epistemologically Marvell's "active Minde" bears a resemblance to Cusanus' *visio intellectualis*. It is enlightening to consider the "active Minde"—that ocean, that annihilating force, that free and creative will whose agent is the Resolved Soul—in the context of Cusanus' thought. I think it can be fairly said that the poet and the theologian shared several conceptions of the mind and soul. Isabel G. MacCaffrey has made the point in the course of her comment on Marvell's reference to "Cardinal Cusanus his treatise *De Docta Ignorantia*." As the chief example of the "affinities of temperament and sensibility" she points to the "[conjoining] of that

* This translation of Cusanus' short work in four "books" has been reprinted, with an introduction by W. R. Dennis, by the Sutro Branch of the California State Library: *Occasional Papers*, Reprint Series No. 19 (San Francisco, 1940).

reliance on divine providence . . . and that confident assertion of the power of intellect" (Some Notes on Marvell's Poetry, Suggested by a Reading of His Prose," *MP*, LXI [1964], 269).

On the basis, chiefly, of Cassirer's study of Cusanus' thought in *The Individual and the Cosmos in Renaissance Philosophy*, trans. Mario Domandi (New York, 1963), I should like to suggest others.

Cusanus developed the doctrine of *docta ignorantia* (knowing ignorance/ ignorant knowledge: is it not of the same family of the ironies as Keats's "Negative Capability"?) as the logical consequence of his chief principle, which was that the finite world and the infinite are, by definition as it were, incommensurate (*finiti et infiniti nulla proportio*). He had turned from the logical method of scholasticism to mathematics because the law of the excluded middle (either/or) made it impossible to discern or represent what was for him the essential character of the universe. Mathematics allows (requires) the possibility of a coincidence of opposites (*coincidentia oppositorum*) which man should neither deny nor try to forget, since "separation itself guarantees the possibility of true participation of the sensible in the ideal" (Cassirer, p. 24). Man has knowledge of God not through mere feeling or by means of a graded apprehension, and certainly not through ecstasy, but by means of intellectual vision (*visio intellectualis*).

These four principles—*docta ignorantia, finiti et infiniti nulla proportio, coincidentia oppositorum, visio intellectualis*—are consonant with the fundamental assumptions that enlivened Marvell's religious convictions, his metaphysical conceptions of nature and love and the mind, his political theory and his sense of history.

1. The separation of the two orders of reality is the cause of corruption, as it is the cause of redemption; it makes possible the opposition which love and contemplation create; it makes obligatory the limits of civil authority in order that liberty of conscience, the guarantor of "every man's eternity

and salvation" (IV, 127), may be protected; it makes possible and necessary the mediating power of man's mind and God's grace.

2. The concept, if not the doctrine, of *docta ignorantia* informs Marvell's understanding of grace as it does his notion of the freedom of the will, best expressed in the passage he cites from Howe: "It cannot be so affrightful a thing to suppose God's foreknowledge of the most contingent future actions, well to consist with our ignorance how He foreknows them . . ." (IV, 203).

3. The coincidence of opposites is the definition of that principle of irony which is omnipresent in Marvell's paradoxical explorations of love, heroic action, and contemplation.

4. The intellectual vision of God's order is one of the chief motives of a poetry which is consistently dedicated to the principles of mediation and correspondence and to transcendence as an act of mind, not as mystic experience. Such intellectual vision is the Resolved Soul's response to temporality, i.e., to the separation of two realms of being and the coincidence of opposites. Temporality for Marvell, as for Cusanus, is providential: *Time is to the soul as the eye is to vision.* (This is Cassirer's redaction [p. 42] of several passages from *De ludo globi* and of *De Mente,* the third book of *Idiota.*)

NOTE 11

"Of flow'rs and herbes this Dial new"

Two explanations of that "pretty device of the gardener . . .
who . . . made a dial out of herbs and flowers" have been
offered. (See pp. 11-12). Either it is a "botanical horologue,"
an invention of Linnaeus himself, in which a variety of herbs
are planted dialwise according to the time of day at which
they open (described by T. J. Buckton in "The Dial of Flow-
ers," *N&Q*, 3rd Series VI [1864], 214-15); or it is simply a dial
whose numerals are planted in flowers. To my knowledge,
there is no sure evidence that a Linnaean clock had been
planted in England by 1650. In support of this notion of a
floral horologue, Bradbrook and Lloyd Thomas quote from
John Rea's *Parthenia Sacra* (1633) a description of the helio-
trope, which is called the "'Gnomon of the Garden, a Dial
artificially made in hearbs, to expresse al the howers of the
day . . . she . . . is turn'd and quite metamorphosed into him,
and now become already in the garden, what he is in his
Zodiack, the true and real flower of the Sun, or Sun of Flow-
ers'" (*Andrew Marvell*, p. 58). But the reference here is to a
single species, described as a "dial" because the heliotropes all
over the garden answer to the sun's progress. In other words,
this "dial" is not a planting shaped like a sundial's face, but a
metaphor. As for the second variety, the clock of flower numer-
als, these authors cite the specimen at Cambridge which is
the subject of a woodcut in *Cantabrigia Illustra*, published in
1690. Is there evidence that it had been planted in Marvell's
Cambridge days? G. W. Johnson's *History of English Garden-
ing* (London, 1829), an annotated, critical catalogue of books
on gardening and horticulture makes no reference to any dial
other than the conventional sundial, the shape of which is

suggested in Markham's phrase, "some Dyall or other Pyramid" (*The Country Farm*, 1615). I have not been able to discover any mention of floral dials in books published at midcentury.

The notion of a rationally designed flower-clock qualifies as an authentically ironic and scientific "metaphysical" image which also substantiates the picture, already formed, of a formal garden. Rather than being appreciated as an allegorical metaphor, Marvell's figure of the dial has been construed as if it were Donne's, an actual phenomenon complexly related to a symbolic meaning in a manner which it is the poet's purpose to demonstrate. But if Marvell's metaphor has a compelling logic of its own, so too, is his habit of mind his own and not George Herbert's. Bradbrook and Lloyd Thomas provide for us an energetic appraisal of the seventeenth-century predisposition for ecstatic contemplation of geometric forms. If Marvell were indeed contemplating formal plantings in "The Garden," rather than being rapt into an ecstasy, surely he would respond as he does in "Upon Appleton House," with gravity and wryness, "allegorizing" in a conventional manner ("For he did, with his utmost skill/ Ambition weed, but Conscience till") and remarking the charm and interest, but not, I think, the mystic beauty of such a garden.

Frequently, the claim that Marvell is describing a formal garden is supported tautologically. For instance, Jim Corder ("Marvell and Nature," *N&Q*, 6 [1958], 58-61), in asserting that Marvell prefers "geometrical nature" and that his gardens "are not momentary attempts to recapture lost innocence, but constant metaphors for order," catalogues references he presumes to be to formal gardens, which include the "gardens" white and red of line 17, but he fails to consider that the "order" acclaimed throughout Marvell's poetry is, precisely, an order "pure and plain."

The English garden in Marvell's lifetime was changing from

decade to decade, a fact which vitiates the arguments proffered by Nicholas A. Salerno, who cites garden manuals from 1679 and 1718 in an attempt to characterize not only the setting of "The Garden" but also Marvell's "own" taste ("Andrew Marvell and the *Furor Hortensis*," *SEL*, VIII [1968], 103-20). (Salerno, like Courthope before him, sets himself the false problem of "reconciling" Damon's views with those allegedly Marvell's. A denunciation, somewhat in the vein of the Mower's, of "gardens of the new model" in *Flora, Ceres and Pomona* (1665) suggests that garden design was indeed a controversial matter. Reginald Blomfield, in one of the more interesting books of the turn of the century on this subject, comments that William Lawson's *A New Orchard and Garden* (1623) was "charming and practical [and expressive of a] subtle delicate instinct" but that it was borne down upon by Bacon's "weight of intellect," so that "the treatises on this subject for the next fifty years follow the lines of *Sylva Sylvarum* rather than *A New Orchard*" (*The Formal Garden in England* [London, 1901], p. 49).

Certainly, critics have not understood the possibilities of mid-seventeenth-century English gardens. Renato Poggioli's delightfully chauvinistic remark can stand as an example: "Marvell still thinks in conventional pastoral terms, as is shown by the sudden metamorphosis of this all too Italian garden—not into an English park, but into an orchard offering its juicy fruits for the asking to the joy of man" ("The Pastoral of the Self," *Daedalus*, 88 [1959], 686-99). Lawson, for instance, offers a plan for "an orchard plot," an elaborate square divided and subdivided into summer and kitchen gardens (which need not be rigidly differentiated, he makes clear); a formal garden of knots; walks, mounts, and what we would call simply an "orchard"; the whole plot being bordered by woods to the east and west, the manor house to the south, and a river flowing at the northern end. It suggests very clearly the kind of

A. All thefe fquares muft bee fet with trees, the Gardens and other ornaments muft ftand in fpaces betwixt the trees, and in the borders and fences.

B. Trees 20. yards a funder.
C. Garden Knots.
D. Kitchin Garden.
E. Bridge.
F. Conduit.
G. Staires.

H. Walkes fet with great wood thick.
I. VValkes fet with great wood round about your Orchard

K. The Out fence.
L. The Out fence fet with ftone fruit.

M. Mount. To force earth for a Mount ot fuch like, fet it round with quick and lay boughes of trees ftrangely intermingled, the tops inward, with the earth in the middle.

N. Still-houfe.
O. Good ftanding for Bees, if you have an houfe.

P. If the river run by your doore, and under your Mount it will be pleafant.

"An Orchard Plot," from William Lawson's *A New Orchard and Garden*, p. 13.

variety Marvell is describing at Nunappleton. Suggested, too, is the kind of garden whose green shade could provide the setting "pure and plain" for the recreating of the "active Minde."

In short, the conceptual resonance of "this Dial new" is a matter of the history of styles—in gardens and in poetry—but it is also a matter of the history of ideas. The recovery of the idiom can assure that larger meaning for us which was clear, for instance, to Emerson, who expressed an understanding consonant with that I am attributing to Marvell. In the first edition of the magazine he and Margaret Fuller produced he wrote (italics mine): "Let ["The Dial"] be such a Dial not as the dead face of a clock, hardly even such as the Gnomon in a garden, but rather *such a Dial as the Garden itself*, in whose leaves and flowers and fruits the suddenly awakened sleeper is instantly apprised not what part of dead time but what state of life and growth is now arrived and arriving" (Cited by Nicholas Joost in " 'The Dial': A Journalistic Emblem," in *Essays in English Literature of the Classical Period presented to Dougald MacMillan*, ed. Daniel W. Patterson and Albrecht B. Strauss, *Studies in Philology*, Extra Series, No. 4 [January, 1967]. Professor Legouis kindly called my attention to this article).

NOTE 12

The *"easie Philosopher"*

SIDNEY REMARKS that Plato, as his abjurations testify, knew well the power of poetry to move and thus it was that he "made mistress *Philosophie* verie often borrow the masking raiment of *Poesie*" (*Defence*, in *Works*, p. 20). Marvell has developed the figure of the *"easie Philosopher"* from this metaphor. The tone of the *"easie Philosopher"* is the key to the metaphysics of the Nunappleton woods; tireless allegorization of the *"Prelat of the Grove"* risks losing one of the most amusing and delightful passages in Marvell's incomparable poem. For the masquer in the woods talks to us confidentially, the way a magician does: "Watch closely and you will see that I am very close to being a bird; and I am already a tree. Watch closely. . . ." A. B. Chambers offers two paraphrases of the poet's announcement of his transformation. First, one of "the apparent sense": "Turn me . . . and you discover that I—a microcosm of my disordered world—was already topsy turvy." Second, the one he considers to convey the correct meaning: " 'Turn me,' and from a tree's point of view my roots will be correctly placed. . . . But [right side up], Marvell is no standing tree, but rather what John Evelyn called its 'inverted symbol' . . . Aristotle's tree, Plato's heavenly plant" (" 'I was But an Inverted Tree,' " pp. 298-99). Chambers discounts "the apparent sense" because he accepts the allegorization of the flood ("England has transformed itself into a world of antediluvian sin . . .") and wishes to claim the woods as "the secluded grove of academe" (p. 291) where the poet can be redeemed by his holy speculations, becoming again that inverted tree whose roots are in heaven, man as he should be, despite a world gone mad.

His survey of the *arbor inversa* topos is full of interest, but Chambers does not include in his lexicon of trees Marvell's own, which is, I think, the Platonic *arbor inversa* taken proleptically. Marvell has characteristically converted an allegorical metaphor to a hyperbolized pastoral commonplace. (Cf. Damon's "Oak leaves tipt with hony due.") The poet (I offer my own paraphrase), playing at philosophy, talking here among the birds and trees, feels himself very close to them; indeed, with very slight changes his conversion would be complete: only give me wings and I could fly, easily; and you could ascertain that I am already a tree, if you turn me upside down so that my "roots" are groundwards. Plato has it that we men are upside-down trees and I, the *"easie Philosopher,"* have discovered that a tree is an upside-down man. (And this is the sense of the passage Chambers cites from Evelyn, who has personified the tree so that "he" refers to tree, not man: "our Tree [like man whose inverted symbol he is] being sown in corruption. . . .") The *"easie Philosopher"* plays between the two metaphors: the poet is so beshaded, so imbarked, so knowledgeable of boughs and branches, roots and leaves, that he can call himself a tree, by the same operation of mind as that by which Damon makes himself the grass; the poet knows that he is an inverted tree because, as Plato has told him, his roots are in heaven, "[to which] the divine part attaches the head or root of us and keeps the whole body upright" (*Timaeus* 90A; cited by Chambers). The echoes of the place "Where my extended Soul is fixt" and of "this Tyrannic Soul . . . Which, stretcht upright, impales me so" ring through the woods.

The *"easie Philosopher,"* this ape of nature, is a poet who enacts his role in the masque with "playful irony," a phrase used by MacQueen and Rockwell (*The Latin Poetry of Andrew Marvell*, p. 29) to describe the tone of Marvell's "Illustrissimo Viro Domino Lanceloto Josepho de Maniban, Grammatomanti," which includes these lines:

> Scilicet & toti subsunt Oracula mundo,
> Dummodo tot foliis una Sibylla foret.

(And no doubt all things in the world are subject to prophecies,/ Provided that one Sibyl be in so many leaves.)

The translators comment: "Marvell seems to be casting doubt on Maniban's ability to comprehend all things in his prophecies and to inject in his allusion to the leaves a note of disorder and confusion" (p. 34). A philosopher who has a lot of material to work with and no one to challenge him does have an easy time of it.

In one of his most amusing attacks on Parker in *The Rehearsal Transpros'd*, Marvell again uses the image of the man who would seeks understanding in "leaves," developing a sequence from the studious attempt to a deliberate game, in this instance unproductive:

> At last, having read it all through with some attention, I resolved, having failed so of anything material, to try my fortune whether it might be more lucky, and to open the book in several places as it chanced. But whereas they say in the *Sortes Virgilianae*, wheresoever you light you will find something that will hit and is proper to your intention; on the contrary here, there was not any leaf that I met with but had something impertinent, so that I resolved to give it over. (III, 113)

In the splendid closing chapter of John Evelyn's *Sylva*, entitled "A Historical Account of the Sacredness and Use of Standing Groves," one may review the kinds of attitudes and expectations, the associations and uses which Marvell is parodying. The mythic character of groves assures a rich stock of metaphors (ark, celebrant, moral creatures, temple, holy music, opulent pattern, etc.), just as their traditional association with secret, personal, and communal rites provides models for these rites of contemplation. Ritually, the poet moves from the hewel homily to "Chance's better Wit," from conference and studies to would-be sacral identification, from the witty exploration of nature's secrets in search of universal analogies to a self-conscious, ironic critique. Thus the *"easie Philosopher"* celebrates the life of nature while he waits for the flooded meadow to drain. The masque of nature will continue by the riverside.

INDEX

INDEX

INDEX